THE ROAD TO ALMOST

THE LEAN YEARS . . . 1950–2024

DARRYL RHOADES

Cover design: Jonathan Patterson
Cover photographs courtesy Mark Kocher: front, 2009; back, 2015
Composition: Anne Richmond Boston

ISBN: 979-8-218-38928-4
ebook ISBN: 979-8-218-41388-0

Contact information:

No Big Deal Records
P.O. Box 190672
Atlanta, GA 31119

www.music-comedy.com
sunglass@mindspring.com

This book is dedicated to my wife, Suzanne Deaton,
who stated early in our relationship that
"we love our friends for their faults."
I've always been outclassed.

Where Rivers Used to Run

Burning embers in the clouds look like shooting stars
Ashes in the moonlight look like snow
I've heard a million prayers are floating in the air
Waiting for the angels to land below

Ten thousand marching footsteps sound like thunder
Rockets look like lighting in the skies
The wind sounds like a train before the smoke and flames
While oceans warm and seas began to rise

Now the water hurts my eyes
And the rain feels like the sun
The weight sits heavy on my chest
Where rivers used to run

One hundred sunsets cast a thousand shadows
As daylight disappears into the night
When green leaves start to rust and streams turn into dust
A brown haze obscures the morning light

But still the water hurts my eyes
And this rain feels like the sun
The weight sits heavy on my chest
Where rivers used to run

These shrines we've built will surely crumble
A testament to how it one day ends
Wash away this barren land as concrete turns to sand
And footsteps disappear into the wind
So I'll close my eyes
And dream one more time . . .
And remember . . . when rivers used to run

"It was like coming *this close* to your dreams . . .
and then watch them brush past you like strangers in a crowd."

MOONLIGHT GRAHAM, *FIELD OF DREAMS*

CONTENTS

ACKNOWLEDGMENTS

*"Every man has two deaths, when he is buried in the ground and the last
time someone says his name. In some ways men can be immortal."*

ERNEST HEMINGWAY

I make it a daily practice to speak the name of at least one friend who
has moved on from this planet. I'm losing friends faster than I can
make them but want to acknowledge some in this section who are
responsible for helping move my story along. If you have any com-
plaints, take it up with them.

From my earliest days of playing music with David Michael, Joe
Neal, Michael Mote, Gary Dockery, Michael Brown, Frank Motes,
Rick Simpson, Ronnie Chamblee, Edward Tanner, David Irwin, Jimm
Neiman, Ken Kinsey, Paul Peek, T Lavitz, Jim Boling, Rick Kurtz,
Mike Garrich, Dean Daughtry, Randy McGill and Claude Gregory,
and those who were instrumental in shaping my path including Doc
Pomus, Joel Dorn, Bruce Hampton, Tom Haines, Buzzy Linhart,
Frank Zappa, Chris Cole, Johnny Sandlin, Bruce Baxter, Jimmy Ginn,
Alex Cooley, Steve Cole, Ken (Hat) Birchfield, Randy Delay, Charles
and Caroline Moore, Robert and Hilda Rhoades, Freddie Caple, Glen
McCubbins, Ben Beall, and Mary Ann Deaton.

The world is less in your absence.

I would also like to thank those who have helped me along the
way with their guidance, suggestions and memories. Special shout out

to Suzanne Deaton, Jimmy Royals, Martin Kearns, Tommy Strain, Murray Silver Jr., Jerry Pece, Michael Simpson, Rick Diamond, Mark Burger, Steve Cheatham, Pat Alger, Ron Norris, Deborah McColl, Dobie Maxwell, Ritch Shydner, Jerry Fields, Jack Bell, Jerry Grillo, Bo Messina, Jerry Farber, June Rennirt, and Eugene Rhoades.

If laughter is good for the soul, Darryl Rhoades is the most soulful human I know.

Court Jester. Musician. Comic. Spoken word poet. Songwriter. Social critic. Author. Performance Artist. Entertainer. But when I think of Darryl, the word that bubbles to the surface above those qualifiers is friend.

I've known Darryl since the Mesozoic period of our lives and he always has had a penchant for making me laugh and making me think, often in the same breath. If quick wit is a pistol, his is drawn faster than anyone I know.

We came of age attending Forest Park Senior High, an average, garden variety way station on the road to adulthood, mostly white and middle class. And being in the south of the 1960s, it included the usual dose of half-wit bullies as well as those who thought bringing Grandpa's Klan robe to school for show and tell was a fun idea.

In school, we were, in different ways, outsiders in our own back eddies, disconnected from the river of rah, rah, sis-boom-bam around us. We didn't hang with the cool kids, or at least the kids who thought they were cool.

I was skinny, shy and introverted, content to cloister with the freaks and geeks of the school's newspaper staff during the day and play music with my first band after the ringing of the bell in the afternoons.

Darryl was as unique then as he is now. There was nothing shy or introverted about the guy.

His family moved to the town later than most of us, so he was a bit of a mystery to our classmates. He seemed to fulfill Jonathan Swift's prophecy "When a true genius appears in the world, you may know him by this sign, that the dunces are all in confederacy against him."

Not that Darryl would ever use or want me to use the word "genius" to describe him, but there was definitely a confederacy of dunces aligned against him, notably our principal who, as detailed in these pages, made a habit of leaning on Darryl the way a one-legged man leans on a crutch.

Often, after a brief appearance in the cafeteria like a hungry-to-be-worshiped god, Principal Kirkland would ferret through the halls in search of Darryl. The burr in his doughy ass was the length of Darryl's hair. Way before kids learned that you had to fight for your right to party, Darryl creatively struggled to keep his hair long. And he excelled at it.

The rule was your locks couldn't touch your shirt collar and Darryl's flowing mane was often long past a casual acquaintance with the cloth. I and others aided Darryl in his evasion of Kirkland's search and destroy missions and I was in line behind Darryl on graduation night and witnessed him pulling off his mortarboard to reveal his banned hair length. I remember the look on Kirkland's face, like the elephant in the room had just farted. Priceless.

The bond Darryl and I shared was our mutual love of music. We had other unspoken lodestones, including our Bible thumping, religious upbringing and fathers who had known poverty and seen war. But mostly, in those days, we submerged ourselves in that harmonious universal language that unified our generation.

Darryl's band, The Celestial Voluptuous Banana, was unlike any other group I knew at the time, and I was in awe of its music. While most high school bands were content to playfully mimic the Top 40, CVB had other ambitions; the earliest performance of a Jimi Hendrix song ("Purple Haze") I heard played live was courtesy of the group.

Darryl, who was in the nascent stages of his I'm-so-hip-I-got-to-wear-shades look, turned me on to The Grateful Dead's self-titled first album. The album had just been released and he was the only person I knew at the time who had heard it. (It would later make *Rolling Stone* magazine's list of the 40 essential albums from 1967, no small feat considering the competition in that landmark year of music.)

Darryl's insistence that it was an important album propelled me to purchase the vinyl.

Days later, he quizzed me about the meaning of the lyrics to "Morning Dew" (side 2, track 1). I was clueless in my response, thinking it was, you know, about dew on grass. After my fumbling answer, Darryl schooled me that the song was about the last woman and man left standing after an apparent nuclear apocalypse.

That's how it was—and still is—with Darryl. His mind has a natural tendency to find the deeper meaning of things.

I've seen Darryl perform countless times. I'm a fan of both his music and comedy. Across twelve albums and counting, Darryl's music careens from satire to heartfelt, and sometimes it punches you in the face when the urgency of his lyrics calls for it. His stand up elevates comedy to performance art. He never works "blue" as they say, but behind the mic he manages to entertain and challenge in equal measure, no matter the stage or his mood.

His skills as a drummer are renowned.

My company had the privilege of producing the Oscar-winning *Crazy Heart*. From our first read of the script, producer (and real-life partner) Judy Cairo and I immediately knew who should play the drummer in the scene where Jeff Bridges' character Bad Blake performs with a bar band. Darryl had breathed the stale oxygen of honky-tonks for years and he had the perfect lived-in face.

When Stephen Bruton, who co-wrote and performed much of the critically acclaimed music for the film with T Bone Burnett, watched the bar scene during the film's sound mix, he nodded to Darryl and the band on screen and said simply: "perfect."

Reading this book, I was reminded of the "rain" monologue of the Replicant Roy Batty in the movie, *Blade Runner*: "I've seen things you people wouldn't believe." Along life's journey, Darryl has known many cultural icons and performed with other extraordinarily talented artists. He's seen things.

The Road to Almost is a testament to an artist's life lived without compromise and with little apology. Darryl's story is at times humorous, even hilarious, and at other turns, it's poignant and heartfelt. The read will be an entertaining one for his many fans and—if there is a god or goddess—it will create new ones.

This book is, in a word, perfect.

Michael A. Simpson
Los Angeles
April 6, 2024

Epitaph Without a Stone

Fear rested on his lips like a half-lit cigarette
He had curb feelers on his heart and a trunk full of regrets
Tail lights look like diamonds shining in the sun
Baby moons kept spinning away in the darkness from everyone

He spent the days boxing shadows and his nights racing ghosts
He threw rocks at the moon and cursed the sun
With a pocket full of almost
He was swimming in the desert in search of a victory
Distance was his friend and words his artillery

He was a story without a hero, an ending without goodbye
Long ago there was someone where dreams went to die

When he couldn't stand any longer and there was no place left to fall
His desires became a ghost town where quitters always go
A footnote to the back page of a book that's seldom read
He blamed his misfortunes on the luck he never had

CHAPTER ONE

The Christian Catch-and-Release Program

*Come on down to discount Jesus, where you'll find everything you need
We've got chains with dangling crosses, and multicolored rosaries
Check out our specials with great prices, plenty of bargains just for you
Printed T-shirts with snappy slogans, Jesus saves and you can too
There's a sale on baseball hats, embroidered with words like "repent"
Order online and use the code word, type in "blessed" and save ten percent*

DISCOUNT JESUS ©2024 DARRYL RHOADES

The hook was set very early when I was bagged, tagged, and entered into the Christian Catch-and-Release Program. The battle between the misery of guilt and the mystery of sin began, and each time I thought I was being released, I realized there was always a piece of me still left on the hook.

Baptism was as much a part of the Nazarene church as the homecomin' dinners after church service on Sundays where women showcased their fried chicken, potato salad, and chocolate cakes. I witnessed quite a few people, including my own family, being dipped in a cloudy backwoods pond by Brother Griffin. I looked forward to the dinners but abstained from participating in the Christian dunking. I never got that thing about being submerged in muddy water to wash away the sins I was unaware of ever committing. I figured if Jesus died for our sins, I was paid up.

The Nazarenes viewed the act of baptism as a demonstration of one's commitment to Christ. Regardless of how you lived your life, without a baptism you were damned to hell for eternity. The game seemed to be rigged against all the other players, without their awareness.

As an eight-year-old, I couldn't wrap my head around the concept of communion (The Lord's Supper). Those who had committed themselves to Christ gathered around the altar, drank fruit nectar, and ate saltines as a remembrance of the sacrifice of the blood and body of Christ. The ritual of eating the body of Christ and drinking his blood seemed cannibalistic. I can't be the only kid who took a hard pass on crackers and grape juice for years after having that image branded into my brain.

Some rituals felt similar to the Masonic handshake, where only members gained entrance and understanding while accessing passwords and secret decoder rings. I questioned why people would put ashes on their foreheads or sit in a booth and confess their sins to some guy on the other side wearing the company uniform. I looked forward to getting wrapped gifts under a decorated tree but was unable to make a connection to celebrating the birth of the baby Jesus. Acknowledging the sacrifice of God's only son by placing chocolate crosses and dyed boiled eggs in a basket lined with fake plastic grass just seemed wacky.

I couldn't reconcile the Old Testament vengeful God with the rebranding of the new and improved, less vindictive New Testament God. Being taught that God is love while seeing signs on the highway ordering me to "Repent or Burn in Hell" and constantly being warned about the "Lake of Fire" weren't persuasive arguments to make me want to join the club. Lake of Fire sounds like a kickass name for a Johnny Cash tribute band, but it also was terrifying to an eight-year-old boy. I believe that was the point. I was confused when I saw hatefulness rationalized through religion. It seemed damned mean-spirited.

I was conditioned to address every elderly man as brother. I thought of it as part of their name. I never questioned a lot of things I was taught in the church until I did, and the mental gymnastics manifested with me obsessively pushing back years later through my music.

I still have my pendant with the wreath and bars, signifying the number of years I attended church without missing a single Sunday morning. Every week, there was a contest with the prize of a silver dollar to the kid who read the most Bible verses that week. I found a way to beat the system. With no rules about what verses to read, I found the shortest verse: "Jesus wept" (Gospel of John, chapter 11, verse 35). I would count the number of times I could recite this on the way to church, and easily won the prize several weeks in a row. I kept hearing about the streets of heaven being paved with gold but figured the money could be better spent while I was still alive. If you were issued a pair of wings in heaven, you don't need a new Schwinn when you get there, but it sure could come in handy for a kid trying to make baseball practice. Only when my mom started getting suspicious did I rethink my get-rich-quick scheme.

I liked the stories about Pharaoh's army, when the seas parted and then suddenly came crashing down and all those people drowning. I figured God had a wicked sense of humor and often played tricks on people when they pissed him off. Having a swarm of locusts at my disposal like He had gave me many ideas, but my prayers went unanswered, ensuring the safety of several club owners years later. There was plenty of vengeance and guilt to go around, and I carried the weight of that guilt while often seeking relief by writing about it over the years. Guilt and revenge seemed to be at the heart of learning about a loving God.

They sing about the blood of the lamb, And blood on the cross
Are you washed in the blood of Jesus, with his blood he paid the cost
They sing about blood a lot; they sing about it night and day
They talk about blood more than they did in the O. J. Simpson case

WHITE GOSPEL MUSIC ©1997 DARRYL RHOADES

Every Sunday, our family could be found standing with the congregation, singing about the power of the blood. Yes, there was power, power, wonder-working power in the precious blood of the lamb.

Blood indeed. There was the blood of Christ, blood on the cross, and blood of the lamb. We were singin' about a lot of blood and Onward Christian Soldiers marching as to war "with the cross of Jesus, going on before."

That's a hell of a leap from "Yes, Jesus Loves Me." With all that action, you'd think a kid would have been more interested. Locusts, women turned into salt, and some guy living inside a whale didn't seem to stick to me.

The fear of Satan, though, was instilled in me early and often. There were many temptations to avoid and traps to steer clear of. He was watching me and waiting for the opportunity to grab me up as kindling to stoke the fires of hell.

Five of us kids stood before the congregation before the Christmas Sunday service. Lined up in order, each kid held a giant letter that together spelled "SANTA." I was the "N" kid who was asked to move next to the second "A." All of a sudden, it became clear . . . SANTA was now SATAN. The evil fat bastard was relentless.

When the church needed more firepower, they'd book a revival, which usually lasted about a week, and we never missed them. Talk about show time! I caught several of the old-school tent revivals packed with sweaty people surrounded by sawdust, with a lot of cryin' and screamin' during altar call. They were workin' the guilt and fear.

We sang a song about Jesus being a fisher of men. I'm thinkin' the bait was the entire congregation singin' mournful songs about being washed in the blood of the lamb. At the same time, the piano would keep repeating the refrain "Oh, Why Not Tonight?" and Brother Griffin would talk over it. Why not give your heart to Jesus tonight? He asked while telling stories about those lost, who had failed to answer the calling.

Sometimes the preacher or a member of his flock would come down to the pew of a possible convert having an emotional breakdown. With nonstop tears and shaky hands, this person would be guided to the altar. This scene was eerily similar to weekly *Wild Kingdom* TV episodes, and referred to as "culling the herd." Lots of snot rags, tears, and testimonies while the congregation kept singin':

My favorite altar call story was about a group of teenagers sittin' in the back pew laughing during church services. They were young and had their whole lives ahead of them, or so they thought. I heard this story told as the piano notes of "Oh, Why Not Tonight" rose to a dark crescendo. Later after they left the church, those zany madcap teenagers were unsuccessful in their attempt to outrun a train and perished. In the wreckage, bodies were strewn all about and "twisted like a jellyroll" while their souls were set adrift and lost for all eternity. Fear was on the hook for anyone listening to this story, and many fish ended up on the stringer that night.

Years later, I reproduced this scenario and evangelistic dance moves quite a few times during Hahavishnu Orchestra performances. The band would sing while I preached about the teenagers lost in space, building the story with suspense and volume while the band would repeat the phrase, "twisted like a jellyroll."

Occasionally when I was growing up, other church members or well-known traveling gospel figures would serve as guest preachers. Some had all the appeal of professional wrestlers, with their trademark raps whipping the crowds into a frenzy. Even the backwoods churches enjoyed a good show before passing the collection plate to pay for the entertainment.

Arthur Blessitt was known as "The Minister of Sunset Strip," where he set up a church next to a strip bar. Blessitt became well known for carrying a giant cross to all parts of the world because he heard the voice of Jesus commanding him to do so. I caught his act while attending DeKalb College, and my mind raced back to my earliest church experiences. Jesus never spoke to me about doing stupid stuff, but if I had heard his voice, I would have at least started lookin' around for the hidden cameras. I stayed clear of burning bushes and dogs named Sam. In the college auditorium, I observed some of the followers entirely absorbed by Blessitt's performance in the same way many of us felt the first time we saw Hendrix play. Blessitt's calling was to straddle the thin line between commitment and being committed. As his age became a factor, I believe he put wheels on his cross as an alternative to asking God to lighten his burden.

One of the locals who made guest appearances in my church, Brother Davidson, provided unintentional comedy. He had a fiery delivery and his face would turn crimson while he lit the fuse with his sermon, in the same way he lit his cigarette before the service. He'd conceal himself behind the church and fight a losing battle with Satan and nicotine. Smoking tobacco and drinking alcohol were deal-breakers in the Nazarene religion.

Keeping in mind that this was in the late 50s when the Cold War loomed large, Brother Davidson preached about the "Kummunists dropping bums" on us because we had turned away from God. Years later, televangelists like Pat Robertson or Jerry Falwell would credit God for punishing gays with AIDS or blame forest fires and natural disasters on those who didn't love Jesus. The contrast between what the church taught and the reality of what I was seeing became fodder for my stage shows years later. Hypocrisy, fearmongering, and other patterns were recognized by people everywhere, and when I put them in my show, the audience immediately connected.

Brother Davidson would attend church every week with his family, who resembled the Waltons with several different sizes of John Boys, only with more Wildroot hair tonic plastered on their heads. I remember all the boys only wearing flannel shirts, and years later, they came to mind when I saw Larry, Darryl, and his other brother Darryl on Newhart.

Warming up in the bullpen was Brother Rayburn, whose specialty was tears, sweat, and volume. He could cry on cue at the right time in any story and work the crowd better than Dusty Rhodes in the squared circle at The Omni on a Friday night in Atlanta. Twenty years later, I would reprise Brother Rayburn by performing "Crybabies for Christ" on stage. The band would start tearing up as I alternated whispering and yelling in a call and response with the audience. I would whip the crowd into a frenzy as I put my hands on my hips, bent over, and danced in a circle as dictated by the baby Jesus.

Equating what I saw as a child to professional wrestling wasn't much of a stretch. There was never any game in making fun of people's faith, but always open season for the scam artist who came up with different angles to access people's wallets and credit cards. In 1987, Oral Roberts claimed if he didn't raise $8 million, God would be calling him home. In 2016, Creflo Dollar pleaded with his congregation to raise $65 million for a jet so he could fly in luxury around the world to save lost souls. Fleecing the flock has been profitable and continuous over the years with the aid of television, a healthy dose of guilt, and promises of eternal life.

My mom used to send money to Billy Graham, and I never said a word because it was her business, her money, and her belief. I remember how much it upset her and many others when everything came out about the Jim and Tammy Faye Bakker gospel con.

In the 1972 documentary *Marjoe* about the religious child prodigy, he explained how the willingness of people to forgive is used against them. Whenever Marjoe was caught scamming people, he would say the devil got a hold on him. He asked and received forgiveness, and then would turn around and do it again. The term "backsliding" was a temporary get-out-of-jail-free card often used by repeat offenders like him before losing its effectiveness. There have been many outstanding gospel thespians, but I believe the award for "Best Fake Apology While Pleading for Forgiveness" goes to Jimmy Swaggart for his teary-eyed, show-stopping 1988 performance of "I have sinned against you, my Lord." It was comedy fodder for humorists on many stages, and surprisingly helped lead to the idea that I could transform my frontman material into a solo performance.

Soon after Swaggart's performance, I saw comedian Richard Belzer at the Punchline Comedy Club, and rather than the intro music most comedians used, he entered the stage to a recording of Swaggart's tearful confession. It was masterful as he stood at the mic for a few minutes, wiping away his fake tears as the audience completely lost it.

There were no limits when it came to going after the scam artist; it was a matter of making it entertaining while twisting the knife, as I had been doing with similar material in rock venues with the aid of videos and a backing band.

The audience was often treated to videos that opened our shows or set up a song during the performances of The Mighty Mighty Men from Glad. With the lights lowered, the TV monitors made great theatre. We overdubbed new audio with a plot that had Jim and Tammy Faye challenging Ernest Angley to a Texas Death Match after Ernest had snuck up on Jim and blindsided him with a folding chair at their previous match at The Omni in Atlanta. Most of the time, these bits were met with overwhelming approval. However, I remember packing up quicker than usual after a show in Bessemer, Alabama, when it was apparent that more than a few in the audience weren't buying it. I surmised that they might want to do us harm after napkins, straws, and a couple of glasses sailed toward the band. I experienced a real fear that I may be getting a lesson about the blood from Onward Christian Soldiers. We watched our rearview mirror for quite a few miles that night, and a few of us even prayed to Jesus to protect us from his followers. Like several of my bands, this one had an excellent show for the wrong venue. Bars didn't always breed an ideal situation for alternative musical presentations.

Jesus is Screamin' on My TV

Well I heard you found yourself a singin' guru
That feels he needs to march around the world
And spread the good news
That I can't be happy unless I choose
To believe in all things you say and do like you do

Don't wanna live on Calvary or die in Guyana
Have a dog for a prophet or move to Miami
You've been born again
You gave your soul to Tammy Faye and Jim
He's comin' back but you don't know when

But when he does you'll show them
You can't be wrong because you're born again
Jesus is screamin' now on my TV
For a donation that can set me free
And save a wretch like me you wash my sins away
Was lost but now I'm found . . . mail in your check today

And you know you're right and everybody's wrong
In a perfect world where only you belong
Make a crippled man see . . . a blind man talk
How does it feel?

Young Christians . . . with gators on their sweaters
They've found a way that's gonna make me better
Get out of my face . . . Potato Head

Fat yellow boys in Cadillacs
A Maharishi wearing turbans never was your style
So kiss the ring of the pontiff and kneel down beneath him
Stand in his sandals for a little while
You'd see the light he showed you was only
A reflection from the diamond that was on his hand
So if you show him your Mastercard
He'll reveal to you the Master Plan

©1987 DARRYL RHOADES

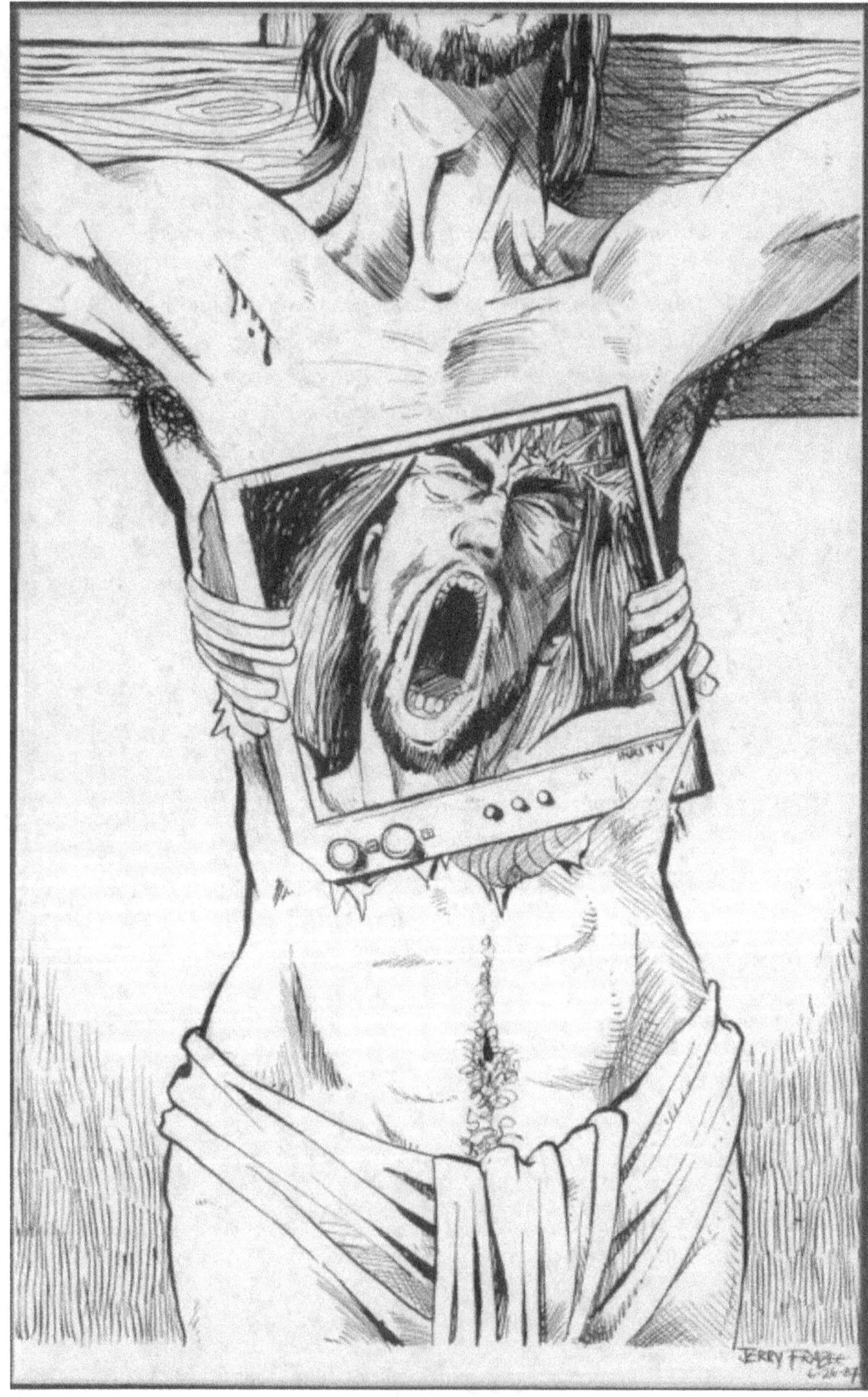

JERRY FRAZE

CHAPTER TWO

The Shadow You Cast
Depends on Where You Stand

The Old Men of War are faded and long since past their youth
They now build shrines to honor the fallen and the few
Who still have their stories of what they did and what they'd seen
And when they all have faded they'll still live in memories

THE OLD MEN OF WAR ©2003 DARRYL RHOADES

Some mornings I could hear him outside by 5 a.m. beating the hell out of the motor because the car wouldn't start . . . and he always figured out exactly where to put the hammer. Kentucky winters were often brutal, and to keep us warm, in zero weather my dad would have to crawl under the house with his blowtorch to thaw out the pipes.

Robert Rhoades grew up in the hills of Kentucky in a place called Cox's Creek and never talked much about his youth, so what I learned came from older relatives. His father, Clarence, and mother divorced when he, his sister, and two brothers were kids. My dad's half-brother, Eugene, was the product of Clarence's second marriage to 13-year-old Ollie Bell Karr. Eugene told me about Clarence picking up his three boys from their mom for ice cream. In reality, he was kidnapping my dad Robert, Lovell (Louis), and Herman (Hilary) to work on his land. They didn't see their mom for a number of years.

Eugene shared several stories about how Clarence would make them work while he sat under a tree and drank moonshine. His moonshine was popular with most locals who often stopped by after church. They'd take a sip from the half-gallon jug kept in the stream by the house, and if they enjoyed that taste, they'd pick up their purchase, which was stored in Aunt Pearl's basement. Eugene would often sneak in to "taste" it from the jug, and the taste started happening more often. As he put it, "It was smooth goin' down but would light your stomach on fire."

Clarence usually had three stills running simultaneously, and they were well hidden. He even had one hidden on the land that became Bernheim Arboretum and Research Forest. This area, designed in 1931 to become a park and opened in 1950, was heavily patrolled by rangers, the most notorious being Cletus Weller. Cletus knew about Clarence's still but could never find it. After playing cat and mouse for a while, Cletus threatened to arrest Clarence, Eugene, and the others if he found it, so Clarence moved the still.

My grandfather cast a darker shadow. He was a pissy little man with a Napoleonic complex and a perpetual mean streak. He often pushed his boys around and severely beat them on occasion. My Uncle June summed it up this way: "He lived by a creek down in a holler, he was a short fella and married a big woman and had a mess of kids." I'd heard the story about Eugene plowing the field when the horse got spooked by a copperhead, which resulted in the plowed line not being straight, so Clarence beat him with a chain. I believe my father ran away shortly after.

When Clarence finally decided to leave his second family, he burned down the house first. Most likely, his diet of greasy food and alcohol played a part in his passing from a stroke in 1952. He lived for 64 years, and the popular consensus was that he overstayed his welcome. My dad never mentioned his name, and until a few years ago, I had never seen a picture of him. I could see the family traits on his face, and thankfully that is where the resemblance starts and ends.

My father was around 12 when he ran away to live in the woods and often slept in the barns where farmers cured their tobacco. Living mainly on the game he hunted, he often raided people's barns for corn, and learned to make do on his own. As a kid, I remember him bringing home one of those old metal Coca-Cola coolers full of rabbits, squirrels, groundhogs, raccoons, fish, or frogs for Mom to cook and feed the family. If he had a rifle and ammo, he knew how to live in the woods and tried to pass along what he knew to me, like how to pick ginseng, yellow root, and slippery elm for medicines. But I was not the best student because I always had other distractions on my mind. I was into playing baseball and catching crawfish and catalpa worms for bait to fish with my buddies.

When my dad was 16, he came home and convinced my grandmother to lie about his age so he could join the army with her blessing. He served in World War II, fighting in Germany, Italy, France, and North Africa. I still have the original article from the *Louisville Courier-Journal*, about my father and his two brothers, Lovell and Herman, serving simultaneously. I never met my Uncle Herman, who was killed at the Battle of the Bulge, but I do remember the framed standard government letter of condolence hung on her living room wall thanking my grandmother for her sacrifice. I get the feeling that my uncle was a good man and a bit of a hell raiser. My favorite story was when Herman was in a barn behind a mule and got kicked so hard he was propelled through the wall and wore the horseshoe imprints on his chest for weeks later.

Like many men of his generation, my father rarely talked about the war and never about the loss of his brother. There would be occasions when I would witness its effect on him, though. I shared a bedroom with my two brothers, Billy and Kenny, in the house my father built by hand in Coral Ridge, Kentucky. We lived by the railroad track close to the Bullitt County line and the brickyard where he had first found work after returning from the war and marrying my mom. More than once, I was awakened in the middle of the night, hearing my dad screaming. One day, I asked my mom what the screaming was all about, and she explained that during the war, my dad was sitting around a campfire with his friends when a bomb went off and killed everyone but my dad and the guy next to him. I never heard him talk about this or other stories I eventually became privy to from my mom or uncles, but I do know when my dad passed in 1996, he still had bits of shrapnel in him which could never be removed.

When I returned from Europe in 1985, I visited my father. When I talked about being in France, he started sharing a memory of Paris, where he would sit under a tree and drink wine, eat bread and cheese all day for a quarter. He had a smile on his face right up until mid-sentence when suddenly he looked up at the ceiling and said, "Yeah, and the limeys were the first to get it. . . ." I saw tears in his eyes and realized he was watching a movie in his head he'd probably seen many times before. At that moment, my father was still captive to those memories, under attack and watching people die around him all over again.

One day during the 1991 Iraqi invasion, I was helping my father pick up some equipment. We were driving down the road in his truck listening to the Neal Boortz talk show on WSB radio when callers were calling in and saying things like, "We should bomb the hell out of 'em" or "We should just send all of our military in and overwhelm them." When a caller commented we should nuke Iraq, my dad, without missing a beat, said, "He's never been in war." With a sorrowful look on his face, he continued, "If some of these callers could see one of their buddies walking across a field with their hand on their stomach trying to hold their guts in, they'd never ask for war again." Yeah, I got that. My dad understood the kind of people who stood outside the circle and rooted for one guy to beat the hell out of the other while they never had to inflict or feel the pain. Most of the time, they never even knew what the fight was about, but it made them feel good to talk tough. My dad, like a lot of men, didn't talk tough. Like most who have fought in a war, he wasn't a cheerleader to repeat that experience.

That was my dad, and I have his Purple Heart. It's a medal most politicians have never held. A couple of years before he passed, he divided up his guns and other items between his three sons. I was given a pistol, a sharpshooter medal, and the Purple Heart. The gun came from a German soldier surrounded by my father and several others. My dad saw the soldier bury something in the foxhole, and when he was left to make sure the hole was clean, he discovered the Belgium Browning and put it in his bag. The pistol and an Italian rifle (he always pronounced it "eye-talian") were smuggled home.

I'll always wonder about how my father divided his personal items and why I got the pistol and war medals. I remember shooting the gun with him in the backyard, and he would instruct me on the correct way to take aim. After holding onto it for years after my father's passing, I gave it to my nephew, Brandon, a Navy veteran from 2001 to 2011 who served aboard the U.S.S. *Cheyenne* when the U.S. returned to Iraq on March 20, 2003. Brandon loved my dad. Dad had a military funeral, and I was offered the flag, but chose to make sure it went to another nephew.

Because my father came up hard, like many returning soldiers, he needed stability. Shortly after his return, he was with a buddy visiting one of my aunts, and my mom happened to be at home. Ever the smooth talker, my dad reportedly asked his buddy, "Who's the chick?" That story sounds questionable because women weren't chicks in the '40s, they were dames with gams, which big palookas took a fancy to, and sometimes the dames would respond if the guy was a lovable mug like my dad. He was a lovable mug with a temper who my Uncle June told me years later was a badass and feared by many. As Eugene would say, my dad was "easy to spark off," and when he was pissed, it was a good idea to find the door and, if there wasn't one, make one. If you saw him bite his tongue, that would signal you to run for your life. With three boys, one in particular, he was often given reasons to be pissed, and it wasn't pretty. Usually I deserved the punishment, a fact that never brought solace to the part of my body that had most recently received his undivided attention.

Once, I threw a shoe at one of my brothers, and it missed him but hit the wall and put a hole in the sheetrock. My dad jumped up and started to take his belt off while I quickly balled up into the fetal position and prepared to meet Jesus. He would only hit me a couple of times, but they were hard enough to hold me over till my next infraction. When any combination of us boys would start fighting, we could expect to hear the dreaded promise yelled from the next room, "You're gonna get a man into it in a minute." That threat was enough for us to give it a rest long enough to make good our escape. We never heard the "this is going to hurt me worse than it will hurt you" bullshit but became very familiar with the promise of "I'm goin' to give you something to cry about."

When I was six years old I went on a hunting trip at Green River with my father and several uncles. I was left alone at the campsite to play while they walked into the woods. I had no concept of time, but later, some guys came into the campsite and didn't notice me standing behind a tree as they started busting out the windows in my dad's truck and throwing stuff around. When they saw me, they jumped back into their green car and drove out. Looking back, I was pretty lucky; that story could have had a different ending, but the actual ending involved my dad coming back later with my uncles, and I told them about those guys. He asked if I would recognize them, and after saying "yes," he grabbed me, and we all jumped in the truck. We ended up at a small grocery store, and one of my uncles told the man behind the counter we were supposed to meet some friends in a green car but must have missed them and wondered if they might have come by. The store manager could not help us, and it was a lucky day for the bastards in the green car. My dad and uncles would likely have been the last thing they saw on their final day on earth.

There were many notorious hunting stories; many died with my father and uncles. My last surviving uncle, June, credits my father with teaching him valuable lessons about hunting deep in the woods, like keep walking when you come across a still because, more often than not, someone was watching through the sights of a gun. The days of stills have pretty much disappeared in the hills of Kentucky and been replaced by portable meth labs and pot fields, but the same rule applies . . . keep on walking.

My dad was good with a gun but a little too quick to pull the trigger, which explains why my uncle, Clarence Mills, ended up with rabbit shot in his ass after he happened to be standing in the line of fire. I went on a couple of hunts with him when I was a kid and listened for the dogs when they'd tree a coon. My dad would shine the flashlight, and then the firing began; surprisingly, more hunters didn't end up picking rabbit shot out of their asses.

I'm amazed at how good of a father my dad became, considering he had such a piss-poor role model. My mom and her entire family likely had much to do with him mellowing out over the years. Eugene mentioned he saw a big change in my dad after his marriage. I remember my mom yelling at him about drinking wine or smoking in front of the kids. After my dad sent me into the store to buy a pack of Camel cigarettes, my mom gave him an earful. I'm sure the need for peace led him to give up both vices shortly after.

He grew up with little and learned to live on it, a lesson that followed him for his entire life, and I often saw the ramifications first-hand. Buying new tires was a foreign concept when retreads or used tires were more affordable, which meant making several unscheduled stops on a trip from Georgia to Kentucky because three tires on his car came apart. When I was a kid, he had an old panel truck for hunting and decided it needed a paint job. With a brush and whatever paint he could find in the garage, we all ended up admiring his work. It was folk art on wheels. He turned old wooden pallets into a swing set for us, and when we became interested in sports, my dad managed to make a pole and backboard from a tree in the backyard. He dug a hole to install it, and mounted a basketball goal for us and the neighborhood kids.

My father made a picnic table as a wedding gift for Suzanne and me on June 4, 1996. The picnic table has been loaded and moved several times, survived exposure to extreme heat, rain, and snow, and still sits in our backyard today. My father was an incredible carpenter, plumber, and builder. Painter of automobiles . . . not so much.

In his later years, a bout with throat cancer left him with a tracheotomy and a weakened immune system. I saw my father's need to be surrounded by family after 1993 when my mom passed away. He became the father he never had, a good man who put his family first and would do anything to ensure they didn't do without. Unlike his dad, my dad chose to stand and cast a shadow that meant something better for all of us. On October 27, 1997, he passed away, and I don't remember crying at his funeral or even for a while after his passing until one day while driving down the road. "In the Living Years" by Mike and the Mechanics came on the radio and then the floodgates opened, and I had to pull over until the storm stopped.

In 2003, I recorded a bluegrass song about my dad titled "The Old Men of War" with a line that describes his influence on anyone who knew him, "The shadow you cast depends on where you stand."

Now I still have his medals and his lessons from the past
He said son it depends on where you stand in the shadow that you cast
Though the old men of war have faded I still find them in my dreams
And they'll always live within my heart and in my memories
And the lessons that he taught I hope will make me a better man
Like the shadows that we cast depends on where we stand

THE OLD MEN OF WAR ©2003 DARRYL RHOADES

CHAPTER THREE

When Pigs Fly

And as you walk, so will your children.
So please teach them this fact
As they struggle just to keep their hearts on track . . .

ON TRACK ©1994 DARRYL RHOADES

Most days, the old man could be found sittin' on his homemade bench out back, murdering a six-pack of Oertels '92. Eventually he'd make his way up the hill to Bear Camp Lodge to continue drinking into the evening before staggering home through the woods.

I'd heard the stories about how my maternal grandfather, Will Rennirt, would get drunk with his brothers and have knife fights, usually ending up cutting hunks out of each other. They also enjoyed hanging targets inside the house to practice their marksmanship, resulting in large gaping holes in the wall.

He'd stagger around the front yard while my brother Kenny and I would throw persimmons at him from the top of a tree. In his drunken rage, he yelled at us to get out of the tree, calling me "Cherry" because he never knew my name. I once mentioned this to my mom Hilda Ruth (Rennirt) Rhoades, and she gave me a sad look and said, "Most of the time, he never knew mine." Will Rennirt would hide his drinking money in the barn, and occasionally one of us kids would find it and hand it over to our grandmother, who'd get excited because she could buy groceries that day. I never felt close to my grandfather, who I only knew as a stubble-faced guy bent over with his mouth on a bottle when he wasn't dodging persimmons.

My mom was one of nine children born at home in Valley Station, Kentucky. The Rennirts came from tough German Irish stock and were kind but stubborn. Luckily, my mom inherited her compassion from her mom Carrie. I can't remember hearing my grandmother complain about the bad hands she'd been dealt, and there were many. Several times, while sitting in the kitchen in the middle of a conversation with her, she would excuse herself to go outside. I'd look out the window to see her wring a chicken's neck as a preview of what was on the menu for supper.

A few years ago, I visited the graveyard where my grandmother is buried alongside the two daughters she'd lost. Roma Jean died in 1943, the first victim of polio in Kentucky that year. Loretta was killed in 1955 after a school Christmas function at a church, when she ran out in front of a car on Dixie Highway. I was five, and vividly remember my father holding me up to see her body in the casket. This was the last time I would ever allow myself to see a lifeless body; I didn't want that to be my last memory of any person. I wouldn't gather around the caskets of my mom or dad with the rest of the family. My grandmother cried so hard at Loretta's funeral her nose bled, and I believe it may be the first time I ever saw what a heart looks like when it's completely broken. I don't think one ever gets over that kind of thing. They try to live each day with unexpected reminders, like what my grandmother found behind the couch: the lamp Loretta had saved up to buy her for Christmas.

My grandmother's religious faith gave her the strength to survive. Even through my grandfather's abuse and pain of losing two children, she told me, "God gave me the best husband, and I've led a good life." I think she seriously felt that way, and while I was hearing her say it, I couldn't help but recall stories from several relatives about bringing her home from church to find that the best husband God gave her had thrown all of her clothes out in the front yard while loudly cursing in one of his drunken rages.

Every Sunday, my grandmother could be found in a pew of Penile Nazarene Church at Valley Station, where I first attended church with my family as a kid. I never considered I had another option. Every Sunday morning, my mom got us up for church, and on occasion, we'd also go that night. Penile Church had been the schoolhouse my mom attended in the 1930s, and by the time we attended, a new school was built next to it. A story shared at my mom's funeral gave me some insight into how she and her siblings were raised.

The family lived in such isolation that there was so much in the world they had not been exposed to or learned. One day, the siblings were returning from school when they saw a blimp in the sky for the first time. They tried to hide by jumping into the ditch, then ran home screaming to my grandmother that they'd seen a flying pig. As funny as that sounds, to me it's no more strange than Christopher Columbus identifying manatees as mermaids while sailing near the Dominican Republic. (I don't know what Chris and the boys were on, but at some point surely there must have been the lesson often learned while playing the honky-tonks—you can't drink 'em pretty.)

My uncle was named after his father William, but since he was junior, we only knew him as Junie, and since he had sisters named Ada Bell, Dot, Sis, Leona, and Dude (Mattie), being called Junie seemed about right.

I regret not talking to my mom more about their upbringing, in a time when most families were more focused on surviving and caring for each other, often overshadowing the importance of formal education. Many like my mom would leave school to work in plants during wartime when the men were fighting overseas.

At her funeral, I learned my mom's favorite movie was *Fried Green Tomatoes*, and as I considered her early years and the people she grew up with, it all made sense.

I grew up hearing the names of some of the characters in Valley Station, like Roy Reisinger, who at age 17 was in the third grade when he got suspended for throwing his teacher out of the window. Drafted out of elementary school when he turned 18, Roy couldn't read or write but was a great artist. When he didn't know how to spell the words for what he wanted, he'd draw it instead.

I was a young boy the first time I saw Robert Earl staggering up and down Stonecreek Road, falling in the ditches. I can't remember ever seeing him standing upright for more than a few seconds. He always seemed like he was barely hanging on to the edge of the world. Robert Earl, who most referred as "The Drunk," would save up his lunch money to buy a half pint of moonshine in the woods on his way to class. He never ate real food, and the liquid diet he chose meant he would sometimes pass out in the front yard for days at a time. He was drafted into the Army around 1948 but got drunk every day while in training. His commanding officer made it his mission to find out where Robert Earl kept his stash, but he was unsuccessful. Robert was eventually thrown out of the military and later revealed his secret to Uncle June: from his barracks on the second floor, he would tie a string around the neck of the moonshine bottle and hang it outside his window, always escaping the attention of the MPs during their search.

Although both of my parents had alcoholic fathers who had done some moonshining, alcohol was never in our house after my father quit drinking wine when I was about five years old.

I suspect my parents, like many parents, sacrificed to ensure that we kids never went without. The baseball field and basketball net existed next to the vegetable garden my dad planted every year, and in pursuit of every foul fly ball, we walked a fine line in fear of trampling the tomatoes.

When the Louisville Army Depot, where my father worked, was closed down, our family was given the choice of transferring to Toledo or Atlanta. Thankfully, we landed in warmer weather down south. No kid wants to be dragged away from his friends, especially at age 13, and I was caught up in my sadness, but my mom never let on how upset she was to be pulled away from her family. Leaving the house my dad built by hand on the land he plowed by the creek where I played, we moved into a sterile new home in a subdivision with small yards of red dirt. It was a huge adjustment. There were no ballfields, crawfish to catch, or friends to ride bicycles with. I felt completely out of my element.

I got into all kinds of trouble, but my mom wouldn't give up on me. She could tell I wasn't doing well, and when no one else was around, she sat me down and asked what was happening. I felt detached for the first several years and only slowly made friends, but things didn't come together until I got interested in music, and my mom was supportive. I bashed drums from when I got in from school until my dad came home from work, and she never complained.

The only critical thing my mother ever said regarding my music was when she saw a televised clip of me singing "Think of Me When You're Under Him" and commented, "We raised you better than that." I came to understand what I wrote and performed were choices I made and was okay with all of it; I don't remember my mom ever attending any of my music or comedy gigs, which was probably for the best.

For years, I labored under the misconception that all my friends had parents like mine. The more I ran around with some kids, the more I understood I had hit the lottery. My parents loved and supported me, and their main concern was my happiness, even if they didn't understand my obsession with music and performing. Their pragmatism was driven by what they had experienced early in their lives, and from that, I learned the difference between telling a story and feeling it. I never heard words like "something to fall back on." With six siblings, there was no falling back on anything. I pursued being an entertainer the same way. I'd like to think I inherited my father's work ethic and my mom's compassion.

My mom would always invite my friends to eat with us. She asked one of my high school friends to live with us for a while when he got into some pretty nasty fights with his dad. I have to believe both my parents had seen enough of all that, knew the pain caused by it, and weren't going to be observers when they had other options.

CHAPTER FOUR

I Wasn't True to My School

It's where the Peckerwoods grow so tall and wide
And leave a lot of room on their fightin' side
The sun beats down on their redneck tan
When the air hangs heavy in Peckerwood Land
It's a Friday night flag flying jamboree
Where the citizens of Peckerwood all agree
That their colors don't run but if you still can
Turn your back and make tracks out of Peckerwood Land . . .

PECKERWOOD LAND ©2018 DARRYL RHOADES (POEM)

No matter how often I heard the Beach Boys sing "Be True to Your School," I wasn't feeling it. The pep rallies and chants of "V-I-C-T-O-R-Y . . . victory is our battle cry" didn't speak to me. It was just another gathering in the 1960s where I attempted to be invisible from Forest Park High School officials enforcing the haircut regulation codes.

One time while the rest of the students filed out to attend the pep rally/indoctrination campaign being held in the gym, I even hid in a cabinet in the classroom.

Between my junior and senior years, I was suspended four or five times and told not to return until I got the "proper haircut," which meant no hair touching my collar or over my ears. I wore enough Wildroot cream oil in my hair to lube up half the cars in the parking lot. Students were suspended regularly, often causing havoc for most of the up-and-coming high school rock bands. I knew several who dropped out because of the relentless harassment.

The authorities' need to impose senseless rules lit a fire in me that fueled my natural inclination to go against it. The more I was pushed, the more I pushed back. I learned quickly that it was easier to go along to get along, but that seemed a little boring, so I went the other way. I came to view my high school experience as less about education and more about indoctrination.

Principal Kirkland and his two assistants, Amick and Turner, attempted to make my high school experience more miserable, and it became a game I often lost.

In between classes, I'd duck into the bathroom and soak down my hair with greasy oil. In class, one of them would stick his head in the door to check on me. Occasionally in journalism class, I'd get a heads-up and my friends would attempt to hide me behind a pile of papers. At this time, I have to give props to Kathy Perkowski and Michael Simpson.

When the hair issue and harassment became unbearable, Michael Simpson, Dennis King, and I made an appointment with Georgia state school superintendent Jack Nix.

Michael was the spokesman and more articulate than Dennis and myself, who sat back as Michael stated our case. Mr. Nix patiently listened and then explained that there were no state regulations regarding hair length for "boys or girls" in schools, and recommended we contact Clayton County superintendent J. E. Edmonds.

I'm unsure how I got Mr. Edmonds on the phone the next day, but our conversation went as I figured it would. I told him about our trip to Atlanta and our discussion with Mr. Nix, and then I asked why it was vital for me to keep my haircut short. His response was the same as Principal Kirkland's explanation: "It's county policy, and I set the policy." End of that conversation, but only the beginning of many similar interactions for years to come.

I understood that many would assert authority simply because they could, without a need to justify it. My inquiries and attempts at understanding the logic behind these rules always felt like pats on the head and condescension. Many of my school experiences became seeds of my pushback and rebellion.

My high school experience was common. Individuality and free thinking are rarely encouraged. More than 50 years later, even the hair issue is still a thing, with Black kids being told how to style their hair. I imagine if most people my age picked up their high school annuals, they'd find many senior boys had the same ambition: "to be half the man my father is." This statement still boggles me. Why would anyone focus on being less? Why would anyone set their sites on being half of anything? I figured I wanted to be twice the man my father was. Even though the likelihood of failure was high, I wasn't going to sandbag my dreams by attempting to be less.

I thought I'd had enough and just wanted to graduate and move on, but couldn't resist one more shot on graduation night. Seated with the other graduates, I wetted down my hair and combed it back, and by the time my name was called to pick up my diploma, my hair had dried out. After getting my diploma, I removed my graduation cap, shook my head, and my long hair flowed down. Friends began laughing and applauding, leaving Principal Kirkland dumbfounded with a scowl. For every graduate, Kirkland simultaneously delivered the diploma from his left hand while extending his right hand for a congratulatory shake. My defiance was topped by my friend, Larry, who spit in his hands at the last second and Kirkland didn't have time to back his hand away, so he shook Larry's spit-filled hand. This was one fantastic night filled with the joy of my parting "kiss my ass" to a high school experience with few high points.

Even though I had friends in high school, I often felt out of place. I wasn't like the kids who were stereotypically running in a pack and usually trying to out-asshole each other with great success. Anyone looking different or standing out in any way was often the target of their bullying.

I never understood the sense of loyalty that led to the rituals and rivalry between Forest Park High and Jonesboro High a few miles down the road. In front of our school was an old cannon by the flagpole. It became a thing where students from Jonesboro would abscond with the cannon, eventually rescued by students from Forest Park. As the wacky shenanigans went on, the rivalry heated up, often resulting in fistfights at late-night hangouts between kids being true to their schools.

One Friday night, I went to a bowling alley with one of my brothers and a guy named Buster. He was the adopted son of another couple who transferred to Georgia with our family from Kentucky. Buster was a funny guy and a little introverted. After we bowled, we were about to get into the car when this well-known alcoholic, Chuck, approached us and started talking smack to Buster. "You must be from Jonesboro cause you got them red socks on," Chuck slurred. Buster tried to appease him, but Chuck took a swing, which was countered with a punch, actually a lot of punches. Buster, we learned in that moment, was a trained fighter. Chuck never stood a chance and went down quickly.

I don't advocate violence, but I am a big fan of karma. In real-time, Buster had treated us to a scene that dreams are made of. There was no "I shoulda done this or said that." Chuck was a dumbass getting schooled about the fact that there's always someone faster and tougher. This experience reminds me of some of the best advice I ever received and wisely took under advisement: "Learn how to fight and then try not to."

Buster eventually joined the Army and was stationed at nearby Fort McPherson. He was on his way to work one predawn morning when a driver, trying to outrun the cops, hit him head-on right in front of the gates at the base, and he died instantly.

Forest Park offered plenty of places where one could get into a fight. Burger joints, bowling alleys, or skating rinks on a weekend night were popular destinations for single-digit-IQ Neanderthals. Their standard mission was to get drunk, talk loud, and engage in a pissing contest to reaffirm their manhood. Most of us preferred to be out with women, so the thought of this bunch of macho guys getting drunk together at Burgerworld is pretty entertaining. Stupid cowboy wannabees.

On a Friday night, after several of us stopped at a Krystal for a hamburger after a gig, I was walking to the car when a guy approached me. I recognized him from high school several years before, but didn't know him. It would be so much easier if assholes wore buttons or name tags; otherwise, they tend to blend into the crowd at late-night places in Forest Park. It would also make it easier to assess the inevitable punch coming. He was drunk and a bit bigger than me, but I never thought for a moment he was about to take a swing and bloody my nose. It happened so quickly that I can only remember hearing someone from another car yelling, "Leave him alone," which distracted the knuckle dragger long enough for me to get in the car and escape.

I went back to a friend's apartment and cleaned off the blood as an unrecognizable anger filled me, along with wondering why I didn't fight back. In my entire life, I can't remember not returning a punch, and size was never a factor. It wasn't fear. In my pocket I had a knife that I hadn't pulled, unlike I had done a couple of times before without using it. The knife hadn't even crossed my mind, and now I was pissed, and couldn't let it go. I never preferred violence, but that night, I felt an unfamiliar rage. Maybe it was the residual effects from all the harassment and constant hammering about what it means to be a man. How do you handle a hungry man, eat a man-size meal, walk like a man, talk like a man, while you stand up and fight like a man? There were always more fans of John Wayne than Mister Rogers.

I knew some tough guys, and I also knew that Mr. Asshole would likely be found at the same place the following night with his Peckerwood Posse. Remember, assholes (e.g., politicians, John Birchers, KKK) always travel in groups of at least two.

I returned, prepared, to the Krystal the next night with a few biker guys I knew. I don't know how the word got out because I certainly hadn't said anything, but greeting us when we pulled into the Krystal parking lot were more Forest Park cops than I had ever seen. We thought better of it and just kept on going. Later, I heard Mr. Asshole and friends had jumped a U.S. Army private who was Black, a detail I'm pretty sure had something to do with the attack, and broke his arm. The U.S. military didn't take kindly to anyone hurting one of their guys since time and tax dollars were spent training them for duty in Vietnam. If he was going to be harmed, it had to be government sanctioned. Mr. Asshole left town until things cooled off, and I never saw him again, but did hear he was working as a correctional officer somewhere. PERFECT. Just knowing he's likely been dealing with erectile dysfunction most of his life is good enough for me. Sons of bitches are like water: they rise to their level, even in the toilet.

I forgot the pep rally cheers and school anthems, and avoid attending any related reunions, lunches, or cross-burnings. You know how some people are so forgiving and move on? I admire their journey in speaking their truth and living their best lives. I'm not one of those guys. Forest Park taught me the stupidity of blind loyalty and the entertaining satisfaction of standing up to authority and conformity. Sue me.

We're Livin' in Cowboy Country

I'm livin' in cowboy country
Got the biggest truck around
With the loudest engine and largest tires
Sittin' fifteen feet off the ground

Balls danglin' from the trailer hitch
Rifle hangin' in the rear gun rack
Gotta double wide with a shed outside
A trampoline for the kids out back

When you're livin' in cowboy country
Where the men gotta talk tough
They carry their courage in their pocket
Just to prove they're big enough
For cowboy country
They dig in their heels and take a stand
And make their point with the back of a hand
That's how people know you're a man
When you're livin' in cowboy country
You're livin' in cowboy country

If you're livin' in cowboy country
There's something you better learn fast
You talk real loud and stand your ground
When somebody threatens to kick your ass

You play the cards you're dealt and place your bets
And don't waste time making idle threats
Cause a man is a man when he owns his debt
When he's livin' in cowboy country

You gotta stand tall when they're callin' you out
And you learn real quick what it's all about
Take it outside or where you stand
And you don't back down cause you're a man
And you're livin' in cowboy country

In cowboy country you can't pretend
Or bluff your way to a winning hand
Play your cards close to the vest
Clinch your fist and stick out your chest
Cause you're livin' in cowboy country
Where a man's gotta talk tough
There's always someone in cowboy country
That's ready to call your bluff
In cowboy country
In cowboy country
In cowboy country
In cowboy country
We're livin' in cowboy country
We're livin' in cowboy country
We're livin' in cowboy country
We're livin' in cowboy country

MARK BURGER 2023

CHAPTER FIVE

If Assholes Were Planes . . .

Don't be kind or waste your time on assholes
They'll say things just to bring you down
Joy is something they can only read about
And there's one thing you can live without

ASSHOLES ©2014 DARRYL RHOADES

My mouth opened, and the words rolled out. The son of a bitch hit me so hard I didn't feel it. I had tunnel vision and an overbearing desire to make him stop breathing.

I'd been sittin' on the side of the stage of a crowded club in San Angelo, Texas, watching my buddy, Scott Kennedy, trying to do his act in front of about 300 people while being heckled by a table of cowboys.

Scott and I had worked together on many C. W. Kendall bar gigs, but on this particular night it must have been "assholes get in free." Many suspected C. W. of routing his tour of one-nighters by blindfolding himself and throwing darts at the map. You'd have to leave right after performing in Texas one night to make the 8 p.m. showtime in New Mexico the following night.

C. W. was a veteran musician who had played piano in the 1950s with Johnny Cash, Buddy Holly, and others. He booked Mexican restaurants, country music honky-tonks, and any place that would carve out a few feet for a comic to stand and perform for an audience that may or may not be aware a show was going on. C. W. was a legendary fixture in the 1980s and 1990s promoting the Texas outlaw comics like Sam Kinison, Bill Hicks, and Ron Shock. Some gigs were rougher than others, but C. W. was easy to do business with. In the beginning of my standup career, I worked any place that would give me stage time and pay me, and C. W.'s gigs kept me on the road and allowed me to work on my act.

On this particular night, after Scott finished his show, he introduced me, handed me the mic, and whispered that the crowd was rough. He didn't need to; I had just witnessed the parade of stupid like they were competing for a prize. I was reminded of an old Southern saying, "If assholes were planes, this place would be an airport." I could almost smell the jet fuel.

After years of performing all over the country, I had plenty of experience dealing with drunks and could defuse most situations, but on this night, I opted for the road that unraveled. Most comics would do whatever they could to disarm the hostility or finish their act and walk away from the anger, but in San Angelo that didn't seem to be my plan, as if I had one. As the saying goes, "fight or flight," and I always preferred to align myself with the Wright Brothers whenever possible. Except for this night.

I used to perform made-up characters in my act, and about five minutes into my performance, I would light a cigarette. On this night, after a few puffs, I flicked it and watched the cigarette bounce right off the forehead of a cowboy sitting closest to me. I'm not sure if he was the loudest heckler, but figured in a crowd of assholes, there were no wrong targets.

After the cigarette toss, I was treated to nonstop verbiage with low-grade articulation, improper English, and a bounty of four-letter words questioning my heritage while directing me to attempt physically impossible acts. Realizing my fate was sealed, I decided to push this train over the cliff with a mind-numbing reply equally well thought out. "After the show, I'm goin' to line every one of you sons a bitches up and kick the shit outta you," I shouted.

I think it was Mose Allison who wrote the song "Don't Write Checks with Your Mouth That Your Body Can't Cash." I'd seen more than my share of bar fights, and this moment in San Angelo took me back to an exciting night in a honky-tonk bar on Stewart Avenue in Atlanta. As two troglodytes squared off, one uttered, "You got an alligator mouth and a hummingbird ass." I've never lost my love for Southern metaphors and similes and the mischief associated with them.

In San Angelo, I made a beeline to the cowboy table and knocked the hat off the man in black, who was still bearing the residue of cigarette ashes on his forehead. Knocking the hat off of a cowboy is a little like covering yourself in honey and throwing rocks at the hornet's nest while rolling around in several ant hills. As one might predict, Mr. Cowfucker jumped up and clocked me, and I immediately felt like I'd just snorted a few lines of meth. There's a point when you're fighting that adrenaline takes over, and you feel as if you're outside your body. I started swinging my fists fast and hard, but when it was all over, I could not recall a thing.

Scott explained that Mr. Stumpbroker swung and landed a punch upside my head, and I charged him while throwing a roundhouse. Instead of hitting the cowboy in the face, I connected behind his neck and threw him down like I was roping a steer. When he hit the ground, I jumped on top of his chest, pinned his shoulders with my knees, grabbed his hair, and started pounding his head into the concrete floor while screaming, "You can't hurt me, motherfucker!" My alleged elocution didn't sound like anything I would have said, but Scott continued filling in the blanks.

I didn't remember being pulled off of him, or him taking a swing at the cop who went to pull him off the floor. When that happened, no one gave me a thought. When the police took the cowboy outside, they had difficulty getting Mr. Cowpoke in the patrol car's backseat.

Seems he kept bumping his head against the top of the car door. Texas cops—same as it ever was, same as it ever was.

Back in my hotel room, I lay awake replaying everything that happened that night. I knew better but had let myself get dragged into stupid, low-rent behavior. Was it all the years of taking shit off disrespecting assholes? Was it the fact that my mom was dying of cancer, coupled with my feelings of being disconnected from anything that resembled order in my life? I couldn't help but feel a familiarity with all of this as a deep depression settled over me.

I had just started dating Suzanne, who several years later would become my wife. The day after the bar fight, I called her and told her what had happened. Years later, she revealed that it gave her pause about seeing me again. She'd been on the other end of anger and wanted to be careful about being put in that position again. She could have decided to end it right there, and I'm thankful she didn't. I had much to learn from her.

Suzanne's words when we first started dating have stayed with me: "You love your friends for their faults." While the words sounded great, I had no idea what they meant until one day, they clicked. Love is most needed when a person is broken and full of doubt. I wouldn't describe myself as broken, but I had a long list of faults, with impatience and anger at the top.

The San Angelo story got out among comics, and for months, when I would work with a new comedian at the beginning of the night, I would hear, "So . . . you're *that* guy." Yeah, I was that guy. Every angry confrontation flashed me back to my teenage years in Forest Park, Georgia. Construction workers, hungry for cheap entertainment, would throw bottles from their pickup trucks at Blacks and longhairs walking on the roadside. Every public swimming pool in Forest Park had at least one pair of government-issued assholes who "just got back from fightin' in Vietnam" and were ready to "whoop the asses of some goddamn hippies." (Editor's note: assholes always come in twos or more, e.g., KKK, Nazis, and television evangelists.)

Meanwhile, as a kid who had moved down to Georgia the summer before I entered the 8th grade, I would also try to interact with kids walking down the street who appeared to be close to my age. I'd yell at them in hopes they would want to play baseball or hang out with me. I felt like I had arrived from a different planet called Fairdale, Kentucky where I had been in sync with all my buddies, playing sports and fishing together. Now I was around people who said, "Come heeeah," and "I carried my mom to the store." In Kentucky, we took people places, but we never carried them.

In Georgia, assholes were never far away. There was an old Civil War museum a few miles away on Highway 41 in Jonesboro featuring a Confederate cemetery. The old railroad station was used in some scenes for *Gone With the Wind*. When I traveled to Europe years later, I realized many still think of the South in those terms. I had some strange conversations with the locals in Amsterdam, Paris, and Brussels. Of course, outspoken segregationists and other racists from the South didn't do a lot to change their minds or anyone else's who was curious or confused about this twisted part of the United States. Even more recently, some in-laws from England visited and were anxious to see the plantations with women wearing hoop skirts. In hindsight, I wish I had the resources to call some friends and punk them. We could have put a spin on it with Black masters whipping white slaves while making the point, "As you can see, the South has gone through some changes."

Until my 8th-grade history class, I had never heard the expression "War of Northern Aggression" to describe the Civil War. My teacher, who used that phrase, also gave the class an assignment to come in and talk about our family history, sort of like a biographical show and tell. One kid came in with a nicely-pressed Ku Klux Klan uniform belonging to his grandfather. Many years later, the same kid said on Facebook that if Barack Obama was elected president, he and others should load up their rifles and pickup trucks and then drive to Washington, D.C. Again, assholes always travel in numbers (anti-Semites, segregationists, and skinheads); on a sad note, this same guy fathered several children. I'd often hear the phrase, "Black is beautiful, and tan is grand, but white is the color of the big boss man," from classmates demonstrating their brilliant comedy chops.

The idiocy and cruelty of racism were relentless. A hundred years after the Civil War, many in Georgia still spoke about it as if it was a recent event. I'd see novelty license plates on cars with a cartoon of an old Confederate soldier and the caption, "Hell, no, I ain't forgettin'." Those license plates served as a much-needed heads-up on people to avoid. When the 1964 federal civil rights bill became law, the most popular peckerwood novelty plate showed a pregnant Aunt Jemima figure with the caption, "I went all the way wif LBJ." A few counties north of Forest Park there were signs at the Forsyth County line that warned Blacks not to be seen there after sundown.

On Sundays, my family often went out for Sunday dinner after church services at East Point Nazarene Church. I was 14 when we went to the Hillbilly Steak House in the Arrowhead Shopping Center close to our home. After the meal, I took one of the cards by the register, and later read the owner's message apologizing to his clientele. He was sorry for having to serve Black people and blamed the government for forcing him under the new civil rights law. He wanted to ensure his white customers didn't hold it against him.

I considered myself apart from the racists and other assholes, but I would often show asshole potential as well. In the 8th grade, I made the basketball team but only played about three minutes the entire season, making it clear that this sport would not be my future. The best advice I ever got but didn't use came from Coach Jay. He gathered the team together after practice one day and said, "Boys, your pecker is an organ, not a muscle, so no matter how much you try to exercise it, it's not going to get bigger." I spent a lot of time and energy in the course of my life attempting to disprove this statement, but to no avail.

With my career as a sports figure in question, the question being just how bad I could suck, I spent serious time hanging out with the local ne'er-do well kids. Two brothers stand out as some of the meanest kids I ever knew. The older one used to beat the hell out of the younger one, and both were always trying to intimidate everyone else. They came by their meanness honestly since both their mom and dad beat them daily for any number of reasons, but in the words of the youngest brother, "My dad did some jail time for beatin' a nigger to death 'cause he threw a brick and cracked the windshield on my dad's truck."

Those boys learned violence well at the hands of their dad, who was known to have a drink or ten, which often preceded the nightly drunken rant many in the neighborhood could not escape. I have to credit the two brothers for helping me build the framework for my character "Buster Love," which I would perform years later. Buster would mispronounce words like sending a special "defecation" to an audience member when performing a song on the radio. He always thanked his fans for sending postcards and letters to him while he was unjustly incarcerated.

Even though I received training early as a kid in Kentucky about the art of speaking "hillbonics," when the brothers threatened to open a can of "whoop ass" on someone, I filed it away for later use by Buster.

I was 14 when I got into trouble with some other kids in the neighborhood for breaking into a junkyard and stealing bicycle parts I didn't need or want; it was an unconscious effort to be accepted by the other punks and an opportunity to prove my stupidity and poor judgment. I ended up in juvie for about a week and got a year's probation, but that wasn't the worst of my punishment. It was having my mom tell me I broke my dad's heart because he thought of me as the kid who would never do that kind of thing. I let him down, and seeing that knocked me back into the reality that I needed to get my act together.

I was 15 when I saw my first live rock concert on November 28, 1965, at the Atlanta Municipal Auditorium. I'd never experienced anything like watching Sonny & Cher, Len Barry, Danny Hutton, and The Enemys that day. All the musicians were partying, laughing, and shooting shaving cream at each other to celebrate their last night of the tour. I'd never seen or felt anything like that kind of joy. People were energized, and I wanted to be on stage, having fun and entertaining a crowd, and years later I did that several times in the same venue.

After my attempt at joining an international bicycle parts smuggling cartel failed, I took a job working at a drug store fountain close to my house. Next to the drugstore was "Buddy's," a slot car business, a fad lasting about 20 minutes in the 1960s, where I hung out on my breaks or after work. Dennis King worked there and also played bass in a local band called The Nightwatchmen. I would talk with Dennis while singing harmonies and keeping a beat by slapping books or the counter. I had no direction at the time, which had been at the heart of my problem, as well as hanging out with other like-mindless kids. Dennis played bass, sang, and worked at a slot car business. This showed me a different world with many possibilities, but I had to act on it.

I hadn't considered playing drums until Dennis suggested it, and within days, I gave $40 to a classmate for a drum set with a rebel flag on the bass drumhead. With no lessons, I practiced all day long, and listened and played along with every bit of music I could get my hands on. Practicing was the first thing on my mind when I wasn't in school, because I was obsessed with music and how it made me feel. To see drummers perform, I attended every dance at the Forest Park skating rink or the recreational center possible, and practiced what I saw every drummer play.

When you read interviews by musicians, most point out the famous names of people who influenced them. My influences were the local bands like The Englishmen, The Apolloes, The Dynamic Five, The Fugitives, The Soul-Jers, and others who stimulated my hope that one day, I could be a successful working musician earning dozens of dollars a night.

The skating rink usually featured local acts, but occasionally, at the rec center, you could see some regional bands like Wayne Logiudice and the Kommotions. Wayne had performed at the Apollo Theatre in New York and the Royal Peacock in Atlanta, and was the closest thing to James Brown I had ever seen in a live performance.

Seeing The Roemans at the rec center was a highlight as well. Years later, I learned that I had seen future Allman Brothers bass player Berry Oakley and drummer Bertie Higgins, who went on to have a solo career with the hit "Key Largo."

I started hanging out less with the other kids in the neighborhood because like many boys at that time, I wanted to be Ringo Starr. Quite by accident, the drummer of The Nightwatchmen, Randy Rivers, was leaving the band, and even though I had never played with any other musicians, I auditioned. Other drummers did too, but I got the gig.

Years later, I learned from The Nightwatchmen's guitar player, Gary Lewis, that my mom had stopped by his house to thank him and the other guys for asking me to join the band. She understood what many politicians fail to grasp these days about music's role in giving direction to kids. School budget cuts have reduced funding for art and music programs even though common sense would dictate it is cost-effective to help kids tap into their creative side for a better sense of self-worth. From personal experience, getting involved with music gave me that feeling of self-worth, drawing me in, and to this day, has never let go. Art and music programs in schools have probably turned around many lives of kids who could have easily turned into the two brothers in my neighborhood.

I remember waking up one night to the sounds of fire trucks and rushing outside to see the flashing lights down at the house where the two brothers lived. The story was that their dad had come home to an empty house, drunk as he had been many times, and fell asleep in bed while smoking. He perished in the fire along with the family dog, and shortly after that, the remaining family members moved away.

For several weeks, all us kids bet each other that we wouldn't walk through the burned-out rubble at night with money on the line. I made a few bucks on that deal but was always terrified and swore I heard noises and voices. My story kept down the competition, and soon the house was demolished and rebuilt for another family to live in.

Several years later, returning from his tour of duty in Vietnam, the younger brother dropped by. I asked him how he felt about serving, and his response was, "We have to be there to Americanize them." I pointed out that the citizens of Vietnam weren't Americans, but then quickly realized I was talking to someone who likely admired Custer's plan to "Cowboyize" the Lakota. So I let it go. Ramming my head into a brick wall was never my favorite activity, although I would do it often in the years ahead.

All the factors that play into, and dictate, your path in life are a roll of the dice. I last heard one of the brothers met a violent death while the other was in prison for murder.

One neighborhood guy I shot pool with hung himself in his family's basement. He couldn't deal with the secret that most of us knew: he was gay, which was a hard thing to handle in those times. One of my best friends in the neighborhood was killed in a car crash while he was still in his teens.

I hung out with some pretty quirky characters, and ran into my share of assholes, and can only conclude that there was something about growing up in that area that often gave way to bad outcomes. One unforgettable example of this involved the pastor in a church we briefly attended. Since there wasn't a Nazarene church close to our new home in Forest Park, we attended Phillips Drive Baptist Church. I didn't know anything about the Baptists other than they weren't Nazarenes, and apparently, that's all I needed to know. There had been a Primitive Baptist church (redundant, don't ya think?) across from our Kentucky house, and while I played in the yard, I'd hear 'em singin', moanin', and sometimes yelling during Wednesday night services. It didn't sound like they were having much fun, and the singin' was horrible.

We only attended the Baptist church on Phillips Drive a few times, and I remember my mom commenting that the preacher was "kinda stuck on himself." My memories were more about what he said from the pulpit, and the eventual lesson that the family that preys together, slays together.

The highly charismatic Rev. Leamond Cooper Stuart Jr. liked to remind everyone of his Native American heritage and most of the congregation referred to him as "a full-blooded Indian." The gossip was that he was a favorite with several women in the flock, but I'm unsure if any actual shearing took place.

He'd go on and on about how he had been victimized in his youth because of his upbringing, and I have no doubt about the credibility of those stories, but I also understand that Rev. Stuart would serve as the poster boy for the mantra that "hurt people . . . hurt people."

On September 26, 1969, Rev. Stuart came up on a couple of kids siphoning gas out of a church bus. The kids jumped in their car, but the good reverend, accompanied by his two sons and son-in-law, caught up with them around the State Farmer's Market. Being a man of God, I'm guessing the Old Testament version, Rev. Stuart apparently didn't see a problem in administering his brand of justice. He smote the kids by sticking a rifle out of his car window and firing off a shot, fatally wounding 17-year-old Terry Pearson.

After both vehicles came to a stop, the occupants in Pearson's car were pulled out, manhandled, and held in place until the cops showed up. The occupants of the reverend's car were arrested, and the reverend charged with manslaughter.

Most of the congregation supported Rev. Stuart, with some taking out second mortgages to help finance his legal defense. His high-powered legal team was led by the infamous F. Lee Bailey and second chaired by a former Grand Dragon of the KKK, James Venable.

Rev. Stuart was given five years for voluntary manslaughter and one year each for two counts of aggravated assault.

Stealing gas out of a church bus had no appeal to me, but I could have just as easily gone down that road while doing other stupid stuff. I could have been in prison or no longer on the planet had it not been for banging on books at Buddy's and singing with Dennis.

After my first gigs with The Nightwatchmen, we added Gary Dockery on guitar. Gary sometimes stayed in his room for days, listening to music in the dark. The walls of his room were covered with the hides of squirrels, rabbits, and foxes either killed while hunting or found on the side of the road. Gary was Ted Nugent before Ted Nugent was uncool. Gary loved playing and fit in well with the band, and I credit him with having the most influence on changing the band's direction and name.

The Celestial Voluptuous Banana came together through suggestions from Dennis and Gary's mom, even though a few people have disputed that. I'm going with my memory. After our name change, we stopped playing Top 40 and were drawn more to The Byrds, Beatles, and more obscure groups like The Chocolate Watchband and Thirteenth Floor Elevator. The press and advertisements described us as "the most psychedelic band in Atlanta." I can't remember if we sounded good, but we rehearsed a lot, and my joy was a feeling I hadn't known before.

Since we didn't have the funds to buy a light show, we would take a fan, put cardboard blades on it, and mount it in a wooden box with a light bulb behind it, and when we hit the footswitch, the strobe light effect could be seen from literally inches away. It might have made more sense to have people look into a light and blink their eyes quickly. As dumb as the homemade strobe light was, I topped it when I took all the heads off my drums and put colored light bulbs inside them. Usually after being pounded on for a set or two, the bulbs would quit working.

We grew our hair, wore Levi jackets, and made out with girls after the gig. I felt like Eddie Haskell getting an all-night pass to Party World, and even without making much money, it was still a well-rewarded night of gainful employment. Now I had a purpose, passion, and a sense of belonging. I fantasized about being on stage and even part of a show hosted by one of the big DJs from WQXI, the most popular radio station in Atlanta, often referred to as "Quixie in Dixie." These DJs were a cast of characters that held the keys to any possible success I saw for myself. Even at venues that were becoming sketchy, any show hosted by one of these DJs would likely be a sell-out. I knew I had arrived when I first performed a show at the Forest Park skating rink hosted by Tony "The Tiger" Taylor, sporting a fake tigerskin sports coat. Other notable Quixie DJs who eventually hosted shows I played were Gary Granger, Patrick "Aloysius" Hughes, Barry Chase, and the one I remember as the most popular, Dr. Don Rose. Dr. Don never held a medical degree but knew how to jumpstart the audience when he hosted the Battle of the Bands at Funtown, an infamous amusement park in an equally notorious area on Stewart Avenue. (As the area became more seedy with crime, the family amusement park's popularity declined and closed as Six Flags over Georgia opened in 1967.) Dr. Don introduced us as "The Celestial Voluptuous Banana . . . the band with appeal," demonstrating the high-brow comedy stylings I expected from the best on-air radio guys.

My favorite DJ at that time was Skinny Bobby Harper, who pushed his humor to the point that he often butted heads with the station managers. His charismatic and off-the-wall personality eventually cost him his job at WQXI. He once called the FBI and made jokes about J. Edgar Hoover, which the law enforcement staff didn't fully appreciate. Skinny Bobby wasn't a "shock jock"; he was just good at his job and one of the few on the AM dial that could hold my interest. Living the nomadic life of a radio personality, Skinny Bobby would go on to land several other radio jobs. The song, WOLD, by Harry Chapin, was indeed on point ("The bright good-morning voice who's heard but never seen / Feeling all of 45 going on 15 / The drinking I did on my last big gig it made my voice go low / They said that they liked the young sound when they let me go") and could describe the lives of many radio guys I've known.

In the late 1960s and early 1970s, most towns had a teen club or place to hear bands. In Atlanta, we played clubs like The Stingray, The Electric Eye, and The Spot, and traveled to surrounding states. Most of the time, we'd drive all night after a show if we didn't have a hotel room. After we played one night in Statesboro, Georgia, bass player Tom Raybon fell asleep while driving us in a van where I was sleeping on our equipment. After I came to, I realized we were upside down in the middle of the highway at 4 a.m. With battery acid dripping on my clothes, I started digging myself out of the rubble. Gary Dockery had been thrown from the van, landing on his leg but still in the path of the van, which then rolled over onto his leg. You hear stories about people having superhuman strength when the adrenalin kicks in, which is the only explanation for Tom lifting the van so Gary Dockery could get his leg out.

The Banana spent a lot of time running down leads on gigs and bookers; the most infamous was Harvey Leech. Depending on who you talk to, Harvey was well thought of or at least a source for many entertaining stories.

Harvey was a bedridden paraplegic who handled the phones. In several meetings with the Banana, he would speculate on various tours he was planning for us that never came to fruition. The tours would always fall apart the week before we were to leave, always after we attempted to get info about the fantasy gigs. We might have established our relationship with Harvey about the same time he was forming his special bond with alcohol. He made several late-night pleas to me to borrow my parent's station wagon and pick him up some liquor at the package store. I always declined.

I'd heard many different stories about how Harvey came to be bedridden, but the most credible and probable account came from Donald Dunlavey, guitarist for The Englishmen.

"When I met Harvey, he lived in a house on West Fayetteville Road in Jonesboro, Georgia, with his mother and stepfather, Mr. Wallace. Harvey had a story on the side of the house with its own entrance. His room consisted of a bed with a lamp table, chest of drawers, and two telephone lines. He made calls almost all day long, booking about seven or eight different bands in Atlanta, and helped us out a great deal when I talked the Englishmen Ltd. into coming to Atlanta. He had a bad argument with his real dad one night and a rifle got in the middle of them arguing and wrestling over it. The gun went off and hit Harvey in the back, which caused his legs to be paralyzed. After a time, his legs began to draw [shrink] uncontrollably, and they decided to amputate about mid-thigh.

"Harvey worked hard and tried to help all us young bands. Money never seemed to be that much of an issue for himself. Never saw any wasted money or up dressing, gold, diamonds, nothing like that. He was tormented though, and sometimes would take pills or drink too much, and if any of the bands were around they had to deal with him."

While the Banana rarely worked any Harvey gigs, one band that did was The Atlanta Vibrations. They won a battle of the bands and the prize was opening up for The Beatles at Atlanta-Fulton County Stadium, but they were limited to playing only instrumentals for a 20-minute set. Their guitarist, Spencer Kirkpatrick, had the best Harvey Leech story.

"Our bass guitarist at the time was a guy named Walter, who we called Tiny. We went over to see Harvey during the holidays, and Tiny gave him his wrapped gift. When Harvey opened it, he saw a nice new pair of shoes." A funny story to be sure, even if deeply rooted in "assholemania." Over the years I've practiced the art of being an asshole, often to perfection. All I know for sure is that today I can laugh about most of these stories and be thankful I didn't end up dead or locked up like several who crossed my path. Music, some well-timed lucky breaks, and the love of friends and family saved me.

CHAPTER SIX

The Man, the Park, & Other Things
(with apologies to The Cowsills)

Trippin' out in Frisco . . . freakin' out by the bay
I spent three days inside a OD tent down in Monterey
One pill made me larger and the other made me small
But the one that Owsley gave me
Didn't do anything at all . . .

I'M GETTIN' BURNED OUT ©1976 DARRYL RHOADES

If ghosts and songs ever lingered in the air of Midtown Atlanta, they were driven away or drowned out long ago by traffic noise and highrise buildings. There are no reminders left as a testament to the existence of The Catacombs or the scene where it played such a large part. The all-night restaurants on the adjacent corners were torn down years ago and replaced with the Colony Square complex advertised as the "Art of Modern Life."

When the Celestial Voluptuous Banana started hearing about The Catacombs, we drove from Forest Park to Atlanta to check it out. As a junior involved with my high school newspaper, I wrote a few stories about the club, which are too embarrassing to reprint here.

While my parents slept, I would sneak out, push their car down the hill, start it, and make my way to 14th Street. Years later, I figured out that my mom likely knew but never mentioned it to my dad so I would live long enough to write these stories.

Located in the basement of Mandorla's art gallery on the corner of 14th and Peachtree Streets, The Catacombs was a "psychedelic dungeon" that typically would spring up in cities larger than Atlanta. The neon paintings on the wall resembled prehistoric cave drawings that came to life under the blacklights, highlighting the exposed furnace pipes, concrete floors, and crudely built tables facing the stage. The basement was musty, moldy, and maxed out at a hundred people, with cops often dropping by looking for underage runaways, drugs, or any number of reasons to close it down.

David Braden (aka Mother David) had opened The Catacombs as a coffee shop in the summer of 1967, the year after he had established the art gallery above. It wasn't long before Braden was busted and charged with occupying a dive along with a few drug charges, and became less visible at the club. I became friends with the manager, Doug Merrell, who was left in charge.

Before The Catacombs, it was all teen clubs, fraternity parties, and high school dances for bands, but this place marked my coming of age. I was still living in Forest Park and had discovered clues that a much bigger scene literally existed just up the road. I had begun listening to The Nasty Lord John show on WBAD, a station located on Main Street in Forest Park. Nasty Lord John (aka John Meeks) was the hippest DJ on the air, or at least in that limited broadcast range. Listening to his show was like taking a class in hipness. He also doubled at night as a drummer playing along with records at The Scene, a dance club on Ponce De Leon. He later played drums in one of the versions of The Second Coming, a band that eventually featured Berry Oakley and Dickie Betts before they became part of the Allman Brothers. By the time we got ourselves to The Catacombs, I was in new territory and felt like I was part of a fraternity with others sharing the same passions, and it was coming right on time.

It's important to understand first that the psychedelic scene of The Catacombs evolved as the 60s folk scene in Atlanta thrived in clubs including The Bottom of the Barrel, The Bistro, and The Crucible, with notable local talent and national touring musicians such as Jimmy Buffett, Jerry Jeff Walker, and John Hammond.

Ron Norris, who led several popular bands, including Chakra and Silverman, talked about performing at the Decatur Drive Inn and basements of churches that would host folk music artists. Often, artists would gather in homes and perform for small gatherings or each other, which was referred to as a hootenanny.

In this era, some iconic venues opened and shaped the entertainer that I would become, even though I barely was aware of that at the time. In retrospect, the musicians I came up with now realize how formative these places were, and the performers who we saw there and the stories we became part of.

The Twelfth Gate, for instance, was founded as a coffeehouse church by a Methodist minister named Rev. Bruce Donnelly and became a popular hangout and a great performance venue. To portray this place and time as accurately and vividly as possible, I asked others who were there for their memories. Songwriter Pat Alger told me, "I knew about the Twelfth Gate and the 'hippie' pastor Rev. Bruce Donnelly. My dorm was just off 10th Street near West Peachtree Street, and I remember walking over to one of his services there at the building on 10th and Spring Street. It was mainly a social club/haven for runaways and lost children like myself—the atmosphere was welcoming and relatable but it was still like going to church, which I was in the process of giving up on. At some point the church stopped sanctioning it or Rev. Donnelly was re-assigned to another church, which happened a lot in the Methodist ministry. . . . Robin Feld, as far as I know, was part of the group that took over the place after Rev. Donnelly departed, and she along with Joe Roman made it into a funky little club with decent affordable food and coffee and soft drinks. Later Ursula Alexander joined them and they turned it into a pretty nice venue. I began to play there around late 1968 or early 1969. It closed in 1973. Unbelievably, I saw Little Feat there on their first national tour for a $1 cover charge. Initially I performed by myself and then with a singer/songwriter named Paul Hansen as Hansen & Alger. I was also in a group called The Hand Band with Ron Norris and Shel Hall, and later a folk-rock band called Milkweed. The Gate was a place where musicians hung out—people like Deborah McColl, Ron Norris, Thom Tollerson, Jeff Espina, Tam Duffill, and many others. Each music club seemed to have its own crowd."

Around 1969, I started going to the Twelfth Gate but only performed at that club once with a loose gathering of friends. It's mainly where I remember seeing some of the most iconic jazz performers of my lifetime, including Elvin Jones, McCoy Tyner, and Weather Report, up close and personal. But it was The Catacombs that offered more variety for folk, rock, jazz, and blues artists to perform and to me was unlike any other club. I became obsessed with hanging out there and checking out the live music.

The energy around The Catacombs often felt contentious because of a cat-and-mouse game with the cops. They'd try to shut down Doug over building code violations, arresting people for being an occupant of a dive or possession of narcotics. Sometimes they would arrest anyone on the corner of Peachtree and 14th Streets for vagrancy. The cops seemed to enjoy harassing for the sake of entertainment while ordering people to move because "you can't stand there," and I noticed that "there" could change quickly. Doug could never appease them.

Even though I was not a drug user, I had to be careful or lucky not to run into a problem during those times. I walked in on two drug busts while visiting friends, but was able to walk away unscathed after being searched. I never had a problem other than often being hassled because of the way I looked. Police wouldn't start using the "we had a report about a suspicious person matching your description" technique until several years later.

I'd heard talk that The Catacombs was a front for drug sales, but I was oblivious to all of that. I was saturated every night with the combined smells of fog, smoke, oils, mold, incense, and cigarettes. I often stayed up all night or crashed on the couches, unaware of any illegal activity if it existed. Being a hyper guy fueled with too much angst, I felt at home playing music and being around other musicians. While many were doing their best to shine a negative light on The Catacombs, it certainly beat hanging out in the neighborhood and getting into trouble with local ne'er do wells as I had done years earlier. After playing there from around 10 p.m. to 4 a.m., I usually went home smelling like a head shop and imagined little tumors having a party inside me to welcome recruits.

The Pennant, an all-night restaurant adjacent to The Catacombs, decided to impose a fifty-cent minimum order per person to keep longhairs from loitering and taking up the booths. Doug thought it would be a good idea to supply about 30 of us with half a dollar and march to The Pennant. In a short time, we filled the place, and almost as short a time, we saw the cops arrive to run us out just because they could. The cops would say things to bait you while hoping you'd give them a reason to handcuff you and throw you in the backseat. The baiting worked on several who were arrested, although I was not among them.

I first saw Ellen McIlwaine, Jimm Neiman, The Hampton Grease Band, Radar, Pale Paradox, The Bag, and Strange Brew at The Catacombs. You could hear various genres of incredible music from 10 p.m. to 4 a.m. every night of the week. It wasn't uncommon to see local celebrities hanging out at the club, like Joe South, Ray Whitley, or any number of successful songwriters then based in Atlanta. It was an electric atmosphere attracting artists from all over the south. There was always a parade of characters hangin' around the club, including dealers, musicians, a Black guy called Spade, bikers named Spider and Samson, and an openly gay man known as Snowball who often wore a white boa.

"Snowball was a hoot," Spencer Kirkpatrick (guitarist for Strange Brew and later Hydra) told me. "She traveled with us for a short while to assist Ken Taylor's wife with their infant daughter while we were out playing. Snowball would be wearing a dress over jeans and a pair of those knee-high fringed moccasin boots, a sweet person who must have had a real hard time being out of the closet in such a visual manner back then."

Ellen McIlwaine was the first woman I ever saw who could belt out a song and play slide guitar as well or better than any man. I'd make my way from Forest Park to Atlanta in the middle of the night when I knew she would be performing. I wasn't alone. "I watched her knock a speaker off the wall with her voice at the Bottom of the Barrel," said Ron Norris of Chakra and Silverman. "She had a large footprint in my world." Pat Alger told me that Ellen "honestly scared the heck out of me sometimes because I never heard or saw anyone like her. . . . She was a strong woman back when that wasn't cool."

Ellen's version of "In My Time of Dying" nailed me every time. Doug Merrell was instrumental in releasing this recording on a 45, and knowing I was a huge fan, gave me a few copies. "In My Time of Dying/Grizzly Bear" was released on the Strange Lights label, and written below the song title are the words "as performed at The Catacombs, Atlanta, Ga." Between the recording quality and the poor mastering job, the record didn't capture Ellen's natural talent, but it's one of my cherished keepsakes. I'd sit and listen to her for hours when the club was packed or empty.

Ellen left Atlanta in 1968 for New York after assembling a band called Fear Itself. They released an album on Dot Records, which garnered a little attention. I remember reading a review when the record came out: "The only thing this band has to fear is itself." I thought it was a mean hack thing to say, but this record did fail to showcase her massive talent.

I contacted Ellen several times after she moved to Canada, where she gained notoriety and success. I'm glad I could send her a copy of the single she didn't have before she passed away in 2021 and ask her about what she remembered from these years at The Catacombs. "Black lights, d'anglophile posters pulsing from the walls, rumors of Bruce Hampton taking a dump onstage (?!), being constantly interrupted by forces filming the audience members for police reference in fear of some kind of uprising," she recalled. "Lots of good music and camaraderie! Met Steve Cook (guitarist, The Soul-Jers) there who became our bass player and went to NYC with us in Fear Itself in 1968. It was exhilarating to be considered part of the 'counterculture'!"

Another performer who inspired me from the first time I saw him performing at The Catacombs was Jimm Neiman. I'd heard he had played bass with the Thirteenth Floor Elevator in Texas but never found any evidence to support that. Jimm was a great musician with a strong voice and a wild sense of humor who sat in with the Banana several times. He also was one of those guys who talked through you instead of to you. He always seemed like a long-distance call away, even when standing beside you. I'd never met anyone with such an insatiable appetite for wildness and self-destructive attraction to the edge.

Several of us in the Banana went to see Jimm play bass at the Atlanta Municipal Auditorium with Dr. Espina's Banana Boat Blues Band and Traveling Freak Show Too with Eddie The Road Manager. The turnout couldn't have been more than 100 people, but through the years, the number grew much like those who said they were at the stadium when Hank Aaron hit home run 715.

I'd often wondered what happened to Jimm and only found out when I started researching this book. He moved back to Florida and joined the recording group Bethlehem Asylum from 1969 to 1973. After he left the band, he became a reasonably successful "rock and roll daredevil." He would sometimes have people shooting darts at him, or he'd lie under 400 lbs. of concrete while someone swung a sledgehammer trying to break through to him. In the book, *History of the Groove* by Bethlehem Asylum drummer Russell Buddy Helm, Jimm was characterized as "very intense but talented. They called him Captain Ego. He wore a superhero outfit before it was fashionable. He killed himself about 1991. He had been taking Prozac. He drove his Ford fastback muscle car late at night on a deserted Pinellas Park road with a garden hose attached to the exhaust and feeding back into his Torino window. He was eventually overcome with fumes, and glided to the side of the road. They found him the next day, a bottle of Jack on the seat beside him. He often talked about The Catacombs."

News like this always feels like a slap in the face. It wasn't that I was a close friend of Jimm's but he had a lot of influence in my development right down to my wearing sunglasses most of the time. It's the feeling of seeing your history slip away when it's attached to clear memories of people you knew and shared times with. Jimm was always an extreme guy, and even knowing that doesn't soften the blow finding out that he ended his own life. My memories from The Catacombs are filled by relationships of people, many who are no longer here or have forgotten those days but those memories are still vivid in my mind.

Joel Maloney was one of the best rock drummers to come out of Atlanta; I loved his finesse, and he had a wicked sense of humor. With the technique of a jazz player, he reminded me of Mitch Mitchell. He joined Atlanta's supergroup, Booger Band, a trio rounded out with keyboard prodigy Will Boulware and guitarist Ted Trombetta. Will and Ted had previously played with the popular blue-eyed soul group The Soul-Jers. Seeing Booger Band in Piedmont Park was mesmerizing. They were as good as any band I'd heard but never got the deal that should have projected them into superstardom.

To this day, a few brag about ownership of the Booger Band tapes, but finding one that isn't a multi-generation recording is difficult. There are also tracks of jams with Duane Allman and Booger Band. Another one of our influences, Ginger Baker, showed up when Cream played at Chastain Park on October 27, 1968. The promoter borrowed several Vox Super Beatle amps from the Banana for monitors, so I got to hang backstage. Joel and I both played double bass drums and were there to watch Ginger, and we were treated to watching him so stoned backstage he kept falling off the drum cases he was sitting on.

I was also inspired by musicians coming from all over the South to join the new music scene. The Bag came up from Florida, knocked me out with their impressive harmonies, and featured a guy on bass whom I would work with many years later. Michael Brown was an incredibly talented musician, but just as impressive to me was that at only 15, Michael could grow a heavy beard. The Bag and The Hampton Grease Band were the resident rock groups of The Catacombs at that time, and around the times the Banana worked there, I saw them more than any other groups.

My earliest memories of Bruce Hampton and the band were guitarists Glenn Phillips and Harold Kelling, both monster players. Bruce wasn't a singer as much as a presence that inspired bizarre stories about what many claimed to have seen him do on stage, some real and some imagined. I'll always wonder why anyone would go out of their way to create fiction when the real stories are as fun and often more interesting.

I experienced my first psychedelic light show, billed as a "phantasmagoria of lights," by The Electric Collage at The Catacombs. The Electric Collage was the first light show in Atlanta. Their immediate popularity and success quickly made them an essential part of the music scene, and founders Frank Hughes and Steve Cheatham exclusively lit the shows at The Catacombs before moving onto larger venues. The two had met at The Catacombs and "connected immediately," Steve Cheatham told me. "Frank is the one who brought in the smoke machine to catch the color as we projected it." More than a few musicians and audience members probably suffered asthmatic attacks when Frank and Steve blew purple fog all over the room each time a band played "Purple Haze," and almost every band did. "I remember the first night The Electric Collage did its thing with us, Frank turned on his fog machine and turned on the purple light when we started 'Purple Haze,' and people freaked out," said Bruce Lowe of The Bag. "Everyone thought the place had caught fire. And I remember I got the crabs from that old sofa they had in there." The fog was so thick that from the stage you couldn't see other band members or the audience. They also used projectors and dishes with oils and food coloring to create amoeba-like figures on a screen behind the band.

Atlanta Vibrations guitarist Spencer Kirkpatrick reminded me how "the primitive fog machines they used smelled like they were spraying for pests, and those damn strobe lights made me fear grand mal seizures! Damn, we lived through some shit!" The fog did remind me of the childhood smell of pesticide trucks spraying roadside ditches, or a Mercedes diesel with leaky gaskets. I've often wondered if years later, some paid a price for ingesting that smoky fog, like 'Nam vets sucking in Agent Orange.

The Banana had our promo picture shot in the latter part of 1968 on the carousel at the base of The Catacombs steps. Around this time, we signed on with the earliest version of Discovery Booking Agency, formed by Frank Hughes and Steve Cole, who were responsible for bringing many Atlanta bands together. Cheatham told me Frank "was the hardest working manager in show business and had the perfect partner with Cole providing ideas as his front man living in hippie land on 8th Street." Discovery promoted us as "Atlanta's Psychedelic Band," making us a natural fit with the Electric Collage, and any show we did together was always an event.

Steve Cheatham recently reminded me of a gig the Banana played at the Marietta National Guard Armory in 1968 with our friends, The Coconut Confetti. During our set, Frank Hughes went into the audience with a fog machine and was grabbed by one of Cobb County's finest because they thought he was spraying LSD into the crowd.

Drug education was still many years away, when they finally referred to it as a war against drugs and bumper stickers featured slogans like "Just say no." Commercials ran on TV showing an egg being fried as a symbol of a brain on drugs. While I'm sure many were confused, I suspect this was a brilliant marketing strategy created by the poultry industry.

Drugs were our new Vietnam, and this battle demonstrated brilliant campaigns such as D.A.R.E. (Drug Abuse Resistance Education). I believe what may have been a little more practical would have been a stuffed wallet with the money being removed as the voiceover said, "This is your wallet, this is your wallet on drugs." Or change the acronym of D.A.R.E. to "Drugs Are Really Expensive." And who could forget the cartoon McGruff the Crime Dog who barked out orders not to do drugs. All these methods proved to be effective in eradicating all the drug problems. They made America completely drug-free and more focused on eating healthy and exercising . . . said no one.

The highways were starting to be littered with billboards sporting a picture of a guy with long hair and the caption "Beautify America . . . Get a Haircut." A national campaign courtesy of John Donnelly & Sons, it was an advertising agency pushback against long hair, which many thought of as a symbol of opposition to the War in Vietnam and resistance to traditional authority, and a symbol of support for drug use and premarital sex. Yes, the Times They Are A-Changin', but it wasn't going down easily for some. It wasn't rare for some asshole to roll down his window and scream, "Get a haircut!" which occasionally served as a warning shot that shit was about to hit the fan. Even though Midtown Atlanta felt a world away from Forest Park, some of the same authority dynamics were still in play, like that day in September 1968 at a headshop called The Middle Earth on 8th Street, when a photographer approached me for permission to be photographed with a 21-year-old guy I had never met.

Jesse Dee Sasser III had recently been in DeKalb County traffic court for driving with an expired license tag and inspection sticker. His long hair angered the judge, who gave him the choice of 60 days in jail or getting a haircut. Jesse chose the latter, which prompted the news story and need for a picture. I was unaware of these facts; I was just a guy with long hair who happened to be at a headshop buying incense or records. I was asked to stand beside Jesse with another long-haired guy named Pat, whom I barely knew from DeKalb College, and we smiled while pointing at his new haircut. When the article came out, Pat and I were "friends making fun of the clean-cut look" of our "buddy," whom neither of us had ever met.

The bass player for the Banana, Michael Mote, ran into a similar situation several years later in Clayton County traffic court. The judge asked Mike why he had long hair, and Mike didn't choose his words wisely. His reply of "It's my business" was meant to explain that he was in a band, and the look was part of it, but the judge heard it as "It's none of your business," and figured he was dealing with another smart-ass punk. Maybe I was reading too much into this, but I saw the exchange as another lesson about the bias of the judicial system and authority to anyone who looked or acted differently.

The generation gap became a popular term for the friction between us and the World War II generation. When The Barbarians recorded "Are You a Boy or Are You a Girl?", that echoed what many of us heard from passing cars filled with peckerwoods. Fathers taunted their boys' long hair, beads, and flowers, saying "If you want to be a girl, wear a dress!" But other than an occasional comment from my dad, I didn't get a lot of flack at home. I did see quite a few who felt lost and confused turning to drugs and often became runaways because of the friction from their parents.

Hollywood flooded the market with cheesy movies to capitalize on the "free love" generation. The unrealistic reflection of those times was portrayed in *The Trip, Billy Jack, Wild in the Streets, Joe,* and *Easy Rider.* I enjoyed the *Dragnet* TV shows where Sgt. Joe Friday busts some kid high on LSD who thinks he's riding a cloud. Check out "The LSD Story" episode featuring "Blue Boy." At the end of those shows, we were always treated to a morality lesson with comments from Jack Webb. It was Hollywood being Hollywood and lookin' for the next box office wave to ride.

When I saw *Easy Rider* in the theatre, I was horrified during the scene when Dennis Hopper was blown off his bike. Years later, I saw an interview with Hopper and couldn't help but laugh. He'd recently viewed the movie again while sitting in the back of a theatre and watched the crowd applaud when he was murdered. Yep, "the times they are a-changin'."

I had no interest in drugs, but it was part of the scene. Occasionally, someone who looked like they had been custom-fitted with the standard police-issued pseudo-hippie undercover narc look would approach me to buy pot. I didn't smoke or carry pot. My fear was being set up, with drugs being planted on me. It was a reality many of us saw happen with friends.

One night, the Banana was playing at The Catacombs when the rest of the band noticed our rhythm guitar player, Gary Dockery, was playing a different song. Or maybe he was trying to speak to aliens through his guitar, because he wasn't exactly hitting musical notes. When we took a break, we discovered someone was putting belladonna in some of the drinks. Belladonna is used medicinally for many treatments, from skin and joint pains to hemorrhoids. It also can be poisonous and hallucinogenic, and that night, it was the latter. Gary was pretty sick for several days, and I was never sure if his story was true or if he was a victim of a bad choice, but for me it was the beginning of the crack in the scene.

When the bikers started hanging around, I could feel more tension fueled by the growth of drugs. Huge guys named Bear and Samson were chill, along with another guy called Spider who wasn't as welcoming, so I kept my distance.

One night, I was visiting a friend on 14th Street and ran into Spider. On a bad acid trip and cowering in the corner, he was screaming like a little girl and terrified of a bug on the wall. There was always a lot of darkness around him, as evidenced by a story told by my friend, Tommy Strain, who was playing with The Perpetual Motion. The door deal with The Catacombs had his band splitting the take equally with the club. When Tommy went to get paid, Spider laid out three unequal piles of money and a pistol. One pile of cash was the Catacombs' share, and the other was split between Spider and the band, meaning the band was getting 25 percent, instead of the half they were promised. Spider then looked at Tommy and said, "Do you have a problem with that?" Tommy, being the quick thinker he is and also possessing a fondness for retaining his balls, replied, "No, I don't have a problem." Few remember Spider, but his scariness never left me, although he looked less menacing when he was freaking out on acid.

Streams of gawkers became more prevalent, driving by in cars with license tags from places outside of Atlanta like Forsyth County and Clayton County. College frat boys and addicts came looking to score drugs and "free love" while some drove by to yell at the longhairs standing by the club. Safety started being a concern for anyone who wandered away from the area unaccompanied. Anything could happen.

I had recently graduated from high school and played at The Catacombs on an extended July 4 weekend. Like most 18-year-old boys, my hormones were raging. I met a girl more beautiful than any I'd known, and her voice on the other end of the phone would make me melt when she told me how much she wanted me. She pursued me, and I never understood it. I felt then, as I have most of my life, that most women were out of my league. Even though I was at the starting line waiting for the gun to go off, I still had some reservations. I was living at home and possessed a good bit of guilt when it came to sex. I'd only had sex once, a couple of years earlier, and had waited for God to strike me dead. I wasn't aware of the hold my early Nazarene indoctrination still had on me until that weekend when we stayed at the Penthouse Hotel, and I wasn't emotionally prepared to deal with it sensibly.

Here I was with this beautiful girl/woman, and it was constant sex. After every time, I would get up and take a shower. I must have looked like a lunatic, not to mention how that made her feel . . . like she was dirty. But that wasn't it at all. I was trying to wash my sins away while knowing that nothing but the blood of Jesus could do that. It was the misery of guilt once more, and I needed a portable baptism right away. After that, I wouldn't answer her calls and she finally quit calling, and my emotions went in several directions at once. When I never received the bolt of lighting I expected, I took that as a sign and began following a mantra that became a fixture in my life: "Anything worth doing is worth overdoing." Moderation was a foreign concept at that point.

While The Catacombs started dying out, the scene around it seemed to explode. Free concerts featuring many bands who had played at the club were being held in nearby Piedmont Park, which is like Atlanta's Central Park. A little research from the archives of *The Great Speckled Bird* (Atlanta's underground press from that period) shows that The Hampton Grease Band started playing free music in Piedmont Park around the fall of 1968. Free music there grew as other bands wanted to play for exposure and by the end of the year, bands like The Allman Brothers, Celestial Voluptuous Banana, The Bag, Strange Brew, and Eric Quincy Tate had followed.

I loved the free concerts in the park, where there was always something going on. You could see Chicago, Santana, Mountain, Boz Scaggs, and others for free on a Sunday afternoon after they had played paid gigs in the area. The audience was receptive to every kind of music; it was the first time I remember playing an "original song." We played a mock country song to entertain ourselves. I would riff from the top of my head about a dog that followed me while I plowed the fields. One fateful day, the dog got too close and was chewed up by the combine harvester. We had the entire crowd laughing and singing along to "My Old Hound Dog Ruff . . . He Was Tough Enough." It was truly stupid and fun, and the song people remembered above all others. Maybe that was a seed being planted, but I wasn't aware.

The Banana started performing more in the park after Discovery signed us. Steve Cole was an intense guy who got a lot out of his 24 hours every day. We would attend meetings at his house on the corner of Juniper and Tenth Streets, where he'd map out upcoming bookings and was always on the hunt for new clubs and bands. Steve was responsible for booking our first appearance at the Atlanta Municipal Auditorium. We were on the bill with The Royal Guardsmen, notorious for their franchise "Snoopy vs. The Red Baron" bubblegum songs. The audience was primarily made up of kids and their parents who were confused when the Guardsmen hurried through their popular songs and then played songs by The Yardbirds and Beatles. It wasn't our audience either, but we were well-received.

At that show, we got to hang around with friends like Orville Davis, the bass player for the opening act, The Fifth Order. I watched Orville jump off the stage to play in the audience, and then after jumping like a crippled frog, he realized he couldn't get back up. It looked like a scene straight out of *Spinal Tap* and was very entertaining to us in the back when some of the stagehands brought a chair and helped him get back on stage. Orville was always a masterful musician and showman. I loved his impulsive energy, which often led to more hilarious moments like when he jumped on top of the bar at Funochios and tried to run the 40 feet with a 25-foot guitar chord.

The auditorium gig was advertised as featuring the "Stars of the Teen Age Fair," which we had performed a month or so before, from August 2 to 11, 1968. Held at the new Atlanta Civic Center, the Teen Age Fair was billed as ten days of music by a plethora of local and national acts, and the Banana appeared with Chet Atkins, Lesley Gore, Soupy Sales, Billy Joe Royal, a teen beauty pageant, light shows, a battle of the bands, car shows, turtle races, dating games, karaoke, and other things oblivious to me. I was in a fog that entire gig. While most of the groups shared their night with other acts, on August 7, The Banana had our own "Flower Power Day." After the first set, I crawled behind my drums and closed my eyes. Even though I had been drinking roughly a case of Cokes a day, I could barely stay awake and had zero strength. I was told later that I was playing every song about half speed.

We were still playing The Catacombs a good bit, and I believe that's where I contracted mononucleosis, also known as "the kissing disease," which, in my case, was probably spot on. My illness sidelined the Banana for almost two months, and dates were canceled. Playing drums or going outside wouldn't be on my to-do list for a while. I lost about 30 pounds and learned later that my mom was crying and worried I might not make it. I literally could not stand up for more than a few minutes. The doctor asked me if I was taking amphetamines because my body was so run down. When I told him about my Coca-Cola addiction, he flatly told me that I had to stop. Between the caffeine abuse and mono, he promised that my body was going to give out. I did slow down, but it would be a couple of years before I got a handle on junk food and caffeine. I became a vegetarian and have remained one for over 50 years.

By the end of 1968, the entire Catacombs experience was dead. Years after I'd moved on to working with other groups, including The Hahavishnu Orchestra, I was contacted to film a scene in the old Catacombs location. *Summer of Love* featured local actors attempting to replicate the look and feel of that time. Incredibly, the room looked much the same as it had ten years earlier. I don't think the film was ever finished, but if so, I hope it was released as a comedy. The roughs I saw were out of sync, like a 1950s Japanese monster movie, including the song we performed. Since we were lip-syncing without music being played, being out of sync was pretty understandable. Later in the studio, I recorded "I'm Gettin' Burned Out" for the film. We performed that song in The Hahavishnu Orchestra with the dancers wearing DayGlo paint under fluorescent lights to mimic the hippie scene.

Most of the movies and documentaries of those times now have a difficult time not coming off as satire, and young people now associate classic songs from that era with stuff to buy. Fifty years later, I go back to this time whenever I hear "Born to Be Wild," "Be My Baby," or "I Can't Get No Satisfaction," even when they're used in commercials for beer, toilet paper, and erectile dysfunction products. Every generation tends to claim the music of their youth as the best, but we can definitely make a strong case for ours. The Beatles are the gold standard for well-crafted songs that will outlive us all. The syrupy songs about teenage heartbreak and having the fastest cars around were ushered out by Street Fighting Men Who Won't Get Fooled Again. Without The Byrds there'd be no Tom Petty. Without Merle Haggard there'd be no Jason Isbell, without Donny Hathaway we wouldn't know John Legend, and without Joni Mitchell there'd be no one.

Redneck Satan

I split the scene when I was 13, I got jammed up by the Good Book
They tried to beat Jesus into me, but them whoopins' never took
I was never scared to take a dare, and fearless I was told
Till late one night under a moonlit light, on a backwoods country road

I was doing 'bout ninety and started redlining, but never gave a damn
I'd cheated death a couple of times, did two tours in Vietnam
I've had my fill of whiskey and pills, but now my heart was racin'
When I heard a voice whisper in my ear, "I'm the redneck Satan"

Some walk the wire of brimstone and fire, to find the god they've forsaken
And I've been told some lose their souls, in a hell of their own makin'
But when I felt his breath on my neck, my hands started shakin'
In all my years I never felt the fear, like I felt with redneck Satan

He said I was in the back of that Cadillac, when Hank took his last ride
Many sold their soul on music row, and there were plenty more who tried
Some seek me out to make a deal, when they find themselves in trouble
There's no shortage of desperate souls, prayin' to Beelzebubba

Now I've seen many things, that I can't explain
When hunger lit the fire, and temptation fanned the flames
But the truth I've learned, when I've been burned
I've only myself to blame
Cause Satan laughs at fools and liars
Who do evil in his name

REDNECK SATAN ©2023 DARRYL RHOADES (SPOKEN WORD)

CHAPTER SEVEN

The Trouble with Guys Like Me

Well I keep on movin' with nowhere to go, I can't seem to settle down
I gotta hunger that I can't escape, it follows me around
No matter where I am right now there's somewhere else I should be
And I don't know what I'm lookin' for
And that's the trouble with guys like me

THE TROUBLE WITH GUYS LIKE ME ©2017 DARRYL RHOADES

When a group disbands, it's similar to your first breakup in any relationship. The Banana was my first band and they were responsible for giving me direction when I had none, and now we were calling it quits. I felt aimless, with all my energy and identity seemingly tied to that group. The band and playing music were my passions; now, I had no plans. I wasn't good with time on my hands. I was always amped up naturally and it wasn't uncommon for me to go without sleep for several days at a time. I would often drive down to the old Rex Mill by the waterfalls of Big Cotton Indian Creek, in the early morning hours to be alone with my thoughts.

If "idle hands are the devil's workshop," I was gonna have to take on a staff to handle all the heavy lifting. I had a fire lookin' for something to burn, and had to be doing something every minute. My struggle with boredom, resulting in questionable choices, had already taken root.

Even though there were offers from other groups, I wasn't interested in endless basement rehearsals. I needed to be busy as a touring musician. I picked up a few temporary gigs before getting a call from my friends in Wingfield. They were touring and needed a drummer, and quickly.

In 1972, I joined Wingfield, who were first working as a house band in a South Georgia nightclub. After a few weeks, we showed up to rehearse and were told we had the night off. The club had a last-minute opportunity to bring in Wayne Cochran and the C.C. Riders, a large show band with a massive setup and following.

Wayne was a native of Thomaston, Georgia, and considered by many as "the white James Brown," whom he befriended as labelmates on King Records. Cochran wore a badass pompadour that looked like a fantastic hood ornament for a 1956 Bel Air, and had some of the same great moves with backup singers. They were one hell of a band, with stage threads like James Brown and his band, The Famous Flames.

I had a conversation with their bass player after their sound check and didn't realize till years later that I had been talking with the man many think of as one of the greatest electric bass players of all time. Jaco Pastorius went on to play with jazz royalty like Miles Davis, Weather Report, and many others. In 1987 Jaco was beaten to death outside a bar in Miami by one of the bouncers who served a total of four months in prison for manslaughter.

Wayne was a music veteran who played bass on Otis Redding's hit, "Shout Bamalama." He also wrote the hit "Last Kiss,' which landed at No. 2 on the *Billboard* Top 100 for J. Frank Wilson and the Cavaliers in 1964 and resurfaced as a hit for Pearl Jam in 1999. Wayne was a great showman and would dance on the bar and pour liquor into the glasses of everyone sitting there. I was spellbound, watching how he had everyone's full attention. I was being schooled and those lessons served me well years later.

A few months after leaving Wingfield, I took a house band job in Johnson City, Tennessee, at the Starlight Club. The club was a honky-tonk bar like the ones I'd played many times, but playing in a house band meant being there for a month.

The club housed the band in a trailer owned by the parents of one of the club's servers, located in a cow pasture miles away. Even though it was not the most comfortable situation, I look back with fondness, except for the fact that the band had to bathe and wash their clothes in the creek as if they were in a third-world country.

My fondness doesn't include an experience with a guy named Eddie who was a semi-pro boxer and seemed to be pretty sane. He hung out at the Starlight every night because his girlfriend was the server who would come to the trailer to make sure we had clean sheets and towels.

One day, the band was sitting by a fire roasting hot dogs (weenies if you're lookin' for a cheap laugh) when Eddie drove up with his girl-friend. As he jumped out of the car, she was crying and begging, and we couldn't figure out what was going on. When Eddie gathered us all together and started yelling, "Who fucked my whore? Who fucked my whore?" . . . It was weird. We were startled, so Johnny Stanley, the guitarist and leader of the group, said, "Eddie, nobody is messing with her." Eddie replied, "You're the first one to speak, so you must have fucked her." I'm sure that was considered sound logic down in the holler or up the crick, but I found it tough to follow. Eddie threw a right hook with a left undercut before Johnny hit the ground. To Johnny's credit and wisdom, he maintained that position as if waiting for someone to count him out. The rest of us stood in disbelief, which didn't include coming to Johnny's defense. Eddie continued ranting about "his whore" and how she was, "the king of lars." Eddie spoke in his native tongue, "hillbonics," but most of us would pronounce the word "liars." Yep, the rest of the night was filled with "if he had done one more thing, I was gonna . . . yeah, me too." Sitting around talking about what we should have done or was going to do reminded me of the joke about the cop who pulled the driver over for speeding, gave him a ticket, and then reached over and smacked the passenger. When the passenger asked, "Why did you slap me?' the cop said, "For you saying what you would have said to me after I drove away.'

The club owner, Gary, told us later that Eddie was a hothead some-times, which might have been a good piece of info to have in the first place. However, it wouldn't have prevented the "who fucked my whore" incident because crazy things usually happen without warning. A couple of days later, Eddie apologized to Johnny, who laughed and complimented Eddie's right hook.

The band had hired my replacement but wanted me to work with him and do some fronting on a few songs. I'd sing the 1950s hit "Blue Moon" while wearing a black leather jacket and twirling a knife. However, I decided to give up the knife twirling after Gary mentioned that some audience members may see that as a challenge to call me out and fight me.

The Johnson City/Kingsport/Bristol triangle was a mystical place that over the years gave birth to several experiences that became fodder for many performances.

I worked some gigs up that way as a fill-in drummer with the Atlanta band Shayde. Every night was filled with musical and social challenges with some of the locals. I wasn't a wild ass on the road, but very capable of making all kinds of bad choices with too much time on my hands.

When the rest of the band pooled their money and challenged me to go to a massage parlor suspected of being a cover for sex activity, I figured it beat the Waffle House. I'd never done anything like that, but the band funded it, so what did I have to lose? We ended up at the Mod Massage Parlor located at Knob Creek (actual name of massage trailer and location). The band waited in the lobby while I lay on a table, staring at the walls and questioning my choices. It was far from being a religious experience, but there was a "laying on of hands" by a novice who put powder on my body and then lotion. She offered "manual relief," and I said yes without grasping what that meant. She sped up the rubbing, and the combination of oil and powder got thicker. I'd never had sex with cake batter before, but feel confident self-rising flour wasn't part of the recipe. I don't know what kept me from laughing when the dam finally broke, but she stood stoic with Betty Crocker-like technique and facial expressions. Upon the conclusion of this activity, I dressed and met the boys in the lobby, who were hungering for details to satisfy their financial investment. All had a good time apparently because all good things do start from scratch.

In September 1973, I road tripped with my high school friends, George Meyers and Jim Bennett, to catch a Frank Zappa concert in Athens, Georgia. His first LP, *Freak Out*, was a game-changer for me, and I got so hooked that my mom often warned that my "brain would rot if I kept it listening to that weird stuff."

With very few places open after the show, we decided to stop at a crowded Waffle House for some fine dining. About the time a table was cleared, we sat down and then noticed Zappa's entourage enter. Some of the band crowded into the booth next to us, but Zappa and his bodyguard, John Smothers, stood waiting. We invited them to join us, so they squeezed in.

Smothers looked like a guy equipped to do his job and not someone to be messed with. He had traveled with Zappa since the incident at the Rainbow Theatre in London in December 1971. A concertgoer snuck backstage and ran up behind Zappa, pushing him off the 10-foot-high stage into a concrete orchestra pit. The guy was deranged and jealous because his girlfriend had commented on how much she loved Zappa. Zappa ended up with a broken rib, fractured leg, and six weeks in the hospital. He was wheelchair-bound for almost a year, leaving the band unable to work.

Even though two years had passed, I could still feel the anger in Zappa's voice. He pointed out how lax the security was, and claimed that his vocalists Flo and Eddie (Howard Kaylan and Mark Volman) stole his band. To shift the conversation, I commented about how great his Athens concert was and how tight his band had played.

Zappa asked if we could give him and Smothers a ride back to the hotel since the rest of the band was still eating. We obliged, with the five people in the backseat including me sitting on Zappa's lap. When we dropped them off, Frank asked if we'd like to be his guests for the following night's concert in Macon, and took our names.

We showed up the next afternoon in time to see the band doing a sound check, rehearsal, and then a few songs to audition the singer Keith, the one-name vocalist eventually known for "98 6." Keith had a great voice, but Zappa was looking for a blues singer, so that day he passed on hiring him.

The show in Macon was just as incredible as the one in Athens. After the concert, I talked to a few players to pick up any information possible. That night, I learned a lesson that has stayed with me throughout my career. When I complimented the keyboardist, George Duke, on how great I thought they sounded, he responded, "I thought we sucked." When I responded, "Okay, you sucked," George looked as if he could have taken my head off.

Maybe I read too much into his comment, but he was pissing on my compliment and I couldn't let it go. I made it a habit of responding to every compliment with appreciation, even if I didn't share the opinion. Thank them instead of insinuating that their opinion is uninformed and without merit.

Early in 1974, Vincent Bugliosi made an appearance on the *Phil Donahue Show* to promote his book, *Helter Skelter*, about the Manson murders. The show was being taped in Atlanta, and friends with an extra ticket invited me along. It was a subject I found interesting enough to make my way into an audience of middle-aged women, at a time when I had a heavy beard and waist-long hair. When the episode aired, friends and relatives from all over the country told me the camera kept panning to me each time some of the hideous murder details were mentioned. I was supposedly representing a side I was unaware of being on, a symbol for what Bugliosi and others were supposedly fighting.

When Phil took questions from the audience, I asked why Manson received the harshest sentence when he hadn't committed any of the murders. Bugliosi answered by comparing Manson with Hitler, that he was the guy who called the shots. But it wasn't the answer that caught my attention; it was his tone. Bugliosi seized my question as the opportunity to work the room and portray me, because of my appearance, as if I were part of the cult.

Around this time, I was playing with a short-lived band called Little Artie and The Green Men when I met keyboardist Michael Barnes. Michael was assembling a four-piece interracial funk group, and I suspected he was down to the Rs in his book of contacts when he offered me the gig. The band was comprised of two white and two black guys, and it always got a laugh when he introduced the band as Oreo. Funk wasn't my forte, but I figured I could use the experience, and the other players were excellent.

We landed a house gig at Scarlett O'Hara's, the most upscale night-club in Underground Atlanta. Scarlett O'Hara's featured popular R&B acts who still had a draw, like Archie Bell and The Drells, The Tams, Little Anthony and The Imperials, Drifters, Platters, and others. While these acts usually had their own backing bands, there were occasions when some of the house band members would be asked to play with them. I was asked to sit in with Bill Pinkney and the Original Drifters the day that their drummer had been thrown in jail for a DUI.

Before Underground Atlanta became unsafe and full of party drunks like those I'd seen in a thousand frat houses, it had a draw for jazz fans and performers like Cannonball Adderley at The Mineshaft or Paul Mitchell in the downstairs room at Dante's Down the Hatch.

Underground Atlanta also had its share of tourist shops, such as the one owned by the former Georgia Governor Lester Maddox. For a time, he did brisk business hawking his albums, clocks that ran backward, and autographed ax handles he nicknamed "Pickrick Toothpicks." The ax handles had gained notoriety when he used them to run black people out of his Pickrick Restaurant in April 1964. In July that year, the day after President Lyndon Johnson signed the Civil Rights Act of 1964, three African American students tried to enter the Pickrick and test the new law, and Maddox escorted them off his property, pistol in hand.

Years later, after he'd walked off the *Dick Cavett Show*, Maddox accumulated massive debt, lost his once profitable restaurant, and became the poster boy sung about by Randy Newman in "Rednecks." Maddox also put together the act "The Governor and the Dishwasher" with an African American, Bobby Lee Fears, whom he had once hired to bus tables and wash dishes at the Pickrick. I think Lester was way ahead of his time—if his time was 1861 to 1865.

At Scarlett O'Hara's, we performed from Wednesday to Saturday, and I made the best of my opportunities to take in as much music as possible, while playing out of my league with more experienced musicians. I enjoyed working with Mike Barnes, Kenny Walker, and Mike Spivey, but I never felt the click I'd felt while playing with most bands. While they were hangin' out together and smokin' pot between breaks, I'd pass the time by sitting in with other bands.

"Smoke on The Water" bellowed out of The Pumphouse, Front Page, Sgt. Pepper's, and every other Underground Atlanta club featuring cover bands. You could stand within earshot of four or five clubs and hear that song simultaneously played by multiple bands.

There were more pleasant distractions, such as standing outside Muhlenbrink's and watching Piano Red, the albino African American, perform in the front window. Piano Red, aka William Lee Perryman, had a long history of playing with blues legend Blind Willie McTell, back to the 1930s. Piano Red later performed as Dr. Feelgood and The Interns, who had a hit "Right String But the Wrong Yo-Yo." Other artists like The Beatles covered his recordings, like the 1962 original version of "Mr. Moonlight" covered on their 1964 LP *Beatles For Sale*. All the heavy hitters, including the Rolling Stones and Dave Clark Five, would stop in to see Piano Red when they were in town. The Brits always seemed more appreciative of American blues and early rock. Artists barely scraping by in the U.S. were pioneering heroes in England.

Scarlett O'Hara's owners, Marvin and Judi Adelman, ran a tight business, packing in audiences dressed to the nines as if they were goin' to church, and in some ways, it often felt like church. Women wearing their Sunday go-to-meeting hats and men in their finest suits would often testify after a few "Flaming Hurricanes," the signature drink.

Marvin always reminded me of the guy in *Monopoly* on the Get Out of Jail Free card, and Judi had big hair that some compared years later to Peg Bundy on *Married with Children*. Marvin and Judi always treated me with respect, and I went out of my way to stay out of the way, a lesson I learned early as a musician. Bartenders make the drinks and servers don't need to have musicians standing in their way while they do their job.

After we finished our opening set, I usually sat in the back and caught the headliner's show. I'd watch Fats Domino finish his set by playing "I'm Walkin'" and bouncing the piano off his stomach as he marched across the stage. I'd watch Cortez Greer work the audience with jokes, like when his pianist played "God Bless America" in the background as Cortez started his monologue: "We live in the greatest country in the world, and we need to learn to live together because to play 'God Bless America' on the piano, it takes the white keys and the darkies." That old joke I'd heard on a Lenny Bruce album years before never failed to bring the house down. Cortez was one of the greatest entertainers I ever saw, and night after night I got to see him doing the same show, every time making it feel like the first time.

I remember Sonny Turner's incredible voice, but I always felt some tension around him. Sonny had replaced the Platters' original lead singer, Tony Williams, and built a large following when he went on his own as Sonny Turner and Sound Unlimited. I was told he was a badass with little patience, but he had a great band including sax player Jay Scott and a drummer I befriended.

On one occasion, Jay approached Sonny and asked for a raise. Even though Jay was a big guy, Sonny picked him up off his feet by his collar and replied, "Is this high enough for ya, motherfucker?" I think that was the extent of Jay's raise. Jay did end up leaving Sonny and worked behind famous acts in Vegas before moving to Atlanta. He got hired by notable producers like Tom Dowd and played on many recordings by artists such as Lynyrd Skynyrd, Alicia Bridges, and Kansas.

Whenever the main act wasn't traveling with their tech crew, the duties of spotlight operator were covered by one Oreo member. I didn't mind, but occasionally, my mind would wander. That's the only way I can explain the night I was spotlighting Chuck Jackson.

I loved Chuck's work with songs like "Any Day Now" and "I Don't Want to Cry." He was great on stage, and during his set, he would always have a song where the music got low, the lights went dim, and he got sexy. The ladies would eat it up. That night as Chuck started getting sexy, I had the spotlight on him as usual, but for some reason I got the bright idea to narrow the focus of the spotlight so slowly that Chuck wouldn't notice it happening. It was the same way with a frog in cold water that doesn't feel you slowly heating it until it's too late.

So, Chuck is talking, the band is playing, the ladies are smiling, and the spotlight is getting smaller . . . and smaller . . . and smaller . . . until it looks like a penlight on Chuck's crotch. Suddenly, Chuck yelled, "Mr. Lightman! Mr. Lightman!" and I quickly broadened the spotlight as wide as it would go. Chuck finished his set and then made a beeline to the light booth that he found unoccupied as I meanwhile watched from behind my drums, preparing for a set with the house band.

Two weeks later, I experienced my first firing as a musician. I'm unsure if the timing was a coincidence or if it was the realization that I wasn't the perfect fit for Oreo. I didn't take it personally and had no problem immediately finding another gig. My time at Scarlett's served many purposes by broadening my drumming skills and receiving a first-rate education about entertainment versus just being a guy who sat behind a set of drums. Or when necessary, hid behind them.

CHAPTER EIGHT

Between Forgotten & Unknown

Just because you said the war was over
Doesn't stop the battles that keep raging on
You gave it a name, and that's where you laid the blame
You brought them back, but they never made it home

BETWEEN FORGOTTEN & UNKNOWN ©2017 DARRYL RHOADES

Upon graduation from high school in 1968, my only plan was to play drums and avoid a government-mandated Asian tour. Between the assassinations of Dr. Martin Luther King Jr. and Robert Kennedy, and the constant clashes between supporters and protesters of the Vietnam War, I was plagued with a feeling of uncertainty about the world and my place in it.

Two years earlier, I was one of the 10,000 people who attended an event called "Affirmation Vietnam" held at the Atlanta-Fulton County Stadium, where the Braves would be playing their first season a few months later. I wasn't pro or con or affirming anything, especially war. I was a 15-year-old kid who came to hear U.S. Army Sgt. Barry Sadler perform his big hit, "The Ballad of the Green Berets." I had accepted the offer from my big brother and his wife to tag along, and I wasn't going to turn down an opportunity to see a real live hero singing a big hit song.

The opening act was a bunch of local and national politicians talking about how "we gotta stop 'em there before they come here" as they worked the crowd into a dull thud. I patiently waited while being treated to the dulcet tones of the well-known former beauty queen "conservative activist" representative for the orange juice industry, Anita Bryant. Finally, it was star time, the man we came to hear . . . Sgt. Barry Sadler sing his hit song responsible for stirring up patriotic sentiment which led many to volunteer for military service. He didn't disappoint while giving a speech that likely ended up on bumper stickers of cars across this great nation for years to come.

One of my best friends enlisted in the Marines with a mutual friend and was eventually kicked out because he couldn't be disciplined and was always getting into fights. I found this comical: a guy getting drummed out of the Marines because he kept getting into fights. It seemed reminiscent of the scene in Dr. Strangelove, where several were reprimanded for fighting in the war room. My friend was undisciplined, so he likely wasn't a good investment of tax dollars. He was drummed out of the military, while our friend who enlisted with him was killed in Vietnam.

I didn't have to look elsewhere to understand the meaning of "collateral damage." I was losing close friends in the war and over philosophical differences about the war. I was not welcome in the homes of a few relatives and friends who associated my look with being anti-war. The heartbreak of losing a son in Vietnam was made more painful by seeing someone like me, while they unsuccessfully grappled for anything resembling reason. Those feeling unimaginable grief said some pretty harsh things, and while the words might have been hurtful, it would have been petty to hang onto my anger. I didn't attend any more rallies after the "Affirmation Vietnam" rally and I changed my tune from "The Battle of the Green Berets" to "War (What Is It Good For)."

Some couldn't wait to enlist in the military, while others did everything possible to avoid the induction. The draft lottery was an interesting piece of history when you think about it. Young men's lives rested on the fate or luck of the number assigned to them depending on their birthdate; in other words, this was the *Hunger Games* over 50 years before its time. A higher number gave you a better chance of not being drafted. I drew lottery number 85, signaling it was time to file for my 2S college student deferment.

I also knew quite a few students, young men my age, who flunked out. They found themselves in the barber's chair and shipped out shortly after that. Every county had a quota for inductees, and the process of taking the physical exams wasn't unlike herding cattle. Around 5 a.m., we were loaded up on the bus in Jonesboro and driven to the old Sears building on Ponce de Leon Avenue in Atlanta, which had been converted into an induction center. We filled out a lot of paperwork and then promptly undressed and were poked, prodded, and told to turn our heads and cough.

There are many stories about the extent some went through to avoid being drafted. Some took amphetamines for days before going in for their exams, all wired, and came off as being psychotic. The "don't ask/don't tell" policy was years away, so being gay was an automatic disqualification that had some confessing their love and desire for other men. I'd even heard of some guys intentionally getting busted for selling pot, getting strung out on heroin, or shooting themselves in the foot, all of which would give them the highly sought-after 4F status. I knew several who filed as conscientious objectors, but that didn't keep them out of the military; it just supposedly kept them from carrying a gun.

It's estimated that between 30,000 and 40,000 U.S. citizens deserted to Canada to avoid the draft. One of my favorite songwriters and recording artists, Jesse Winchester, moved to Canada and built a promising career before finally returning to the U.S. when President Carter pardoned him in 1977.

Almost 50 years after the last helicopter left Saigon, I'm still losing friends from the poisons used in the jungles of Vietnam. For years, the seriousness of their claims was denied. I had friends who returned but couldn't adjust and became the "one in twenty veterans" who commit suicide daily. The government brought 'em back, but they never made it home. There's a wall in D.C. with over 58,000 names of soldiers we lost in a war that most didn't understand.

Those years influenced my development as a performer in many ways. Anita Bryant would loom large in my shows in the 1970s with the Hahavishnu Orchestra as we lampooned her Bible-based stance against gays. I was going for the laughs, but anger and resentment always bubbled under the surface. I had a giant picture of Anita with a perforated mouth during our earliest shows at The Bistro in Atlanta. During the show, I would shove cucumbers, zucchini squash, bananas, or whatever cylindrical food item was at my disposal, through her mouth from the backside while the band played "God Bless America." Satire was a passion made more exciting with targets like her. People who proclaim their faith while holding a flag and attacking the rights of others are begging to be mocked, and it has become a lifelong passion of mine to accommodate them.

Not all satire from those years was well received. The Uptown Cafe was a late-night venue on Peachtree Road across from Peaches Records and Tapes store in the trendy Buckhead neighborhood. Open till 4 or 5 a.m., the club attracted local musicians, bartenders, and often big-name acts after they performed a concert in Atlanta.

One night, the club was packed as we went into our version of "I Left My Heart in San Francisco":

> I *left my legs in South Cambodia*
> *I left my arms in Cam Ranh Bay*
> *And when I crossed the DMZ*
> *I lost the biggest part of me*
> *My mind was stolen by the CIA*

We had fans in the audience who would hang with us no matter how far out we went; however, the four Marines sitting in the room were not among them. They were overheard making plans to rearrange my body parts, and to this day, I don't know exactly how they were persuaded to abandon their project, but Sue Schell, one of our dancers, suggested that it was a bad idea, and I'm glad they agreed. Also in attendance was a local news personality who made his objection noted when he vacated his table in disgust, and made sure to draw attention to his departure to everyone seated around him. I assumed there would always be some who could be offended by what I do, but pulling back wasn't an option. I wasn't a fan of this guy anyway, so when people like him became pissed and felt the need to draw out their performance while leaving, I leaned into mine even more.

Pissing off people wasn't the goal, but I came to understand this as a natural consequence of the material I chose to perform. Some people are easily offended and even angered to the point of violence. It was that way in the 1970s, and it remains the same now. Some will scream "free speech" while attempting to silence yours. There are names for people like that, but the one that comes to mind is "target."

My approach was always balls to the wall with almost no limits. Satire requires teeth, and if you're holding back, you've compromised the art of the performance. An ass beating by those Marines may not have been out of line, although it would have likely resulted in me pushing back even more. Pissing off people was never the goal, but one of the most satisfying fringe benefits.

CHAPTER NINE

Diamonds in the Rough

Well they wrote about me in Rolling Stone
They said I couldn't miss but I proved 'em wrong
Well it just goes to show you, you can make your plans
But the bottom line it's out of your hands
Some said I couldn't make and I never will
Didn't listen to them then and I ain't listening still

BIOGRAPHY ©2003 DARRYL RHOADES

In 1972, I played drums with Dear John, a group that included my friends Jimmy Royals, Al Storey, Mike Smith, and Pat Robertson. Those guys' collective sense of humor and my typical smart-ass compulsion to be entertained showed up at a strip club in Macon.

The band played songs by Uriah Heep, Yes, and other groups you wouldn't expect to hear at a strip club. The club owner didn't expect or want to hear those songs either. When we played the instrumental, "Night Train," the dancers would shake their breasts to the beat, so I started speeding up the tempo of the song, which made them complain to the owner about how their tits hurt.

After the first night, the owner said he would give us one more opportunity to salvage the gig, and we had that night to learn some new songs.

We returned to our hotel room, worked up six new songs, and after the second night, were promptly fired with time off for bad behavior. At this time, I'd like to be on the record as apologizing to all the dancers for the pain that I may have unintentionally inflicted on their breasts.

I picked up a road gig working in a house band for a few weeks with several guys I didn't know in Bumfuck, Indiana. After several days, I started bouncing off the walls in my head. On a day off, I decided to walk to a bowling alley with the guitarist, Lewis Varnedoe IV, and on our way back to the condo, I found a dead snake in the ditch. The snake was still pliable, so I decided it would be a good idea to place it between the sheet and mattress of another band member. Very early in the morning, we heard a shrieking sound coming from his bedroom and were informed he had found a dead snake in his bed, which he surmised must have been killed when he rolled over in his sleep. Yeah, let's go with that. I love imagining that he thought that for years until he read this story. Seems the clock was always tickin' with a countdown for how long it would be before I would succumb to boredom and create mischief and mayhem that entertained some in the band if they didn't wake up with a dead snake under their sheets.

Occasionally, I would play upscale country clubs where the band was not allowed to eat with the patrons, and I always felt like I was one step away from being called "boy." The more I saw of that part of society, the less I cared about anyone else's opinion.

For a time, I worked with a lounge act and was required to wear a wig by the bandleader, who felt my long hair would present a problem. So, I wore a wig and formal wear, and since the band got to eat for free at the buffet, I would fill my pockets with dinner rolls to eat while playing that night. "I remember looking back and seeing Darryl playing his snare and cymbals with one hand," said our pianist Jimmy Royals, "while the other one was busy grabbing dinner rolls from his jacket pocket and stuffing them into his mouth, looking like a chipmunk."

Being booked into lounges for extended periods meant getting a weekly paycheck and having to learn how to play with brushes and more stick control instead of bashing. I took the opportunity to interact with audiences whenever possible by playing drum solos on tables, plates, and sometimes the audience members themselves. In my attempts to keep from being bored, I was encouraged each time I felt the audience was being snapped out of a coma. This technique was also helpful in keeping me awake while playing, "Bad Bad Leroy Brown, baddest man in the whole damn town." My understanding was that Leroy Brown was badder than a junkyard dog.

My need to escape boredom soon led me to songwriting, and I became obsessed. I would write during the breaks at the clubs, and even when I was performing on drums, sometimes my mind searched for lyrics to whatever song I was writing. I felt alive with a purpose that led me to get together with friends and record. I found it constructive and therapeutic, and the energy and freedom to write about whatever crossed my mind eventually evolved into my stage performances.

My early songwriting was a mixture of rock, country, and a new influence I experienced while playing in the lounges. I started thinking melodically along the lines of artists like The Mills Brothers; Lambert, Hendricks & Ross; and others from the 1940s and 1950s. During the lounge years, I wrote my first song to receive radio airplay, "My Leprosy Queen." Modeled after one of those corny songs in a Dick Powell movie, "Leprosy Queen" was about a guy who fell in love with a woman who kept coming apart.

When we're walkin' through the park
I know she can do me no harm
I take my leprosy queen by the hand
But it comes off at her arm

MY LEPROSY QUEEN ©1974 DARRYL RHOADES

For a time, my fear of being typecast as a schmaltzy balladeer would be alleviated, and the immediate response from the humorous songs was all the encouragement I needed to keep doing what I was doing. The earliest recordings of songs like "My Leprosy Queen," "I'm In With the Zen Crowd," and the new dance craze, "Suicide," took place wherever equipment and people could be assembled. Years later, I would get a better handle on discipline, but at this point, I felt a joy in music that I'd been lacking. I began to sit in with other bands and try new ideas, fronting the groups instead of sitting behind a drum kit.

Around 1974, I went on stage with a giant stuffed rabbit at a club called Hot 'Lanta and sat in with friends in the band Looney Tunes. I placed a mic stand and a can of shaving cream between the rabbit's legs and shook the can until its contents launched all over the audience. I felt uncontrollable energy when I saw the crowd go wild and the band laughing so hard they could barely get through the song. I played a kazoo when the band went into "Purple Haze" and then burned it at the end of the song, a la Jimi Hendrix. After that set, the band across the room, Road Turkey, came over, laughing at what they'd just witnessed. It was a moment I relived years later when their drummer, Stan Lynch, attended one of my standup shows in St. Augustine, Florida, after he'd left Tom Petty's Heartbreakers.

I had never seen an audience respond so enthusiastically, and knew I'd stumbled onto something that felt like home. I began to sit in with local bands like Cary Nation at Alex Cooley's Electric Ballroom and perform over-the-top stage antics. These appearances became transformative for me as I realized they were about more than entertaining myself. I was so encouraged that I started envisioning a live show. It would be another year before I assembled The Hahavishnu Orchestra, which was less of a plan than a destiny of characters coming together by happenstance.

In the latter part of 1974, I recorded "My Leprosy Queen" and other songs on a cheesy two-track recorder in my drum room with my high school friend David Michaels. WIIN, an AM radio station featuring radically new programming appealing to my taste, inspired me. When I recorded "My Leprosy Queen," I got the idea to take it to the station because an early morning DJ, Ross Brittain, had a reputation for playing off-the-wall songs. I timidly called, asked to speak with him, and was told to send a tape for review. I dropped off the tape at the reception desk the next day and figured that would likely be the end of it, but the following day, I got a call that my song would be played on-air around 6 a.m. I went through my phone book and called everyone I'd ever known without actually understanding most musicians never see 6 a.m. unless they're up all night.

Apparently, many people were up early driving to work, hearing this poorly recorded song, and were amused. I was told a few callers commented that their parents hated the song, so the callers requested it to be played several more times that day and for many days following it.

I started dropping tapes off anywhere to anyone who might consider playing them. A fire was lit, and I continued to write songs for radio play. Next up was "Suicide," a parody of classic R&B dance songs, but the horn parts were played with kazoos.

> *Well I gotta new dance some people have tried*
> *The ones that can do it have already died*
> *The name of the dance is suicide (hit me band)*
> *Now hold out your hand and ball up your fist*
> *Bring the razor right down on your wrist*
> *Yeah slip the rope on over your head*
> *Get into it till your face turns red*
> *Yeah slip in on your neck and put your head right through it*
> *Hang on in there I know you can do it*
> *Good gawd*

SUICIDE ©1975 DARRYL RHOADES

The morning that "Suicide" was first played on the radio, the response was over the top, and I was invited to appear live on the show. I took advantage of every opportunity to be on whenever possible. Those appearances on the 6-10 a.m. morning show with Ross Brittain sharpened my radio skills, and introduced me to Rex Patton, Glen Howard, Marianne Pace, and others who did characters on the show. It was unlike anything else I'd heard before.

Rex was working at a gas station at that time but found his niche on the radio with characters such as the effeminate Charles Chastain, who regularly spit out double entendres, Carlton Quaalude the III, and the all-American redneck Roy Dean Epps. Glen Howard, who was employed as a federal law clerk in real life and looked like the guy who probably does your taxes, doubled as Dr. Damon Hokey and Grandpa Timothy. Marianne Pace always slayed me with her alter ego, Marilou Sou Sou, who was young and too hip for the room.

Ross played everything I brought in and even wrote a cover letter for me to send songs to the nationally syndicated "Dr. Demento Show," which was also carried on WIIN. I was always hopeful but never expected anything to come from any tape I sent out, but the good Doctor finally got back to me and let me know he would be playing my songs. Excited and encouraged, I began sending crudely recorded songs to agents and record companies and racked up over a dozen rejection letters, some being funny while others were weak attempts at humor. I framed them for my wall of negative reinforcement. I would not be dissuaded.

Without even thinking about it, I was building my fan base at WIIN, with a family with loyal listeners who would often stop by the station. Several of those who stopped by were musicians with a similar sense of humor and taste in music, including future band members Jonny Hibbert and David Irwin. As I entertained the idea of putting a band together, I wanted it to be a band I'd go see if I weren't in it. Everyone would be enthusiastic on stage, have a good sense of humor, and could pull off various genres of music. I was looking to put together a musical theatrical group, and my only template was performers like Zappa, The Fugs, and Bonzo Dog Band.

Little by little, new people enlisted into recording sessions, which seemed more like a party than anything to be taken seriously. Rex suggested high school friend Debbie Thompson, who brought in her friend, Susan Kirkpatrick, as a background vocalist. I immediately thought of my friend Jimmy Royals to round out the singers. I had played some gigs with guitarist Marvin Jackson, who had been around Atlanta for years. When the idea of doing a live show started to materialize, I knew I would be out front, so I contacted my high school friend, Joey Dukes.

Every link connected to another and eventually included bass player Keith Christopher, who played with Orpheum Circuit and had a keyboard-playing friend, Jimmy Walker. Marvin brought in his girlfriend Gina Grant, and she contacted her friend, Sue Schell; both rounded out the group with their very talented and creatively trained dance skills.

Wearing outrageous costumes and masks were by design. We immediately had the audience's attention and they reciprocated the energy we brought to the stage. This was a new experience for several in the band who had never played in a group before, but I think people tend to be less inhibited in costumes, and nobody was holding back. As the lineup came together, we were invited to play our first show at Lakewood Fairgrounds on August 24, 1975, with several other groups from the area.

Billed as "the only intentionally funny band," we were not referred to as The Hahavishnu Orchestra yet; only my name appeared on the poster. We were unlike anyone else on the bill, although some other unique groups were taking the stage that day. Everyone in Thermos Greenwood and the Colored People were painted different colors, The Hampton Geese Band with Bruce Hampton (formally of the Hampton Grease band and later to become notorious as Colonel Bruce Hampton), and Eric Quincy Tate were enormously popular and had an album out on Capricorn Records.

The concert was organized by local radio personality Mike Malloy, who was currently surrounded by several people trying to help him through a panic attack in his trailer. Mike faced many challenges, including people who had figured out ways to get in without paying. Gatecrashers wasn't a new thing; it happened at Woodstock and other festivals, including those held in Atlanta. Mike was definitely going to take a bath on this one. Chalk this gig up to experience and promotion because money wouldn't be in the mix. Yeah, baby, it was show business without the elephants, mop, and buckets.

Some of the smarter people in the group thought ahead in their wardrobe choices, but I was not among them. We took the stage wearing masks, welding suits, Boy Scout uniforms, maternity dresses, evening gowns, gas station attendant shirts, Tarzan outfits, and whatever else the shelves at Goodwill had to offer. The stage was set with a mannequin wearing a Richard Nixon mask and props laying at our feet.

We performed what would become our signature opener, "Suicide," while parodying James Brown's stage entrance on *Live at the Apollo*. The song was an instant attention-getter with its pseudo big band intro and the backup singers' kazoo horn section when I sang, "Bring dem funky horn parts in." Everybody was sweating, and I was counting off every song at hyper-speed.

We performed about 15 songs in a set lasting about 75 minutes and closed out with "Surfin' Shark," a timely song parody of Jan and Dean's "Dead Man's Curve" based on the movie *Jaws*, released that year. The song had gotten a lot of airplay on WIIN, and on stage, I played a taxidermied sailfish Marvin's father caught on his Cuban honeymoon in 1941. I'm unsure what kept us from going down with heat exhaustion; it was brutal, with no place or time to escape the heat, but we finished the set with a tremendous response. Everyone regarded our show as a success.

We played a blistering set where I ranted on stage with setups way longer than needed while the band waited for me in the scorching 100-degree heat to hit the cues for them to start playing. Hundreds of people didn't know what to expect, and after we were off the stage, some were unsure what they'd just witnessed.

We would soon become The Hahavishnu Orchestra, a play on the popular jazz fusion group John McLaughlin and the Mahavishnu Orchestra. I'm unsure who came up with the name, but when McLaughlin appeared at the Great Southeast Music Hall in Atlanta, I was told that he pulled down a couple of posters promoting our upcoming appearance there. I later read an interview with Mahavishnu drummer Billy Cobham in which his occasional references to The Hahavishnu Orchestra needled McLaughlin.

Our rehearsals were long and often but a lot of fun. The singers worked out the harmonies and choreography in one room, and the rest of us went over the music in the next room.

We took inspiration wherever we found it. Our bass player, Keith, came to one rehearsal while apparently battling flatulence, to the displeasure of nearby band members. I inquired about his nutritional choices and learned that broccoli was the culprit. Later that evening, after the rest of the band left, he and I sat down and wrote a jazz instrumental titled "Broccoli for Two," which became a crowd favorite in our shows.

Going into the Lakewood show, we had no idea where this ride was heading, but everyone had vowed to be on board for future dates. I booked the following Monday to Wednesday at The Bistro at 1102 West Peachtree Street. The legendary Bistro stage was more suited for a trio, so it took some work to make room for ten musicians and two dancers to perform without bumping into each other. Anticipating the singers' choreography and guitars swinging into faces, everyone marked their area. The dancers were forced to do their steps before the stage, but somehow, it all worked.

We packed the sold-out room all three nights and improvised new material off the cuff, which became a regular part of the show. We did two sets instead of the 15-song Lakewood set, with a lot of crowd interaction, bringing friends up on stage, and thinking on our feet. The band played off each other, and the audience met us at every turn. We evolved as musicians and performers, and I felt as if I was doing speed on and off stage.

Weaker songs would be replaced, but the early material had its place at that time. The blues parody, "I Be Gwine on Down to Da Watermelon Patch," about the bitch of being a white guy with a mood ring turned dark from depression, was short-lived. During a sound system glitch in an early Bistro show, we performed the "Helen Keller Boogie" one night on the cuff. I would mime the lyrics and move around like Mike Jagger on stage with the band while the backup singers performed choreography and mimed the background lyrics. The longer we did it, the more berserk it became. The band would stop when I pointed to Marvin, who got down on his knees and played a muted solo on guitar with his tongue. Everybody got in on it, including Joey, taking an air drum solo. The song became longer, and the audience was more engaged. Throughout our history, there was never a shortage of ideas coming from any band member at any time.

"Ooh Baby, Baby, Baby" was mainly a takeoff on bland pop songs and the artists who recorded them. I would talk about how we were cleaning up our image while I sprayed underarm deodorant. The lyrics were insipid, but the song was performed with smooth harmonies and tight choreography. The band simulated a skip in the record, which we repeated several times.

> *Before I met you I couldn't forget you*
> *Baby baby you're so fine*
> *And you're drivin' me out of my mind*
> *I was home all alone you called me up on the telephone*
> *Now sweet darlin' I want you for my own*
> *I love you only please believe me*
> *Hold me tight and never leave me*

OOH BABY, BABY, BABY ©1976 DARRYL RHOADES

Each night, we would ask the crowd to try to stump the band. They'd put written song requests in a box, and whatever slip of paper was pulled out, the request would always be "Brandy" by Looking Glass. We acted as if we weren't sure how the song went and were trying to figure it out on stage. I would count it off, and then magically, we executed the harmonies perfectly and sounded exactly like the record.

We always understood the importance of making it a show and built in time for me to leave the stage to change and re-enter as the next character. To give myself time to put on a wrestling robe, redneck attire, or cowboy outfit, I had to figure out how to keep the show moving while I wasn't on stage. Sometimes, I simply picked up a guitar and played "Everybody Loves a Clown" straight-faced and almost monotone, walking away while the band went into the next song's intro. We kept a rapid pace without giving the audience a lot of time to digest what they just saw for fear of missing what was quickly coming at them afterward. We also learned to incorporate songs featuring other band members, many of whom became fan favorites.

While I was never a big fan of parody songs and fought to keep us from being described as a parody band, some of the earliest parts of the show were built around parodies. One of the most popular parody pieces was "I'm Commercial," a take-off of the Helen Reddy song

"I Am Woman." The song provided me an exit for another costume change while Jimmy blew the roof off with his performance, which sometimes included a vacuum cleaner as a prop. As soon as the lyrics "I am woman hear me bitch / buy my records and make me rich" were sung, it was full game on, and that song would be mentioned in every review, local and national. It was also performed by *Saturday Night Live* alumni Jan Hooks in 1980 when she was part of the cast on the WTBS show *Tush*, which highlighted an incredible ensemble built around the personality of comic and journalist Bill Tush. When that show's producers objected to the word "bitch," writer Terry Turner came up with, "I am woman, hear me whine / and my jeans are Calvin Klein." Being a verb and a noun, "bitch" was a word I loved, but someone bitched about it, so the lyrics were altered, which was a bitch to me.

I appeared on the *Tush* show three times, playing drums behind Jan in one and lip-synching "Burgers from Heaven" and "I'm In With the Zen Crowd" in the others.

I often wrote songs based on current events or a theme that might grab the audience's attention and work in the context of the show. I classified them as funny, musical, or even shocking, but eventually, a few went into the "what in the hell was I thinking" category.

A few months before the band was assembled, one of the biggest stories in the news was the "right to die" fight in the court case of Karen Ann Quinlan. Quinlan was on a breathing tube after chasing valium with several gin and tonics and lapsed into a coma. When the test showed irreversible brain damage, her parents fought to have her disconnected from the machine. She was disconnected, and then fed through a tube for nine years before passing away from respiratory failure.

In a temporary lapse of reason, I wrote a pretty song with sweet harmonies titled "Euthanasia." The odd stage theatre portrayed a guy in an oxygen tank, fully understanding what was happening and desiring to have the machines unplugged but unable to speak. We thought it would be nice to have me wheeled in on stage in a shopping cart covered in broccoli, celery, and other produce while Jimmy shouted, "Vegetables! Vegetables! Get your fresh vegetables here!"

Fortunately, that part of the show was short-lived, as was the related "We're Eatin' Bacon" segment. I remained oblivious while Gina, at the side of the stage, was frying bacon on a hotplate. We set up a cue for the band to go into a riff while singin' "We're eatin' bacon," and then I would continue to pick up where I left off to set up the next song. I'm not sure who could claim credit for this turd, which thankfully laid on the stage for a far shorter time than Karen Ann Quinlan did before dying a horrible death in a trail of vapors. While this was a genuinely forgettable moment in the history of the band, it was about trying new ideas, which on occasion went over like farting in church.

We tried many ideas without holding back because they cracked us up at rehearsal. Some were truly funny, and some were just stupid, like my parody of the "Have a Tampa" cigar commercial, which became "Have a Tampax" while I lit a tampon in my mouth. It got laughs, but then again, I could have likely pissed on somebody's leg to get the same reaction. My attitude was pretty much if I'm hittin' a nerve, I'm hittin' the mark: great soundbite but stupid logic.

Outrageousness gained us much attention, and we took every opportunity to showcase it. We showed up one night in full-stage garb at the iconic Film Forum in Ansley Mall in Atlanta. The Film Forum was a popular theatre known for underground films and midnight movies, and it was owned by longtime Atlanta actor George Ellis, who hosted Friday night fright films on local TV as a character named Bestoink Dooley. When we asked to do a surprise short set before the movie played, Mr. Ellis didn't bat an eye before saying yes. In the dark, with everyone seated to catch the film, we walked in wearing women's dresses, masks, makeup, and more. The lights came on, and we went right into "Leprosy Queen." A surprised audience immediately responded enthusiastically, and our set was talked about for days, helping to ensure the next round of sellouts at The Bistro.

When The Bistro owner, Jimmy Ginn, approached me about "working with the group," I didn't understand clearly what that would entail. Jimmy was an enigma. Several band members would go to his office with me, and after a meeting, we'd all scratch our heads trying to figure out what we had just heard. He was difficult to pin down on specifics, but he felt we had promise and was in our corner, whatever that meant. Jimmy financed some studio time at Lefevre Studios for us to record our only 45 rpm, with "Burgers from Heaven" on the A-side and "Surfin' Shark" on the B-side. It was released on his label, Wonder Records. There was no contract other than my signing over the publishing, which I eventually bought back. Jimmy always seemed to be a little high and hanging around some strange characters I didn't need to know, but at the same time, "working with the group" meant that he was there for us if we needed a few bucks or even if there were legal issues facing some of the band members. Jimmy knew people who knew people. Years later, a few of his associates from Jamaica flew in looking for the president of Wonder Records because they "wondered" where their money was. Apparently, Mr. Ginn had financial partners in his agricultural pursuits.

During a special Halloween midnight show at Peaches Records and Tapes on Peachtree Road, I learned how quickly a bit can go sideways. One of the more popular segments in our show was our performance of "Yikes! Here Comes the Negroes," which resulted in several stories that would come up later. It was a biting piece meant to hit some right between the eyes.

I would enter the stage wearing a homemade Klan uniform while the band played "Theme from Shaft." I yelled at the band to stop playing while screaming some of the most guttural redneck phrases I'd heard growing up in the South. On this particular night, I had a few Black friends attending the show, and to spice it up, I asked them to jump in and start beating me up. The band was in on it; I was in on it, and my Black friends were in on it, but the audience didn't have the script. WHAT A STUPID IDEA!! When it went down, the fans decided they would jump in and help the less-than-sensible big palooka on stage, resulting in an unplanned break in the show.

Blame it on excellent theatre, fans coming to the rescue, or maybe an opportunity for some to entertain their own violent tendencies, but a situation like this could get out of hand quickly. We eventually got back to the show after having to explain to a few that it was theater and the Black guys were friends.

One night, I was watching Tom Snyder's *The Tomorrow Show* with an appearance by rock impresario Bill Graham, who didn't mention us by name but said that no performer should be dressing up in a KKK costume. I wasn't aware of any other groups matching that description. Knowing that Graham had escaped Nazi Germany, I understood his attitude even though it didn't impact my direction at the time. There would be several times his point would be validated when the performance of that song would be misinterpreted as support for racist attitudes instead of in-your-face satire.

The show constantly evolved, with occasional personnel changes. Our original multi-instrumentalist, David Irvin, left, and his replacement, Edward Tanner, added so much on every level that it's difficult to describe his contributions adequately. He was brilliantly funny and brought a different approach through his style of guitar playing.

Great bands are always going to be about chemistry. All the players were good, some very good, but our chemistry made it click. I instantly liked Edward, and we hung out a bit away from the band and rehearsals. He had been working with School Kids Records, which had a store in Bloomington, Indiana, home of Indiana University. Having friends there, Edward invited me to make the trip to catch Charles Mingus performing in a college bar. It wasn't a place I'd expect to see a jazz legend, but I was a huge fan and had recently read his autobiography, *Beneath the Underdog: His World as Composed by Mingus*.

In his book, Mingus had a reputation for being a demanding bandleader, and I saw that again that night. After playing several songs, he took a piece of paper out of his pocket and announced that someone had told him there was a young kid in the audience who was a great sax player and hoping to sit in. Mingus asked for the kid by name (we'll call him Freddy), and I never took my eyes off this young sax player as he stood up with his instrument in hand while his excited friends high-fived each other. Freddy stepped on stage, and the band started playing. The kid started blowing, and blowing, and blowing while the band kept playing and staring at each other. After about six or seven minutes, the song ended with Mingus announcing the kid's name. The crowd went wild, and Freddy returned to his friends, who were still high-fiving and showing him all kinds of love. Everyone is so proud of their talented friend, hero, and star.

And then . . . Mingus approaches the mic and says, "Hey Freddy, next time you sit in to play with a band, play with the band. Some of these guys might wanna play, so listen to them. Now go home and shave that shit off your face and do something with your hair."

I couldn't take my eyes off Freddy as the smile melted off his face. I figure he either hocked his sax the next day or became a world-class sax player who got a free lesson from one of the greatest jazz musicians and composers who ever walked the face of the earth.

We soon experienced our first national press when Rich Bryant wrote a short piece in *Oui* magazine titled "Big Banned Sound." We were described as "sort of a musical contemporary Lenny Bruce who makes fun of subjects that would be off limits to The Fugs." The piece played up the outrageous bizarreness, and the picture captured our low-budget thrift store look, which seemed out of place in a skin rag. Of course you never know what pervs might be reading about you anywhere, and God knows we had some pervs who were fans of the band.

At every turn, our audience was growing along with support from local writers such as Jeff Cochran, Jim Pettigrew, Tony Paris, and Russell Shaw, who also had national connections. Writers would talk about us to other writers, and the local journalists met me at almost every gig on the road. We were good copy because there were very few acts to compare us to. "You don't have to waste any time wondering if you've seen Darryl Rhoades & The Hahavishnu Orchestra before," a review began of our opening at Exit/In in Nashville in July 1976. The following nights and every subsequent appearance, there were sellouts. We had a loyal following in the country music capital, and it wasn't uncommon to see major stars in the audience.

In November 1975, we set out for our first road trip to perform at the Performance Art Center in Tampa. When we arrived in Tampa, I was promptly flown back to Atlanta for a meeting with Frank Fenter, executive vice president of Capricorn Records.

Frank was aware of the press we were generating, and the frequent comparisons to acts on major labels with large budgets, such as The Tubes. The conversation between him and Jimmy Ginn was like trying to keep up with Yogi Berra's doublespeak. It felt like we were running in place, although I was amused by the phrase used to describe the band as "diamonds in the rough." Apparently, without seeing the band, Frank thought we were "diamonds in the rough," I accurately translated that phrase as "not right for our label." Part of our charm was the rustic look, and it was never our plan to hire a hair/wardrobe stylist or choreographer. Without powerful representation or a record label deal, we could rock the Goodwill look, and had to.

I returned to Tampa with little news to report to the band. Concentrating on what I could control would be a better use of my energy. Word had already spread, and from the first night, the club was packed, and it seemed we could do no wrong. The band was clicking, and we were making fans. Well, mostly.

I usually did my homework when I went into any town to get the lowdown on local characters. Politicians, stump-breakin' peckerwoods, and disgraced religious figures turned drug addicts were always targets, and the slimier, the better. When the opportunity arose, I would incorporate references to local rock stars, which would usually get a great response unless some of their friends were in the audience. You may know the Outlaws were from Tampa, but I did not. I was unfamiliar with their hit, "There Goes Another Love Song," until Edward played it on guitar for me. Somewhere in our show that night, we went into an unrehearsed version where everyone played it in different keys while I "sang" some improvised lyrics on top. We cracked ourselves up along with most of the crowd. However, the friends of the Outlaws who were in the crowd told them about what we did, and years later it came back to bite me when I submitted a song to their record producer, Johnny Sandlin.

Johnny had played with Gregg and Duane in The Hourglass, which predated the Allman Brothers Band, which he later produced. Johnny's girlfriend, Jana Vickers, was a good friend of my girlfriend at that time, and because Johnny was shopping for material for the Outlaws' new LP, it was suggested that I send one of my songs. I sent him a four-track demo of "The Lights Are On (But Nobody's Home)," and he gave it a thumbs up before playing it for the band. They loved the song until finding out I had written it. Mutiny was afoot, and the foot was about the same size as the one I was nibbling on when Johnny told me the story. He eventually got around to "What in the hell did you do to the Outlaws?" I told Johnny about the bit in Tampa, and he laughed and said he thought he could smooth it over. I'm unsure if he pulled rank, but The Outlaws went on to record my song and, on the insistence of Arista Records President Clive Davis, was placed the first song on the record. The LP, *In the Eye of the Storm,* only made it to No. 55 on the *Billboard* chart, and my name was misspelled in the credits, but the sales did generate enough money for me to finance the recording of my first LP, *Burgers from Heaven.*

I had much to learn, but to this day, I thank Doc Pomus for directing me to set up my publishing company and signing with The Harry Fox Agency to collect royalties from overseas. I still get checks from HFA, which range from 1 cent to 73 cents, and one day hope to collect enough checks to wallpaper my drum room. When I posted that idea on social media, Butch Trucks of the Allman Brothers offered to send me some of his royalty checks in the same range. A member of one of the most popular and successful groups in rock history was getting royalty checks amounting to pocket change. In the phrase "music business," the word "business" has more letters.

A year after the LP release, I got a call from Outlaws guitarist Hughie Thomasson, complimenting "The Lights Are On," and asked if I had anything else. If that happened now or even 20 years ago, I would have answered yes and written something, but I didn't have the chops or confidence then, so I answered no. The LP Hughie was looking for songs to record, was *Ghost Riders,* which charted at No. 31 on *Billboard.* Opportunities missed or ignored, I gotta bunch of 'em.

In November 1975, we performed our first gig at the iconic Great Southeast Music Hall, opening up for one of my heroes, Martin Mull.

Martin performed solo, with his stage set resembling a furnished living room with a couch, lamp, table, and plant as part of his promotional tour of his newly released Capricorn Records LP, *Days of Wine and Neuroses.*

My first time meeting Martin was a year earlier in Atlanta when I nervously approached him at his promotional appearance at Turtle's Records. I gave him a tape of my home recordings, which were getting airplay on local radio. I didn't know if he'd listen to them, but years later, Howard Kaylan, founding member and lead singer of the 1960s rock band The Turtles, mentioned that Martin and he listened to them together.

The concept of doing a show together seemed like a great marriage, even though it wasn't sensible for a solo act to follow a large ensemble of local musicians starting to amass a considerable fanbase. Sitting in the wings and watching the audience's response to our show might explain why he commented, "And now for the adult portion of the show," when he took the stage after us. Martin could come off as smug and condescending, and in many ways, it was part of his charm if you acted as if you didn't notice it.

When I had lunch with him the next day, his exact words were, "I've never been so humiliated in my life." While it didn't make me feel good, I understood where he was coming from. Opening acts were about setting the table for the headliner and warming up the crowd. Our balls-to-the-wall approach was a little over the top as a warm-up act. He was very complimentary about our performance, but following a band like ours was challenging, and I saw that several times while we were in the beginning stages of opening shows for others.

If I was riding a high from the sudden regional notoriety and following, I was about to learn how little that might mean on a tour to new markets. We traveled to Fort Myers, Florida, for a five-day gig in December 1975 at The Rolling Stone Club. The owners were two brothers, Lee and Sal, who looked like extras on *The Sopranos*. Marketing wasn't their strong suit, so we played to small audiences, including a few frequented by some vice cops who had heard about our shows. As soon as we arrived, we got the heads-up about the cops and figured making a few lyric changes might be a good idea. If we had to rewrite lyrics, at the bare minimum we had to entertain ourselves.

In one popular bit called "Disco Shit," we would string several disco songs together and change the lyrics. We would sing "Shit! Goddamn! Get off your ass and jam!" from a Funkadelic song being played on the radio, but singing the uncensored version popular in dance clubs could be a problem in Fort Myers. The logical thing to do was insert some idiotic alternate lyrics, so it became "Heck! Gosh darn! Get off your tails and yarn!" OK, not clever or funny, but our inside joke entertained the band every time we did it, which counted for something since the small attendance in Fort Myers did little for our morale. The week was uneventful, other than meeting a female contortionist who entertained several band members. The variety of entertainment often made touring less painful and sometimes downright festive.

We did have a brief encounter involving the law. On Saturday night after the gig, Jimmy Royals and I went to Lee and Sal's office with the contract in hand to collect our money. Lee, the slimiest guy in the room other than his brother, made it a point to show a large pistol on his desk while claiming that he hadn't made enough money to pay us. He then suggested we would have to "pay our dues," while he offered considerably less. "I've paid my fuckin' dues and want our money," I responded. I understood the gun wasn't placed on the desk as an office decor statement. After a few tense moments, we decided that leaving was in our best interest. On our way out, we spotted our guitarist Marvin and asked him to have the band stall by taking their time loading out. We were heading to the police station.

I have no idea what the cops thought, but when I entered the station wearing a Boy Scout uniform, and Jimmy sporting a Fu Manchu and drag outfit, we were quickly dismissed and advised to contact an attorney.

Around 2 a.m., we called Jack Tarver, a practicing attorney and owner of the Great Southeast Music Hall, and received some sound advice. He figured that Lee and Sal likely knew the cops, and we might want to get the hell out of there ASAP and reconsider our options later.

When we returned to the club, we discovered that the band had sped up loading after Sal pulled a shotgun on Marvin, who yelled,

"What are you gonna do, shoot me?" Thankfully, cooler heads prevailed, the vans were loaded, and we hit the road.

I still have that worthless contract as a backup in the event another toilet paper shortage occurs, but the lesson was clear to me about how meaningless a contract is if it's unenforceable. Contracts are only good if both parties are honorable or someone has the muscle to make the other party live up to the agreement.

The bottom line: We performed a few days in Fort Myers, Florida, to small crowds who didn't get what we did, several of the guys in the band got screwed by the yoga queen, and then the entire band received the same treatment from Sal and his brother—without the benefit of a reach around.

After our experience in Ft. Myers two months earlier, we were looking forward to performing in a friendlier atmosphere. In January 1976, we appeared at Memorial Hall at the University of Georgia to a packed audience of fans and hopefully soon to be converts. While our parody of the Allman Brothers' "Whipping Post" was a fan favorite, our decision to perform it that night was probably less than sensible. Our lyrics have been reprinted in the book *Midnight Rider* by Scott Freeman, *Rolling Stone*, and plenty of interviews and show reviews.

> *I've been OD'd, I've been on speed*
> *I don't know why Cher took all of my weed*
> *Took all my quaaludes and my skag too*
> *Now my cocaine stash is empty, and I don't know what I'll do*
> *Sometimes I feel, sometimes I feel*
> *Like I've been tied to a Harley-Davidson*
> *Tied to a Harley-Davidson, tied to a Harley-Davidson*
> *Good Lord, my whole band is dying*

The band played the music spot on, right down to the instrumental section, where I'd fall to the stage and do my best whimpering, strung out Gregg Allman impression. The audience went berserk, even more so when Jimmy Royals entered the stage behind a giant cardboard

Cher, I'd beg for "her" forgiveness while we bantered for a few minutes before the band came back in.

This bit would always bring the house down, but not so much for the people from Capricorn Records there checking us out. I wondered, as they likely did, if we would be a good fit among their roster of Southern rock acts. The Allmans were their main act, but Capricorn needed to understand what we were about. They found out that night in Athens, which may be the reason why negotiations never went further. If an adult had been in the room, a more intelligent decision may have been made. I believe Marvin explained it very eloquently when he said, "We were 26 years old and stoned on hormones."

I did feel better later when Martin Mull implied that the partying atmosphere at Capricorn took precedence over his career. The demise of that label can probably be blamed on many things, but when that discussion came up, drug use seemed to take center stage.

With every new Gregg episode, our Allman Brothers bit grew and was mentioned in every press notice. The Allman Brothers' roadie, Scooter Herring, was targeted in a drug investigation for furnishing drugs to the band. When Gregg was popped for possession, he faced prison time unless he turned witness for the state and testified against Scooter. This situation caused a major riff among the band members, who claimed they would never work with him again, and they didn't for a long time. In my stoned-out Gregg impression on stage, I would drool and whine, "Scooter done it . . . Scooter done it," while the band would yell, "Testify Gregg! Tell it! Testify!"

Even the Texas Tower sniper shooting provided fodder for us. In an interview for the University of Texas school paper, I explained the lyrics to "Only in America," which referenced the Kennedy assassination, Patty Hearst, and the Symbionese Liberation Army killings, along with the University of Texas Tower sniper murders in 1966. I met several people who had been on site that day. The song wasn't written to be funny; it was done with anger. The song intro included a U.S. flag held by the dancers as I talked about America's greatness proven with products like K-tel Records, Captain Kelly Smoke Detectors, and Popeil's

Pocket Fishermen. Then we sang about gun violence, a theme revisited in my songwriting over the years.

Singing "Only in America" would have been much more challenging if I were closely attached to that event or the people involved, just as if I'd had a personal connection to the Allmans, it would have likely been more challenging to perform satire about Gregg's drug issues. It's a tricky dance to collect the right amount of info about touchy subjects while not getting too close to any of them. You want a connection but not investment to the point where the humor gets lost. I didn't worry about insensitivity back then and still don't on most subjects.

By February 1976, our mostly positive press reviews were getting us offers for dates and opportunities in showcase clubs. One key performance was in front of the Radio and Records Convention held in Atlanta in February 1976.

The R&R convention was an opportunity for record company executives to excessively indulge together in the vices of their choice while claiming it all as a business expense. Many of those execs chose to bring their party to Alex Cooley's Electric Ballroom on February 20. Alex was a force in the business as a promoter and among the contingent responsible for both Atlanta Pop Festivals. He came through several times for the band and opened doors for us; what happened after those doors were opened was out of his control.

Alex thought adding us to the bill that night with rhythm guitarist Bob Weir, one of the founders of The Grateful Dead, might be helpful, even if it was a strange matchup. At no time did I entertain the fantasy that we would be discovered and signed, but we figured it would be an excellent opportunity to make ourselves memorable. That show was especially memorable for those partying with Buddah Record Company.

We always got a great crowd response when we performed "Burgers from Heaven." Jimmy Ginn paid for 70 dozen hamburger buns dropped from the ceiling light platform on cue when I sang the opening lyrics. The buns landed on unsuspecting audience members, spilling drinks on inebriated record company people, most of whom were from Buddah Records. Buddah didn't sign us, and I was told that its president wasn't amused, but I still felt it was important for the record companies to know what they were getting and if we were on the same page. As it turns out, we weren't even in the same book.

Working the showcase clubs wouldn't make anyone rich, but often led to bigger opportunities. Nashville's Exit/In was and still remains one of those clubs. The promotional poster from July 1976 advertised our first gig there as well as John Prine, Richie Havens, Dixie Dregs, and several other performers who went on to the prominence and success that we were seeking. Anyone could enter Exit/In and change an entertainer's career path at any given time. We had not met that person yet, but we did become a favorite among some of the most iconic artists of this era.

In the summer of 1976, Rex Patton and I loaded up his car and headed to Los Angeles. Armed with video copies from low-budget local public access TV appearances, press kits, and contact info from Alex Cooley, we had no strategy other than knocking on doors and making calls.

But first, we went out of our way to see all the remnants of Route 66 as we could, which explains why we ended up at a cheap hotel in Seligman, Arizona. After settling in, we went to the little bar next door to shoot pool, where two older guys, on drums and guitar, were playing Creedence Clearwater Revival songs. A little piece of paper hanging on the door advertised that night's talent, Zeb Turner and Bob Dilley.

I would eventually learn that Zeb Turner was a rockabilly pioneer who played guitar for Hank Williams and Red Foley after World War II. Zeb's songs, written for legendary music publishers Fred Rose and Ernest Tubb, were recorded by Tex Williams and Willie Nelson. On that night, Zeb was a middle-aged guy playing cover songs badly from the corner of the room in a small Arizona town pool hall while being ignored by locals more interested in drinking and sinking the eight ball in the corner pocket. I regret not introducing myself. I may have missed out on some great stories.

We made it to L.A. in several days, found a cheap hotel, and started making calls. We met with the contacts Alex Cooley set up and were refamiliarized with the term "diamonds in the rough." What they weren't saying out loud was the difficulty of keeping a large band like ours on the road, even though we had been doing it for a couple of years while establishing a large following.

I was always torn when we were called a "comedy band." I must have sounded confused when I protested, however. It's sort of like a clown saying, "Yeah, I know I'm wearing floppy shoes, a big red nose, and just got out of a little car with 15 other guys who look like me, but I'm an actor and want to be taken seriously dammit!"

I had witnessed good and bad marketing and understood the challenges. The Dixie Dregs once told me about the time they picked up their label's promotions guy at the airport after the release of their new LP. He commented that he was excited about the album and especially liked the instrumental they recorded. That comment would have been considered a great compliment if the Dregs weren't an instrumental group, discovering that their record promoter wasn't familiar with the album or what they were about.

When the Dregs were on Capricorn, I remember a commercial for their LP spouting, "If Lynyrd Skynyrd and John McLaughlin had a baby, it would sound something like this," then a few seconds from the newest Dreg's recording was played. What a corny ad that said nothing about the music, but then again, the public relates to things that are familiar. Praising originality is a lost cause if you're caught up in making comparisons to an established artist.

As much as I wanted to sell our concept to record companies or booking agents, I never wanted to turn on the radio one day and hear, "If Soupy Sales and Pink Floyd had a bastard child who was an acid casualty, it would look and sound like this" and then play one of my songs.

We met with several agents, executives, and various people in the business who were loaded up with words and empty of ideas. But the conversation was promising with Herb Cohen, Frank Zappa's manager for the first ten years of his career. Herb watched our videos, making some priceless comments like "that guy looks like he should be sitting on the hood of a '57 Chevy" when he saw Jonny Hibbert playing sax. Herb had a reputation as a tough guy who had connections and could make things happen. He also had managed Tom Waits, Tim Buckley, Lenny Bruce, and quite a few other acts who made me feel like Herb could be a good fit. He spent time with us and showed us where Tom Waits stayed and his favorite breakfast hangout. As he showed interest, we started talking about making plans, and would be in touch. I was comfortable with him, but at the same time, I'd heard stories and was naturally cautious when signing contracts. I wasn't asked for any commitment at that point, and didn't feel I was being blown off after our meeting like I did with the others.

We returned to Atlanta in a week or so and had a band meeting, during which I shared our experience and the possibilities for the future. Herb started calling me at all hours from Europe or wherever he was conducting business. He discussed different possible scenarios but eventually booked us into New York City. Even with all the press we were getting, I was still a little tentative, but as several band members stated, we needed to make some headway to keep this thing together.

In October 1976, I got a call from Herb informing me that he had booked us at the iconic Other End (formerly The Bitter End) in Greenwich Village. We were scheduled to make our NYC debut with a two-week run in early 1977, from January 18–22, and January 25–29. The first few nights were closed to the public, and the club was packed with press, a brilliant strategy. The prestigious Barbara Dewitt Agency lined up so many interviews that by the time I performed in front of a packed room every night, I struggled with losing my voice.

We didn't draw a paycheck, but Herb allowed a $5-a-day stipend for each band member, a great weight loss program. Everyone learned how to budget that $5 with pizza slices being $1.25 each, and depending on how many subway rides were required from the Chelsea Hotel, where Herb housed most of us, we might be able to eat two slices.

Between the pizza slices, drinks bought by fans, and the one daily meal provided by club owner Paul Colby, we were hangin' onto a dream by a thread. I was familiar with how writers often condescended toward Southerners, which lit a little fire under several of us. New York City can be intimidating, but we had something to prove.

Our opening act was Mississippi folk singer Steve Forbert, who'd been making the rounds in the city. From the first night, the club was packed, and on the weekend, we got word that some record company guys were in the audience. Could this be the night talked about years later on late-night talk shows when asked, "Do you remember when all hell broke loose and your band hit it big?" Yes, that night led to Steve Forbert's record deal and the release of his first LP later that year. Marketing one guy on guitar proved to be more appealing than the possibility of supporting a traveling circus band.

The history of The Bitter End/Other End and its place in folk music history wasn't lost on me. I longed for some behind-the-scenes stories, and would engage Paul Colby in conversations about Phil Ochs and several other heroes to me. One night, Paul introduced me to Dave Van Ronk, a folk legend from the 1960s who influenced and performed with some of the greatest musicians of that generation, including Ochs, Bob Dylan, and Joan Baez. I looked Dave in the eye and shook his hand, and he looked right past me into another galaxy where he was most likely residing at that moment. Later, I heard a story from Tom, the soundman at the club, about the time Dave was playing on stage and stopped in the middle of a song, bent his head, and just sat there. In a short time, Tom realized that Dave had fallen asleep, and with only a few in the audience, he went on stage, woke Dave up, and thanked everyone for coming.

Before any show, I would usually scan the audience to figure out the best way to navigate through the crowd during the performance. One night at The Other End, I saw a man in a wheelchair wearing a black Stetson hat, whom a band member identified as Doc Pomus. Doc was a legendary songwriter of over 1,500 songs, including hits like "Save the Last Dance for Me," "Viva Las Vegas," and "This Magic Moment." I occasionally glanced at him during the show and noticed he was engaged, laughing, and having a good time. He attended several of our shows during that run, and I'd hang out with him afterward when I could. We often ended up at an all-night deli where I was treated to great stories and comments like, "Bagels killed more Jews than Hitler."

Later in my solo visits to New York for meetings, I spent time with Doc visiting the Songwriters Hall of Fame, which would open up for him to have a private tour. At every New York show we attended, artists made their way over to introduce themselves. Doc usually knew most of them and after catching Mose Allison at The Bottom Line, I asked him what Mose was like. Doc replied, "He lives in New Jersey and drives into the city to play his gigs, then drives back home to the family and cuts his grass." I can't imagine a more perfect way to describe someone.

Everyone loved Doc, and if he liked you, he had no problem letting you know, and if he didn't, you'd figure it out quickly. I slept on his couch a couple of times and spent hours talking with him about his early history as a white Jewish blues singer in predominantly Black surroundings. One day, he had me pull out a shoebox full of pictures and it was the first time I saw a picture of him standing, with the aid of crutches, while singing in front of a band. He mainly had used a wheelchair from childhood polio.

Brought up tough, Doc talked about playing poker with some street-savvy guys in a private backroom game. A couple of punks interrupted one game with guns and robbed everyone. I asked Doc if they ever found the guys, and he told me they were found—and never seen again.

One of my favorite Doc stories was confirmed by music producer Joel Dorn and speaks to friendship and loyalty. Doc worked with a large blues band during *The Blues Brothers* era. I'd heard about how some blues players who considered themselves purists took offense to stars like Dan Aykroyd and John Belushi appropriating the art form as "The Blues Brothers." I thought that attitude was incredibly short-sighted; as the saying goes, "a rising tide lifts all boats." When the Blues Brothers' *Saturday Night Live* skit turned into a movie, that exposure gave many artists' songs a second life, which should have been recognized as a gift.

One of Doc's oldest and best friends was Big Joe Turner, who Doc viewed as the founder of rock and roll based on a history of 1950s recordings, including "Shake, Rattle and Roll." Joe mentioned to Doc that he was interested in hiring the band Doc was working with to back him on some dates. When Doc mentioned it to one of the band members, he was met with, "We're not going to have him ride our coattails," to which Doc responded by putting a derringer in the guy's face and screaming, "I'll blow your motherfucking brains out!" That was the Doc I knew, so loyal to his friends that he wouldn't idly stand by when they were disrespected.

Doc and I stayed in touch until he passed away in 1991. Most things people hold onto will eventually end up in somebody else's yard sale, but I've accrued a few things that have value because of the giver or the memories. Doc gave me the book, *Doc Pomus & Mort Shuman Song Folio*, with an inscription, "To Darryl, It's all in front of you. You've got the talent & intelligence to nail all of it. Best of Everything, Doc." Years later, I pulled it out, read it, and instantly felt depressed, as if I'd let him down. I found it difficult to reconcile his words of hope with the reality I was feeling that I was coming up short.

I'm not sure I'm worthy of being listed as a contributor in the 2012 documentary *AKA Doc Pomus*, but watching that movie was healing. I bought the biography *Lonely Avenue: The Unlikely Life and Times of Doc Pomus*, which I've never been able to open. Maybe one day.

Getting to know Doc was one of the many positives from being in NYC, but it wasn't an easy time for the band. We were packing the room and Herb was impressed with the show. If he wasn't impressed by a band surviving in the city on $5 a day, he should have been. Herb would take me out to lunch for a meeting, and at the time, I never thought about how the rest of the band felt about it while they were starving. Maybe I couldn't get a doggy bag for twelve, but I get the point. While giving everything they had on stage to make it work, they were starving.

Each time I reminded Herb of this, he made plans and talked a good game. The two-week run bolstered his confidence in us, but when he alluded to sidestepping the plan of signing with a label in favor of releasing a double LP on his label, I was cautious and concerned. It was the same model he had used for Zappa's debut record, but I questioned whether a single LP would be stronger debut release.

In NYC, we also experienced one of the worst blizzards in the city's history. The Other End was closed for a few nights, taxis quit running, and people skied down Bleecker Street. A real New York experience wouldn't be complete without the mandatory van theft. One of our vans was parked on a side street, stolen, and then found a couple of days later on blocks in a lot several miles away.

Herb's plan of bringing us to New York to create a buzz was working. Shortly after our run at The Other End, an interview with owner Paul Colby ran in the special edition of the *International Talent Weekly Performance* magazine. "The reception for Darryl Rhoades and his merry band of co-conspirators, with their incredible energy and sparkling wit, led to perhaps the best club act I've ever seen," Paul stated. "The Hahavishnu's jokes remain with the staff." Considering the roster of entertainers who have appeared there, this was a hell of a compliment.

On the heels of our exposure in New York, we were booked at one of my favorite venues of all time, The Armadillo World Headquarters in Austin, Texas.

With a capacity of 1500, the AWHQ was created from an old abandoned National Guard armory, and featured iconic musicians from AC/DC to Zappa and everybody in between. Frequented by cowboys, hippies, and businessmen, the club had a clientele as varied as the genres of music.

We came in as the opening act for local favorites, The Uranium Savages. The Savages were a collection of artists, poets, musicians, and actors; it was uncanny how similar their concept was to ours. They were loose and spontaneous, and we loved hanging out and performing with them. It was a circus, and I felt like I was home again.

Austin remains one of my favorite cities, but in the 1970s, it was extraordinary. The AWHQ was legendary; even today, you'll find many who can talk about it for hours, and its original posters are highly sought after by collectors. I still have copies of all the Hahavishnu posters from our appearances there with The Uranium Savages, Balcones Fault, and Andy Pratt.

Some lunatic fringe fans danced on the edge, but I loved being around them. I was never into drugs, nor was most of the band, but on occasion, several members didn't mind experimenting. A fan in Austin decided to show her love for the band by supplying them with some original Owsley acid kept in her refrigerator for a year or two. It would be a vast understatement to say this 1960s holdover chemical was strong; it was the Dom Perignon of Acid. Under this influence one night, some of the band decided to travel to Tulsa to hear Pablo Cruise. I viewed that trip as an argument for abstaining from drugs on many levels. When they shared their experience, which included watching a cowboy kick the shit out of a guy in slow motion, I wondered where's a good strobe light when you need it?

A couple of days later, the band checked into a roadside motel in Tulsa to perform at Cain's Ballroom. The housekeeper, sporting a fine set of sparkplug earrings, was still readying our rooms, so we went across the street to a greasy spoon restaurant for breakfast. The absence of one band member wasn't noticed until 20 minutes later when he walked in, zipping up his pants. He was the vagina whisperer, skilled in one and done, hit and run, wham bam, thank you, ma'am. He was the guy who attracted scabies and crabs and nailed everything in sight. I'm unsure if it was strong magic or low standards, but that talent co-existed with his vast musical abilities. I can't swear to it, but I think he got extra towels and a couple of bars of soap for his efforts.

We generally attached a rider to all contracts to specify our needs for sound, lights, and sometimes catering. Jimmy Royals typically handled those details along with most of the bookings. Most of the time, our rider requirements were met, but there were a few times when a 40-watt bulb was called a "lighting system," and a Shure amp with small speakers was referred to as a "sound system." Issues like these are why Van Halen famously included the "no brown M&M's" clause in their rider, and Todd Rundgren demanded one toy monkey smoking a cigarette in the dressing room. Failure to pay attention to those details leads to speculation that other important guidelines might be ignored, which could be anything from production values to safety requirements.

For some reason, Coors beer was placed on the rider in our contract sent to the Armadillo. Not being a beer drinker, I never understood the fascination with Coors other than that it wasn't available east of the Mississippi. When we arrived that afternoon to set up, Jimmy went over the details with the Armadillo manager, Hank Alrich, and when it came to the rider, Hank said, "We don't drink Coors beer here; we drink Lone Star beer. We consider Coors to be horse piss. Is that okay?"

Beer was a club staple, and anything other than Lone Star wasn't up for debate. At one time, the Armadillo came in second only to the Houston Astrodome for the most Lone Star beer sold. A beer garden/restaurant was attached to the Armadillo, where several band members came up with one of the best cons ever. Our creativity and ingenuity weren't limited to the stage, and empty stomachs with empty pockets can be demanding.

While several of the guys were nursing some beers one afternoon at the beer garden, they came up with the story that they'd never seen a tostada before and wanted to know if they could get several free ones to decoupage and take home. Genius!!!!

The Austin scene was unlike any other we had experienced before. We were invited into people's homes, cookouts, and lake parties, while several other clubs contacted us to extend our stay by working their rooms.

Touring was an ambitious undertaking made less complicated by having one of the best tour managers I've ever worked with. Jerry Pece joined the Hahavishnu crew early on and played a large part in figuring out the logistics of transporting 12 to 14 people who required food, lodging, and sometimes therapy. He was loyal to a fault, and turned down job offers from other groups we worked with on the road who had record deals.

Most four- to five-piece bands would have an actual road crew, but we traveled with Jerry and our light guy, Farrell Roberts. Farrell had worked with us several times as the house guy at the Great Southeast Music Hall, but came with us for about a year when we hit the road, and then he returned to the Music Hall.

Along with many moving parts, we had multiple personalities that could become contentious. Factoring in the attempt to survive on a slim budget, you get your drama wherever you can, and we had plenty.

Jed's was another highlight on our itinerary when we traveled to New Orleans. The club was owned and operated by a character named Jed Palmer, the subject of more than a few great stories.

Jed always treated our band well, but then again, we appealed to his taste, which might have been more indictment than praise. Rumor had it that Jed Palmer was a disbarred lawyer who had killed a man. I have no idea if it's entirely true, but my many conversations with him about his knowledge of the underbelly of New Orleans nightlife led me to believe it was a strong possibility.

Allegedly, an Atlanta club owner called for a meeting of clubs to form a cartel for block-booking bands to get better prices. As the story goes, Jed took exception to the fact that the invitation offered no free beer or accommodations for the other out-of-town club owners. He decided for payback to be in the form of stealing cocaine from the Atlanta club owner's ashtray and replacing it with dog shit. The Atlanta club owner denied this story, while Jed swore by it. Both men have left the planet, but knowing them both as I did, I tend to go with Jed's version.

When we performed at Jed's, we stayed at the Travel Inn motel located on Airline Highway, better known years later as where TV evangelist Jimmy Swaggart was discovered in Room 7 with Debra Murphee, a known prostitute. The common perception was that the good reverend was laying hands in an attempt to heal her while talking in tongues.

The Travel Inn was a favorite place for bands because of its hooker chic ambiance and affordable price. On our first trip to New Orleans, we checked in at the motel and ran into George Thorogood and the Delaware Destroyers, and invited them to that night's show.

On this particular evening, I was in the middle of singing "Yikes Here Comes the Negroes" while donning a Ku Klux Klan costume. The song satirized and attacked the Klan (which was very strong in New Orleans at the time), but that fact was not known to guitar legend Clarence "Gatemouth" Brown as he stepped into the club and saw me in complete Klan regalia. I thought I recognized him from the stage but lost sight of him, so I asked George to confirm if it was

Gatemouth. I was told it was, and he did a 180 toward the door, utter-ing profanities and not hiding his anger. I imagine Clarence had seen enough of it in his day and wasn't amused on any level, even if we were making fun of it.

After seeing rave reviews in the New Orleans press about our shows at Jed's, we were contacted by a guy named Jim, who worked in a cor-porate affairs business and booked local cruise ships. The money was decent, but we were the wrong choice. Most tourists on a boat cruise aren't typically expecting or looking forward to hearing a band sing about necrophilia or suicide. We performed, got paid, left, and heard nothing from Jim.

In the interim, Jim was assisting *Saturday Night Live* producer Lorne Michaels and his crew in their preparation for a live show from New Orleans. After we had performed on the boat, Jimmy Royals had called Jim at least 10 to 20 times but couldn't get him on the phone because Jim was 1. out of town, 2. off today, 3. at lunch, 4. in bed with the flu, 5. had to see a man about a large dog, or 6. was scheduled for a lengthy enema that day. (I made up two of these excuses and leave it to the reader to figure out which ones are real dodges used by our man of the hour).

We had the bright idea for Jimmy to call Jim's office and say he was Lorne Michaels. So when Jimmy was asked by the receptionist who was calling, his reply was Lorne Michaels. Jim came on and said, "Lorne baby, how ya doing?" and was not pleased to find Jimmy on the other end. At this point, I learned a valuable lesson about the entertainment business: Just because someone won't take your calls doesn't mean you should take it personally; it only means they don't want to talk to you. It's a lesson that I have had the pleasure of relearning many times.

Other helpful hints to decoding rejection include, "We're goin' a different way," "You're not right for my room," "We are switching up the way we do things," and "Our demographics have changed." All are wording variations for ways to say "no."

Around this time, I was contacted by Charles M. Young from *Rolling Stone*, who said he was interested in doing a story on the band. In our conversation, he referenced the bit we did on Gregg Allman, and I replied, "If Dickey Betts sees this, he'll probably cut my balls off." Of course, that quote was printed in the random notes section in the next edition of *Rolling Stone* and later in the book *Midnight Riders* by Scott Freeman.

As much as we loved playing the showcase venues, we still had to make a living. Sometimes, we worked in rooms more known for using standard Southern rock boogie bands. Even working in those rooms, we won over many fans, packed the clubs, and drew more new converts when we returned.

The first time we played the Whipping Post in Augusta, a rock bar with a wild reputation that it lived up to, I had my suspicions. Our friends, The Dixie Dregs, had lived there for some time and came out to see us, but most of the audience had no idea what to expect. The manager and booker, Randy Powell, had driven to Atlanta to catch a show and pursued us to do some dates.

Connected to the bar was Lucifer's Follies, a "gentlemen's club," a term that always makes me picture the little Monopoly guy wearing a top hat and sipping on a martini while watching women do gymnastics on a pole. Missed it by a mile! While we were singin' about necrophilia and leprosy, some locals were in the adjoining room watching the infamous snake lady dance with a python around her neck.

Usually, a regional boogie band would open up for us at the Whipping Post, while I would hang out in the makeshift green room, also known as the beer storage room. I guess that's why I didn't hear the gunfire blending in with the crowd noise that night. As the story goes, while one guy was watching the opening act, another guy thought it would be a good idea to pull out a pistol and put a slug in his stomach. Jimmy Royals was sitting nearby with guitarist Michael Colford, and the reality didn't sink in until Colford grabbed him, and they hit the floor. I've heard several different accounts about what led up to the shooting. The most consistent one was about a drug dealer who got stiffed and decided gunfire would be the best way to handle this business deal gone awry. Turns out the guy who got shot didn't make it. Good times in Augusta!!!

We performed at the Whipping Post several times, but we had to figure out how to extricate ourselves from one weekend gig there. We mentioned the opportunity to perform in D.C. during the inauguration that was translated as "playing for the inauguration." After being let out of our obligation, we accepted an offer to perform at the "Anti Inaugural Ball" held by the Yippies during Jimmy Carter's January 1977 inauguration. Not only would it be lucrative, but it would also be attended by legendary counter-revolutionary figures from the 1960s.

The Yippies (Youth International Party) was a counter-revolutionary group that referred to themselves as "Groucho Marxist." I loved their sense of humor and street theater. They weren't about changing policy as much as being a thorn in the establishment's side while mostly protesting drug laws. Popular tactics included chaining themselves to the White House fence and, my favorite, lining up on the Georgia-Florida border with shovels so they could dig a trench and separate Florida from the rest of the country.

In 1967, a few of the Yippies, including Abbie Hoffman, got on a tour of the New York Stock Exchange. They threw real and fake money down on the trading floor and were booed by some traders while others scrambled to pick up the cash. After that, the stock exchange installed a glass barrier. In 1968, the Yippies advanced a pig called "Pigasus the Immortal" for President. Our band was a perfect fit for the Yippies even if we weren't overtly political, because we shared their zest for outrageousness and getting a reaction.

The Yippies struggled to be recognized as a legitimate movement dealing with the issues of the day. When Abbie Hoffman jumped on stage at Woodstock during The Who's performance and ranted about John Sinclair's incarceration for giving two joints to an undercover agent, Pete Townshend introduced the butt of his guitar to Hoffman's head. Perhaps that blow to the head, which knocked Hoffman off the stage, possibly explains his behavior over the years that followed.

The entire Anti Inaugural Ball was mysterious. Our connection with the Yippies came from a drug dealer (herein referred to as D.D.). D.D. was a fan who plied his trade to help finance the Yippies and was responsible for paying us to perform in D.C. We were housed in a home owned by members of the Yippies, who also felt a need to post guards outside our bedrooms. We were paid before we hit the stage, and they treated us better than most of the clubs we had played. During the performance, someone slipped into our dressing room and stole a few hundred dollars out of a dancer's purse. The Yippies replaced the money. Who does that anymore?

The Yippies were outrageous but had a lot of heart, and even more importantly, they had a great sense of humor. We met a founding Yippie member, Paul Krassner, and the show's host, Hugh Romney (aka Wavy Gravy). Before introducing us, Wavy Gravy engaged the audience with a call and response, chanting, "Who do we want for President?" The crowd would respond, "Nobody!" The atmosphere was charged.

Wavy Gravy was best remembered for his hosting appearance at Woodstock and receiving his moniker from B. B. King at the 1969 Texas International Pop Festival. He was a pleasant enough guy who could easily have been the official poster boy for acid burnouts.

We performed without a hitch at the legendary Warner Theatre with a packed audience of mainly drug and alcohol casualties. They loved our show and were ready to party, even when they didn't get some of the things we did. We were booed when we brought out a U.S. flag at the beginning of the song "Only in America," which featured one of the best opening verses of any song I've ever written:

A few months later, D.D. contacted me about going to New York City for a photo shoot because *High Times* magazine wanted to do a story on me. I had never read that publication, but I figured I would take all the press I could get.

D.D. bought the plane tickets and, before we got to the airport, informed me that I was not to sit with him or acknowledge him in any way at the airport. Color me naïve; I didn't understand what was happening but complied. When we got to NYC, I was also told to go to baggage claim for my bags but not to stand close to D.D. or acknowledge him until we got outside to catch a taxi. I was starting to figure it out, and it was later confirmed that he was carrying a couple of suitcases filled with hash. I assumed the drug sales proceeds would likely help finance more concerts or shenanigans, roguishness, and tomfoolery.

When we landed in NYC, I met D.D. outside at the cab stand as instructed. We were taken to a building where someone gave me a shirt that read "Eat the Rich." I wore it under my Levi jacket and posed while shaking my hair and jumping up and down. The magazine came out in September 1977 (Issue #25), with author Hunter S. Thompson on the cover and one of those pictures of me in their "Cult Hero" section. Occasionally, I will see a copy of the magazine for sale on eBay.

The story in *High Times* about the band was very flattering, but I learned a valuable lesson that still applies today. You can do an interview and articulate exactly what you mean, but there's no guarantee your words will translate into print. If the publication subscribes to a particular agenda, your interview will likely be shaped to fit that agenda.

High Times was a magazine about the legalization of pot and had a large number of subscribers. In the article, my words were rewritten to reflect enthusiasm about drug legalization, even though I never proclaimed it or ever smoked pot. I didn't recognize the interview in print. I wasn't angry about it; I understood it, and I always thought if people were talking about you, then you were at least on their minds. I've done quite a few interviews and always try to be careful with how I phrase my words, but at the end of it, I realize I only have so much control. I've learned to relax and go with it while offering up as many soundbites as I could squeeze in. That's what most interviewers were more interested in. I've often had fun with it while hinting at certain things or occasionally lying, and then the lie would be printed, and I would quote it.

For the record, even though I was not outspoken about the legalization of pot, I thought it being illegal was silly. Over the years, I've known several with terminal diseases, and smoking pot was the only relief from their pain, even if temporary.

I don't know what it was about the band that attracted drug dealers and some of their crazy ideas to help promote us. A couple of guys in Charlottesville, Virginia, wanted to pay to place a giant shark head on top of a large truck and drive it all over Manhattan. We took a hard pass, although it would have been an adventure, possibly a great story, and couldn't have hurt us.

When I was interviewed by the *Atlanta Journal* preceding the release of my second LP, *Better Dead than Mellow*, with The Mighty Mighty Men from Glad, I implied that I played minor league baseball and was friends with Los Angeles Dodgers manager Tommy Lasorda, who would also appear on the LP. The truth is, I had a part-time job setting up party themes in various locations, and had just returned from New Orleans, where record producer Brendan O'Brien and I set up a corporate Halloween party with a woman dressed as a mermaid lying on a table surrounded by shrimp and seafood. (Yes, insert any number of jokes here). The celebrity of the evening was Lasorda. Since it was a Halloween event, I wore a tiger-striped suit, and Brendan wore a sparkly outfit when we posed with Tommy. The picture ran with the *Atlanta Journal* preview story and fit perfectly for the inside cover of the LP.

If you pick up a copy of this LP/CD, you'll see Tommy also credited for singing backup on the record. This is in keeping with my long-held philosophy of "anything worth doing is worth overdoing." Other than posing once for that photo, I had never had contact with Tommy Lasorda, who also didn't sing on the LP.

Joel Dorn once told me that he would occasionally credit serial murderers and obscure historical figures on LPs. That inspired me to give credit on my LPs to deceased family members for playing orchestral instruments such as violins, cellos, and glockenspiels. Soon more creative liberties were taken. When The Men from Glad appeared at the University of Alabama at Birmingham, I implied that I had worked with Eric Clapton and other legendary musicians. It was printed, and then I quoted it. When I introduced the band members at the end of our show, I always referred to drummer Danny Begay as Bobby Buntrock. Young Bobby was the kid who played Harold "Sport" Baxter on the TV show *Hazel*. Eventually, radio DJs would mention they'd met our drummer before when they hosted events featuring child actors. It was a beautiful thing unfolding: in the mid-1980s, we were touring with Danny "the fake Bobby Buntrock" Begay, while in 1974 the real Buntrock had left the planet due to an automobile accident.

Now that I think about it, it's a little scary, similar to Joseph Goebbels' technique. State the lie, repeat the lie, print the lie, and the lie becomes the truth. I was having fun with my fakery because it was humorous, as opposed to how this technique now is being played out, with the news being reported as subjective rather than factual, resulting in anger and division on a national level. Probably no one was surprised when I wrote about this trend in a song called "Stupid":

You think it's a conspiracy, and you don't believe a word
God's gotta plan to thin the herd of stupid
So grab your remote and your cigarettes
If you don't know nuthin' there's less to forget
Don't stand in the rain complainin' bout gettin' wet and be stupid
Some people say stupid stuff wrapped in a flag
Or while they're drinkin' their lunch from a brown paper bag
But when they call it their faith, I start to gag
They're stupid

STUPID ©2021 DARRYL RHOADES

In May 1977, when we performed our first booking outside of the U.S. at the Horseshoe Tavern in Toronto, I wondered if the audience would get all of our references. That concern went away as I quickly recognized the Canadian audience was getting the same preparation as Americans, with an advertisement that promised, "The Tubes Will Drop Dead When They See This Show."

The lineup on our promo poster included Etta James, Richard Hell, The Steve Kuhn Jazz Quartet featuring Bob Moses and Weather Report's Miroslav Vitous, and a few other performers as a testament to the variety of music you could hear at this venue. Our friends Howard Kaylan and Mark Volman (The Turtles, Flo & Eddie) were in town working on a TV show and took the stage with us at the beginning of our set to sing "God Bless America" as a lead in to "Only in America." Several of us joined them after the show for a late-night meal, and I held out hope that we might tour together. Since Howard and Herb Cohen were cousins, it seemed doable and an obvious match. We wanted that because often we found ourselves on a bill that had me wondering what the booker was thinking. Boogie bands, comedians, ventriloquists, folk singers, jazz bands, and country bands opened for us. Some acts were decent, and others were downright mediocre. However, the worst pairing was at The Kingfish in Baton Rouge when the Hahavishnu opened for blues legends Sonny Terry and Brownie McGee.

I can't imagine what either of these gentlemen thought as a bunch of white guys wore hosiery, wedding dresses, and masks, and women wore cheerleading uniforms and military camouflage. I'm sure these two blues icons had seen just about everything since their pairing in the early 1940s but I have to think we were new ground for them. Their music and stage presence was serious and raw, as opposed to our over-the-top satirical presentation. To their credit, they never said anything to us or even to each other. They just sat back and watched the circus.

When we hit the stage, I pointed out and joked about the obvious to the audience: we probably weren't what they came to see. We won them over and were rebooked to headline several months later. On our return date, the club manager, Danny, stiffed us with a bad check.

However, the story has a happy ending. Danny did a lot of drugs, OD'd, and died a couple of years later, so everything worked out.

We headed back to Austin to open for Balcones Fault, a local band that had signed a national record deal. I was unfamiliar with them but was told they had a good following and shared similarities with us. I didn't see that, but when we took the stage, it felt like old home week. Many who had caught us several months earlier were back with friends. Venues like the Armadillo, where the band felt accepted and part of the Austin family, always recharged our batteries and helped remove the bad taste in our mouths from some roadhouses and pool halls.

We were on the road and trying to fill every night possible. On tour, a night off means spending money you're not making. We worked in Austin, Houston, Longview, Dallas, and many smaller rooms. Even when the stages were built for five, we figured out a way to get 12 on it. The love from the audience would go a long way in keeping up our spirits, but that was never guaranteed. At times, it could go south in a hurry.

In the latter part of May 1977, we performed a show at the Texas Electric Ballroom in Dallas, opening for Brownsville Station. I was a fan of their music and their guitarist, Cub Koda. The venue was huge and packed, and the crowd was ready . . . for Brownsville Station.

On stage, we instantly felt resistance, which crescendoed when a bottle sailed toward Jimmy Royals' head as he was singing our popular parody of Helen Reddy's "I Am Woman." I was changing costumes on the side and amazed when I saw Jimmy catch the bottle in midair, throw it down, and walk off stage. I quickly headed toward the asshole suspect among a group of fellow assholes. Beating me there were our road manager, Jerry Pece, and soundman, Keith Everett, armed with large lead flashlights cops used for attitude adjustments. Keith, ordinarily a docile guy, had the target by the collar and was about to instruct him on correct rock concert etiquette just as security arrived to break it up. The band had left the stage, and our show was over. Within minutes, I found myself backstage with Cub, who proceeded to hold "rock 'n' roll court" (his words) to inject his wisdom on how to prevent such situations. I wasn't up for the lecture of woulda, coulda, shoulda. I was still pissed.

I had forgotten this unpleasant incident until years later when I was doing standup before an oldies concert in Michigan, and one group on the bill was Brownsville Station. I briefly spoke with Cub; his memory was sharp, and it was funnier the second time around—sort of.

We were glad to be working but had little to show for all the miles we were putting in. It was costly to maintain the traveling rock circus tour. Moving 14 people and all that equipment required at least three shoddy vehicles, usually two vans and the station wagon my father gave us, which wasn't in great shape since it had been plowed into while we were loading out at a gig in Philadelphia.

"We had one old station wagon with a messed-up passenger door that wouldn't close, so Darryl's dad drilled into the car and rigged it with a padlock hasp lock to keep the door shut," guitarist Michael Colford recalled. "We had relatively few automotive mishaps, considering the shape of the vehicles we were in, although, I do remember one time where the battery in Darryl's old blue Ford van started leaking some kind of toxic vapors, and everyone in the van had to hang their heads out the windows to finish the trip home."

Road manager Jerry Pece told a story about driving the station wagon my dad had given us. Broken down on the side of the road, Jerry managed to have the station wagon towed to a mechanic at a gas station. The mechanic popped the hood and immediately identified the problem, while also recognizing that the water pump in the car came from a clothes washer. The genius of my father was not lost on me. From the time he was a child, he was always figuring out a way.

In June 1977, we drove from Texas to Nashville for a three-day gig at Exit/In, where we had an established fanbase. Friends drove up from Atlanta to celebrate my 27th birthday as well. Most of the band stayed at the legendary Loveless Inn, known for its hospitality, biscuits, and blackberry jam. The motel was operated by a family, including a son who was a fan and would open the kitchen at 2 a.m. to feed us.

I was still in contact with Herb Cohen and on the fence about where that relationship was going, so I put in a call to Zappa to get his advice. I was out when he returned my call and left this message with

Jerry: "Tell Darryl if he wants to sign a contract and have it shoved up his ass, then sign with Herb." I took his words under advisement.

Herb had persuaded Howard Smith from the *Village Voice* to come to Atlanta to review our show at the Great Southeast Music Hall on July 4 to promote our return gig at the Other End in July 1977. Chuck Young was coming to the same show for a *Rolling Stone* story. I don't think I've ever been more nervous. So much was on the line, to the point where I forgot the lyrics to "American Luv" and started playing with the mic cord while mouthing words, any words. After the set, our soundman Keith approached me and apologized for giving me a bad mic cable. I laughed and explained what was really happening, and over the years, I've reprised that trick several times.

The *Village Voice* review came out on July 18, 1977, the first day of our 10-day run in New York. "Not only do their parodies exquisitely humiliate superstars like Barry Manilow, Kiss, Greg Allman, the Beach Boys, Helen Reddy, John Denver, and Jimi Hendrix, they include endearingly vicious assaults on disco and punk rock," wrote Howard Smith and Brian Van der Horst, adding, "they are also one helluva tight band."

We were a lot more confident and relaxed on our return, and along with the press, some of our musical heroes showed up in force. Iggy Pop came to see us one night and, not being one who was ever shy about being on stage, joined us while we performed "Boot in Your Face." He wore fishnet pantyhose with a cowbell stuffed between his legs, laid down on stage, and rolled around while I stood on top of him, singing and doing my Joey Ramone pose.

Iggy loved the band and talked incessantly about wanting our band to tour with him. At the time, he was being handled by Herb Cohen, and when I brought up the subject of joining Iggy in Italy, Herb quickly dismissed anything Iggy said. I was still trying to get a reading on Herb, and seeing this didn't look good.

For all of my hesitancy about coming to NYC, I was being insecure for no reason. We were killin' it, and the audiences weren't jaded as I had feared. The word was spreading, and we were drawing some interesting crowds. Our sax player Tim Bernard remembered what happened one night during the song "Surfing Shark." "The routine called for Darryl to wear a large papier-mâché shark head and chase me through the club while I was playing the sax solo," Tim said. "Meanwhile, I knew Ace Frehley of the rock group Kiss was 'in the house,' at a table with two women and a couple of bottles of Dom Perignon champagne. Wearing a mish-mash costume comprised of a white matador jacket and gold lamé turban, I climbed up on Ace's table as Darryl was right there comically, furiously engaged in the "shark attack," biting at my legs. One of the bottles of the expensive bubbly went crashing to the floor, all to the delight and encouragement of Ace and his dates."

Joel had begun to work with Robert Palmer on his next LP, and they dropped by. Robert never had a clue about what we were doing, and when I was introduced to him, he had one of those limp wet bread handshakes. If you're going to shake my hand, at least pretend you are present.

Martin Mull was enjoying success from *Fernwood Tonight* and dropped by one night to witness the band completely blowing the place apart with a standing ovation and a couple of encores. When it was over, he came to the dressing room, looked me straight in the sunglasses, and said, "Nice try." As usual, he was killin' me.

There was a buzz about our show, and it didn't hurt that Chuck Young was bringing other journalists like David Fricke and Legs McNeil in to check us out. We hung out a good bit, including Chuck, Jimmy Royals, Handsome Dick Manitoba, and myself taking in the Dead Boys at CBGB, "the undisputed birthplace of punk." I was looking forward to checking out the scene that Chuck couldn't stop talking about. I appreciated the energy and rebellious attitude, but it didn't move me musically, though I must confess that watching Dead Boy Stiv Bators smash a guy in the head with a mic stand was inspirational. I incorporated that move several times years later.

We won converts in NYC but still retained the ability to piss people off on occasion. One night, songwriter Buzzy Linhardt invited Phoebe Snow to catch our show. I was familiar with her recordings (she wrote and sang "Poetry Man") but not her personal life, which seemed to have some bearing on why she was disgusted with me singing "Coathanger."

This was a song sung in character, against type, where I suggested the girl I impregnated should get an abortion, and it wasn't my problem.

> *It worked for Mary, but Joseph was a fool*
> *You're carrying a baby since I last saw you*
> *It's been two years you claim immaculate conception*
> *You've got the problem, but I got the connection*
> *Coathanger*

COATHANGER ©1975 DARRYL RHOADES

I went at it hard, and Phoebe, who had a daughter born with brain damage, took it personally. I had no interaction with her, but Buzzy told me she was distraught and left in a huff before our set ended. Phoebe also advised him not to get mixed up with our group. I was sorry she left, but I'd seen this before, and it wouldn't be the last time by a long shot.

For the record, I've always been pro-choice and understand the passion on both sides. Less than five years before this 1977 performance, *Roe v. Wade* was passed and was still a hot topic targeted by religious and political groups, making the subject even more attractive to me, then and now.

Pro-choice means precisely that, and "pro-life" means someone else can make the choice for the woman, and that someone is usually a man. Pro-choice vs. No-choice. I can see it no other way.

I'd never heard the term "misogynist" until the writer Robert Palmer called me that in an article. I'm not sure what song set him off, but there were many candidates. I could see how a critic could find a lot of reasons to object or criticize and wasn't concerned about it. You take the praise and criticisms equally and also consider the source. Paraphrased, one of my favorite sayings is, "Critics are legless men who teach jogging." Still, it might have been this criticism that gave me the idea to write a song to feature women demeaning chauvinist pigs. The duet was performed by Debbie Thompson and Susan Kirkpatrick while several of us guys sang background and did dance steps to "You're So Impotent, Baby." It wasn't one of my gems but it went a long way to amuse some women in the crowd while my sexual prowess took a beating.

Everything was coming together, and Paul Colby talked to us about working at The Other End on New Year's Eve 1977. I'll never know what opportunities or exposure we missed from turning down that gig, but we were loyal to what we called our home club, Great Southeast Music Hall in Atlanta. Our New Year's Eve holiday show there was an established tradition.

My relationship with Joel grew while the one with Herb stalled. Joel was openly talking to some labels after discovering I hadn't signed any papers with Herb. He would attend our shows when we were in the area, including a club called The Other Side in Wilmington, Delaware.

Some bands went wild on the road by wrecking hotel rooms, throwing TVs out of their windows, and having orgies. In Wilmington, we stayed in a motel by a horse track, which attracted the biggest flies I'd ever seen, and we bet on who could kill the most flies in their rooms. Yes, this was some of the wild partying to pass the time before we would retake the stage. We bought bags of giant rubber flies, put them all over the stage at night, then threw them into the audience.

Quite a few times, our opening acts had significant record deals while we were still the country's most highly publicized unsigned touring band. Zappa once mentioned to me that the early Mothers of Invention experienced the same plight, and even after their records were released, groups with much higher record sales still opened for them because they were the live concert draw. I always appreciated opening acts with character, and the more we performed in showcase clubs, the more I was exposed to some fun groups, or at least interesting ones.

One of our opening acts at The Other Side was the Australian group with a major record deal, The Dingoes. We also worked a few nights at that club with a well-known rocker from Philadelphia, Ken Kweeder, and his band, "The Secret Kids." The S.K. had a militaristic look, including matching uniforms and armbands, and when they took the stage, it looked more like an invasion. Their most popular song,

"Man in the Moon," was catchy, and we would parody it right in front of them.

Most of the time, the bands we worked with had a good sense of humor and were in on the jokes we pulled on stage. When the Mighty Mighty Men from Glad performed with Kansas, and played snippets of their songs in "This Song Is Boring" right in front of them, they laughed and got into the spirit of it. "This Song Is Boring" was one of my earliest and a Hahavishnu's favorite where we repeated the title over and over while burning a guitar, doing mock rockstar poses, and showcasing occasional licks from other band's songs. Like the rest of our show, this was all done in great fun and usually brought the house down, and if the nerves of a few musicians were frayed and their butts puckered it wasn't my concern.

After a solo meeting with Joel, he invited me to drop by the studio during a Steve Goodman session. I had never met Steve and was only mildly familiar with his music, so I was a quiet spectator in the back of the room. Joel and Steve were working on a song titled "You Better Watch Out" with an incredible string arrangement by the legendary Jimmy Haskell. A session with Joel meant he was in control but not dictatorial. He listened to suggestions and Steve's concerns. Steve and I stayed in touch, and he would contact me when he performed in Atlanta, and when time permitted, we hung out. He'd play me songs he was working on, and one in particular, "In Real Life," was one of those songs that felt like a sucker punch to the gut. Great songwriters like Steve have a way of connecting, and I was learning just how talented he was.

I also ran into him in Austin on a night off, and he invited me to an *Austin City Limits* taping. Afterward, we played poker at our hotel with some of the band and a few locals before heading out for breakfast. The radio was playing during breakfast, and we both heard the news about Zero Mostel's death. Steve looked at me and blurted out, "Wow, somebody just took a lot of air out of the world." I had never heard that phrase before but instantly felt the words. When I dropped him off at his hotel, he wrote down his phone number and the names of his wife and children. That said a lot about Steve. He was hilarious, sensitive, and intelligent, and in 1984 when I received a call from Joel informing me of his passing, I immediately felt, "Wow, somebody just took a lot of air out of the world."

After Austin, we worked a show at The Bayou in Washington, D.C., with Root Boy Slim and the Sex Change Band with the Rootettes and our friends, The Nighthawks. I'd heard the comparisons and knew Root Boy had a following, a story, and a reputation.

Born Foster MacKenzie III, Root Boy was a Harvard grad with a fondness for LSD, which likely played a part in his schizophrenia diagnosis. He was brilliantly talented, and while I didn't get to know him as well as I'd wished, I'll always admire the fact that he was kicked out of, and banned, from his Delta Kappa Epsilon fraternity house at Harvard by his fraternity brother, George W. Bush.

Root Boy and the band were signed by Warner Brothers and recorded a well-produced LP featuring the song "Boogie 'Til You Puke," a phrase that ended up on T-shirts and bumper stickers while the record was less successful. For the next several years, record company execs reminded me of this in negotiation meetings.

Root Boy wrote off-kilter songs, dressed wildly on stage, and was backed by a large band. While he had a considerable following, he didn't sell enough records to turn a decent profit for the record company's efforts. I was painted with the same brush and never dealt with a record company that could get past that bit of logic. Being compared with a group that wasn't turning a profit for their record label gave pause for other labels to take a chance and that was a tough obstacle to overcome.

There were several suggestions made in these meetings. The most popular was cutting the band's size and fine-tuning the songwriting to consider increasing commercial appeal. There was no second-guessing the size of the band. I never considered it, and as far as songwriting direction, I can't even guess what that would have led to, and I wonder if those who made the suggestions had a clue, either.

On a side note, I was contacted by legendary record producer Jerry Wexler. He alluded to the possibility of bringing me to Muscle Shoals to record with the in-house band responsible for the soundtracks of so many 1960s classics. Hindsight is a bitch, and maybe I should have been more excited, but I figured the band who starved, worked their asses off, and sometimes argued with me deserved to be the band on the record. There are no regrets or second-guessing because this idea never went far beyond a few conversations. Along with the expense of a group our size and no apparent hits, we were viewed as a great live show with explosive energy and incredible visual appeal, which would be challenging to capture on vinyl.

Chuck Young's piece on us came out in *Rolling Stone* on August 25, 1977. Being the *Star Wars* issue with the cast on the cover was a lucky placement for us as a collector's edition. The high we experiencd from the article was short-lived.

The following day, we pulled into the gravel parking lot at The Warehouse in Conroe, Texas, with wiring so lousy we blew the circuits all night long. Our assigned dressing room was the beauty salon next door. We soon found comedy in the screams from the audience to play ZZ Top songs. To keep our spirits up and find joy wherever possible, I hung upside down from the rafters in my underwear, screamin', "I'm Just Lookin' for Some Tush."

On August 31, 1977, we worked our third date at the Armadillo with opening act Andy Pratt, who had written a song, "Avenging Annie," covered by Roger Daltrey. A couple of nights before we worked together, Andy and his band were in Houston when a mugger ran up to him and yelled, "I'm on acid, give me all your money!" then stabbed him in the hand. I still can't believe he was onstage playing piano at the Armadillo two nights later, but he wouldn't miss that gig.

While I was writing this story, I was reminded by Jimmy Royals about the time I stabbed him in the hand, although I wasn't on acid. When I was re-entering the stage dressed in 1950s leather jacket garb for the intro to "Burgers from Heaven," I would twirl a knife while yelling at the band to quit playing that "cock rock" and make a mock attack on some of the band members. On this particular night, Jimmy raised his hand at the perfect time and my knife was in the perfect angle to stab him, and I did. I stayed in character, and we went through the song; Jimmy exited the stage at his usual time, but I found out later the cut was deep and bleeding profusely. Somehow, he got through the performance, and I realized that the band members who had voiced concerns about the knife were right. A smarter Darryl would have thought to wrap tape around the blade, use a fake rubber knife, or abandon any prop that would send someone to the emergency room.

Our gig with Andy was the first time headlining the Armadillo, and it was pretty rare for an unsigned group to headline. It was also the first time the "Burgers from Heaven" artwork appeared on a poster created by legendary Austin artist Rick Turner. Rick had accompanied us to NYC and painted the same artwork in the dressing room, admired by everyone backstage.

I've experienced many surreal moments, but few could top performing a takeoff of an iconic musician while he's watching.

A teaser for the WTBS variety show *Future Shock* had host James Brown entering some swinging doors with "Soul Brother #1" written on them. He then grabbed the mic and screamed, "I love you!" and did a split. When the show offered us the opportunity to perform, we wanted to make a big entrance. Parodying Mr. Dynamite's commercial was a good idea. Marvin and Gena bought a ton of brown butcher paper, taped it together, painted a record on it, wrote "Soul Brother #2" underneath the record, and then perforated it so I could bust through after the intro into the arms of dancers Gina Grant and Sue Schell. I grabbed the mic while the band jammed on the intro of "Suicide," attempted this white man's version of a split, and did the mic stand drop-catch that James had made famous. I grew up watching the Godfather push the stand away from himself and with his foot on the stand's base he'd jerk it back into position with the mic landing in his hands.

After the performance was shot, I went to one of the cameramen who was shooting next to "the hardest workin' man in show business," James Brown. The camera guy told me he had a difficult time holding the camera steady. James watched the performance as if he didn't understand what we were doing and then commented out loud, "Is that a trick on me?"

After the shoot, I introduced myself to Mr. Brown and was met with the dreaded "wet bread handshake." I told him what an honor it was to appear on his show and how much his music meant to me, which is still true today. He looked at me as if I was a hologram, and his loss for words was puzzling. I'd heard Mr. Brown speak several times, including a ceremony where he took the stage, accepted an award, and said, "I'm speechless, I'm speechless," and 45 minutes later he was still talking. To this day, I'm not sure if he heard me, saw me, or was even there, as he appeared to be circling the cosmos.

A TV or movie is often shot out of sequence, and the timeline is adjusted during editing. Our appearance on *Future Shock* was shot without an introduction. I stuck around long enough to watch The Godfather of Soul struggling to pronounce "Hahavishnu," and when our appearance aired on Christmas Eve, 1976, his intro was, "Now ladies and gentlemen, Darryl Roe and the Hahavishnew." I was told later that even getting this took seven takes. *Future Shock* went off the air in 1979, and other than my copy with the missing intro from Mr. Brown, our appearance and most of the others epidsodes have been either destroyed or placed in a vault somewhere.

Our New Year's Eve shows at the Great Southeast Music Hall opened as a Holiday Inn lounge act, and Jonny Hibbert played the host who told cheesy jokes like "Hey, did you hear about India? They have a new deli." Yeah, I said cheesy. The band would perform several holiday songs like "Jingle Bell Rock," and then all hell would break loose from the back of the room, which led to an unexpected stage entrance. One of my favorite showpieces of all time, often brought up 50 years later by those who saw it performed live, is "Santa Claus on the Cross."

The cross and foot brace was made by nailing 2x8 wood pieces, with large, embedded spikes for a handhold, and I took my place on it dressed in a Santa Claus costume. Four big guys would lift me and, on cue, walk from the back of the room toward the stage. "Something is happening!" a surprised and confused Jonny Hibbert would yell. "What's going on in the back of the room?"

"You've got the wrong guy!" I continued to scream, till I got close enough to pick up a mic and then get dumped onto the stage.

Eating lit cigarettes was always a nice touch too, especially when we went into "Think of Me When You're Under Him," a take-off on the lounge acts like those I'd played drums behind for years. All the years of playing in country clubs, Holiday Inns, country bar dives, and backing lounge lizards were paying off; none of those experiences were going to waste.

The American debut of the Sex Pistols was a media circus in a room with a capacity of 523, which several thousand still claim to have witnessed. I've been interviewed many times about the Pistols' debut at the Great Southeast Music Hall in Atlanta. On January 5, 1978, I was there.

My part of the show was small; I was only sitting in with the opening act, Cruise-O-Matic, for a song with Hahavishnu bandmate Marvin Jackson. None of us about to take the stage felt any pressure; we were prepared to have fun and figured on getting some pushback from the crowd.

The crowd was there for the Pistols, so beach music and British 60s pop weren't going to play well. Cruise-O-Matic was a 1960s cover band started by two ex-Hahavishnu members, Edward Tanner and Jonny Hibbert. There are different versions of why they were chosen to open up for the Pistols. I prefer to believe they were picked as mood-setters to piss off the crowd, a job they did perfectly. The idea of adding me on stage to perform a song satirizing the evening was the perfect way to end that part of the show. The idea of taking any of this seriously never occurred.

At the end of Cruise-O-Matic's set, I took the stage with Marvin, sitting in with the band to perform "Boot in Your Face," a short song satirizing the punk scene in much the same way that I made fun of disco, gospel, and other genres of music. The fact that it hit a nerve with some of the punk fans was a bonus.

I wore a 4-foot metal safety pin that looked like it ran through my stomach. I sprayed "Kill Me" on my jersey, spat at the audience, and occasionally received a response in kind with tomatoes bouncing off my chest.

BOOT IN YOUR FACE ©1977 DARRYL RHOADES, REX PATTON

The thought that some idiots brought produce to a rock show was comical. My theatrics were equally matched by the band's posing all over the stage. Some of the audience likely got what we were doing, but subtleties and humor were not that crowd's strong suit. The joke some missed was when the song ended, I would introduce another song for "My Fadda," a shorter version of the same song.

Cruise-O-Matic's set ended, and now the audience was ready for anyone not named Cruise-O-Matic. In the dressing room before the show, the Pistols were nervous. There was some small talk, but it was crowded with the press trying to get in and their handlers trying to keep them separated and focused. Our friend, Glenn Allison, was helping provide their security. His size was intimidating, but he was the proverbial "gentle giant."

The Pistols hit the stage, opening with "God Save the Queen," and the crowd predictably went wild. Depending on who you talk to, the show was either fantastic or nothing special. I found them to be the Monkees without the musicality. I appreciated their energy and ability to make people respond, but I didn't find their music to be anything I hadn't heard before. Drummer Paul Cook and guitarist Steve Jones were decent. Sid Vicious was a poser holding the bass, and Johnny Rotten (John Lydon) was the ringmaster.

The most talented person in that circus wasn't on stage.

The guy who pushed the right buttons and pulled the right strings was their manager, Malcolm McLaren. McLaren was a clothing designer and boutique owner who understood the value of shock and outrageousness. He fancied himself as an artist and songwriter, but he gained traction as a promoter and manager through his short stint with the New York Dolls and then putting the Pistols together. With his business savvy, he set the media in motion and the country talking about punk music, specifically the Sex Pistols.

I certainly wasn't in camp with most of the glowing critiques from the press. Rock journalist Robert Christgau favorably reviewed the show for the *Village Voice*, but with a condescension toward the South that I found familiar with many Northern journalists.

"The rock and rollers who opened the show, a good-time 60s copy band from Georgia Tech who will be referred to here as the Shitheads," Christgau wrote in a review published Janary 16, 1978. "About 40 minutes into the set the Shitheads brought out a special guest, 'Atlanta's leading punk.' This turned out to be an exceptionally hirsute person wearing a 'Kill Me' T-shirt and carrying a large papier-mâché safety pin who sang two almost identical two-chord songs—both called, apparently, 'Boot in Your Face.' He also spat at the audience, but the cops, praise the Lord, restrained themselves."

Leaving out the band's name in a failed attempt at humor and not mentioning my name weren't minor details. They put this reviewer into ass-kicking territory. Somebody worked hard to make me a four-foot metal safety pin, not a "papier-mâché" one. Hell yeah, I spat on the audience only because I didn't know where you were sitting, Mr. Christgau.

My appearance on stage that night lasted no more than five minutes, but the visibility and its use as a promotional tool lasted way beyond the Sex Pistols' existence. Reviews from that show ended up in the foreign press, and the national and international press was more than I'd had in a long time. While my name rarely popped up, my image appeared in my favorite article from the supermarket tabloid *National Examiner.*

In the February 14, 1978, issue, this story about punk music and the musicians returning to England is titled "Good Riddance Punks." I read the article and never understood the point, but appreciated all the pictures, including mine on stage wearing the "Kill Me" shirt. The caption: "Another punk at a concert with a request many music fans would like to fulfill."

Yep, that McLaren boy knew what he was doing. It didn't stop there.

I'd heard about a punk documentary, *D.O.A.: A Rite of Passage*, not to be confused with the 1950 Edmund O'Brien flick of the same name. By coincidence, my music attorney, Scott Sanders, and I were in NYC when the movie premiered and went to see it. My appearance in the film was edited to short portions of "Boot in Your Face" between edited segments of an interview with record store owner Bleeker Bob. I stayed for the credits, which didn't include Cruise-O-Matic, Marvin, or myself. The song wasn't even in the music credits.

Since I was never contacted for permission, I called Doc Pomus for advice, and he recommended that I call his brother, famed divorce attorney Raoul Felder.

Mr. Felder explained while I had a case, it would cost a ton of money to take to court and would net much less from my claim. In other words, save yourself a lot of worry, time, and cash, and forget it. I contacted the company that released the movie and discovered they had edited out my scenes rather than respond. Only the edited version of the film was made available for several years. I eventually got a call explaining that the Pistols were thinking of getting back together, and if their trial shows were successful, they wanted to re-release the movie with my scenes.

As I understand it, the Pistols did a few shows, and nobody cared. The buzz was gone.

Around 2018, a friend told me a BluRay version of *D.O.A.: A Rite of Passage* was being released with my scenes back in, so I tracked down the law firm handling the contracts, and negotiated a check for myself and "Boot in Your Face" co-writer Rex Patton.

In 1980, my friends, The Nighthawks, were in the studio recording their self-titled debut LP for Mercury Records. They recorded their version of "Boot in Your Face," which I still have yet to hear, but I saw the listing on the promo track sheet. They explained that it was recorded, but their producer vetoed its release, leaving it off the album. Its inclusion could have led to a Grammy and being referred to as part of the soundtrack of our lives. But since the song wasn't recorded, the LP didn't get a Grammy and its modest sales led to The Nighthawks losing their record deal, I was spared the task of having to write an acceptance speech.

Quite a few bands had been signed based on their performance at The Main Point in Bryn Mawr, Pennsylvania, and as we prepared for our first appearance there in January 1978, a snowstorm was starting that we worried would affect the crowd size. We were all running on empty as Jackson Browne sat at the bar, watching us go through our sound-check. The band always rose to the occasion, though. There were no slackers on that stage, and everyone played off of each other's energy.

We had one of those nights where everything clicked. Of course there was tension from the staff when I filled my mouth with ham-burger buns, jumped on a table, and started spitting them all over the crowd during "Burgers from Heaven." The mood was kicked up a notch when I worked my way over to the club owner, who didn't par-ticularly appreciate it.

On this run of Northeast clubs, we broke into new areas and several legendary rooms, including Paul's Mall in Boston. I had never been to Boston, and was unfamiliar with that club and its history as an upscale jazz venue. The snowstorm didn't do us any favors, and the enthusiastic audience could have likely fit in our van. At the same time, the *National Lampoon* touring show we were favorably compared to played down the street. I felt like we were sitting at the adult table but eating from the kid's menu.

Bad weather on the road wasn't a new challenge, but the North-east snowstorm of 1978 was more severe. We slowly made our way to Woodstock, New York, to perform at Joyous Lake and stay ahead of the whiteouts. The road can, and often does, bring out the strange in us all, between the lack of sleep, bad diets and low income and many miles traveling in crowded vans, it was taking a toll on several in the band, and I'll use that as an excuse for how bizarre things could get sometimes.

We finished our set at Joyous Lake and were told that a major ice storm was coming, so we decided to leave in a few hours. The weather was so cold that the people who walked out with heads sweaty from the load out found their hair frozen. As we returned to the condo, some guy from the audience attached himself to us without saying much, which was a little awkward. No one addressed why he was there, so another band member and I figured we should freak him out. We went into the next room, stripped off our clothes, sprayed shaving cream all over our bodies, then walked back into the room where the band was hanging and acted as if this was normal. The other band member, still covered in shaving cream, started moving back and forth in his chair, and when he got up, there was a shaving cream landing strip where his ass had been. I'm not sure how anyone kept a straight face, but the stranger had a weird look on his face and, within a few minutes, calmly declared he needed to go.

On our way to appear at My Father's Place in Long Island, the ice storm was so blinding that we had a semi brush up against the van and knock off the side mirror. We played with hometown favorites, The Good Rats, and my New York music attorney, David Sonnenberg, caught our show for the first time. David was Meat Loaf's manager and the go-between in negotiations with Joel and me. Joel understood my hesitancy in business dealings and paid David to represent me. It was an odd arrangement and an apparent conflict of interest although I had complete trust in Joel. I'd heard so many horror stories about working relationships going south that I wanted to ensure I was covered and this arrangement was the only choice I had. David was intelligent, and his conversations with Joel would occasionally turn contentious. Sitting there and listening to them talk about me as if I wasn't in the room was unpleasant, but I figured it was part of the process.

We were working our way back home when we performed at The Elbow Room in Harrisonburg, Virginia, with a popular regional blues band, the Charlottesville Allstars. We were hired on a recommendation by Rev. Billy C. Wirtz, and we became friends and would go on to work together on several projects, including me producing his first LP, *Salvation Through Polyester.* The album was crudely recorded on a small budget, but captures his magic at the time. I'd produced a few recordings but was never comfortable doing that, especially after working with people who were great at it.

In early 1978, we performed at the National Association for Campus Activities (NACA) convention in Atlanta and received some incredible offers for college dates. At the end of our set, I jumped off the stage to go into the audience wearing my papier-mâché shark head but landed on the side of my foot, which instantly sent pain looking for many places to land in my body. I fought back the urge to throw up, and hobbled around in the crowd till I made my way back to the stage and finished the last song. That injury sidelined me for several weeks and knocked the band out of performing some critical dates for much-needed income. This event wasn't the death knell but signaled more bad luck coming our way.

We eventually fulfilled several college dates, which were often lucrative but not necessarily a perfect match for what we did. Responding to a short notice request, we made our way in the dead of winter to Ferris State University in Big Rapids, Michigan, to fill in for Dan Hill.

Dan had to make a TV appearance to promote his new hit, "Sometimes When We Touch," a syrupy love song about a guy who would cry and get emotional when he described his love to his girlfriend. The music sounded perfect for a hormone replacement commercial, but like other songs of its ilk, it worked for radio.

Lured by the need to pay bills, and feed our addiction to food, we didn't stop to ask, "What in the hell are they thinkin'?" We figured the money was good and who knows, maybe we'll pick up some new fans (or not). When an audience is expecting to hear love songs but is treated instead to songs about abortion, necrophilia, euthanasia, and instrumentals inspired by flatulence, performed by a band dressed in drag queen chic, Ku Klux Klan costumes, and security guard uniforms, well, let's just say it was a little confusing. Neither they nor we had any idea what was in store, and we quickly realized that someone didn't do their research and was just focused on filling the vacancy.

The band was never big on contract riders, but we made a few modest demands, such as cheese, bread, crackers, cokes, etc. Upon our arrival in the dressing room in Big Rapids, we discovered a pathetic tray of semi-ripened fruit and white bread. The kicker was Cheez Whiz in plastic bottles. So, as we learned that night, a rider can't prevent one from still being served a large bowl of disrespect or indifference.

The great thing about Cheez Whiz, besides being able to seal your prostate, is its versatility. As demonstrated that night by our bass player, Ronnie Chamblee, who possessed excellent penmanship, it can be used to write one's name on the wall. Yet, I don't think this had anything to do with the less-than-stellar review of the show we received in the college paper the following week, claiming we were offensive. The review featured a picture of me eating a hamburger bun from the tray Gena held in front of her hips, just outside her crotch. The review described some songs as insulting and the band as over the top, offending many in the audience.

While I took pride in hitting the target, I had to respond to the paper, so I wrote them a letter explaining our plight. Here we were, a band coming from Georgia in the dead of winter, filling in on short notice for a megastar like Dan Hill, who wrote a romantic anthem that will live on in the hearts and anuses of America.

So a college got stuck with a band that wasn't appropriate for their "taste." We had experienced it a couple of times, but this example was more extreme and likely booked by an agent more concerned about his commission than supplying a suitable replacement for Mr. "Sometimes When We Touch."

This song lives on among the thorns residing up my ass. To drive that disgust further up the tunnel, it was re-recorded by a man I consider to be one of the greatest rockers in the 1970s, Rod Stewart. I may never be able to claim to have a hit or to have tons of sex with supermodels, but I can commit to never recording a version of "Sometimes When We Touch," so I guess things even out sometimes.

There's something about frozen swimming pools in the dead of a Michigan winter that brings out the stupidity in all of us. Okay, maybe just me, which would explain why I jumped in the pool and broke through the ice on a $5 bet. When I climbed out of the pool, there were scratches all over my back from the ice, and when I got back to Atlanta, my girlfriend accused me of sleeping with someone who in the height of ecstasy put their nails in my back. While the accusation really fed my ego, I laughed and thought it was crazy that she came up with something like that. I later learned the definition of "projection."

I bet Dan Hill never wrote a song about that.

On March 5, 1978, we opened for Sha Na Na at the Duluth Arena in Minnesota. The 9500-seat capacity was primarily filled with kids and their parents waiting to see the wacky headliners with the sophomoric TV show filled with lame-ass jokes. Bowser had already split, and the band seemed to be playing out the string as crowd-pleasers and friendly guys. Still, they sandbagged us by only letting us use half the sound and lights, a common practice by some headliners. They even explained we were getting more than most bands. No matter their rationale, I saw it similar to someone running a race but telling the other runner you would only cut off a few of their toes instead of a foot. I never understood the practice, although I've seen several versions of this in comedy where the headliners would cut the time of acts in front of them if they felt insecure, or limit subjects the support acts could talk about, and of course refuse to permit the opening acts to sell merchandise because they feared it would affect their sales. But that wasn't the only thing that stunk at the Duluth Arena, the largest venue we'd played to date. Downstairs from the concert, the arena was hosting the The Ringling Bros. and Barnum & Bailey Circus, and the smell of elephant dung wafted up to the delight of concertgoers and musicians gagging on stage.

Even as college dates were coming in for us, it seemed like too little too late for some band members. I was starting to hear about possible defections; several band members were being offered other jobs, and I couldn't blame them. We were fed with hopes that always seemed just outside our grasp with the next showcase from the record company A&R man who either didn't show up, or if they did, they didn't get us. We lived on promises and a $5 per diem while traveling all over the country in two vans with no air conditioning through heat and blizzards. We existed on quotes from every magazine predicting big things with accolades not handed out to popular groups with huge success, record support, and an income.

Things were starting to get wacky in the asylum. On April 20, 1978, we were booked for a show at Mississippi State University and drove to the wrong venue in the wrong town before making it to Starkville and finding another band setting up for their show that night.

From the wings, I watched our opening act, a comic named Kelley Monteith. I was familiar with Kelley from his appearances on *The Tonight Show Starring Johnny Carson*. While watching him, I wondered how anyone could get up on stage alone and keep the attention of any audience, much less a room full of college students, for an hour. The irony isn't lost on me.

We limped through several gigs and personnel changes before calling it quits in May 1978. After almost three years of non-stop touring, and putting Band-Aids on problems that required major surgery, I had to step back.

Oddly enough, a month after we all decided to call it quits, I got a call from Sha Na Na's management asking if we were available to tour with them. I gave it a day and then declined. I would have had to work in several new members, and my heart wasn't into it. It would have been more about the money, and every time I've been in that place, the results weren't something that made me proud.

Throughout the showcases, prominent national write-ups, a huge growing fanbase, and well-intentioned attempts by entrepreneurs to manage the group and secure a record deal for us, nothing of real substance ever manifested.

Jimmy Ginn dropped out of the picture when Rex Patton and I made our trip to the West Coast and made connections with Herb Cohen. Herb's budget in NYC, with the high-powered press machine and $5-a-day per diem, evaporated; months later the hotel where we stayed phoned me wondering who would pay the hotel bill because Herb didn't take care of it. Joel Dorn's attempts to get us signed, while bringing record company presidents in to see us, flatlined. He was hanging his hopes on Island Records founder Chris Blackwell, who decided to go with another Georgia-based group starting to make waves at the time, The B-52s.

The manager for a recording group called Nector flew into Atlanta, stayed at my house, then rode with us to one of our last gigs, at Georgia Southern University in Statesboro. It was genuinely forgettable.

I got a call in November 1978 from Alex Cooley, asking if I would emcee a show at The Omni in Atlanta. It wasn't a big deal, and I could use the bread since I wasn't working. The concert lineup was the Ramones/Van Halen/Black Sabbath show on November 13.

One of the roadies for Van Halen recognized me from a performance we did at the Armadillo in Austin and wanted to introduce me to David Lee Roth, who shook my hand and never looked at me once while he scanned the crowd coming in. The only thing worse than a wet bread limp handshake is the one where the person is looking past you as if you weren't there. My mood quickly turned to dread, and then I met the tour manager, who also happened to be Van Halen's manager. He looked at me with some familiarity, and when told I was emceeing, he squashed that plan immediately by saying an emcee wasn't needed. I faked my best "I'm so let down" look while feeling a huge relief. I later realized I had met Noel Monk briefly before the Sex Pistols show when he was working as their tour manager, and I'm so glad he decided my services weren't needed. I was even more thankful when I saw the crowd turn on the opening act, The Ramones, booing and pelting them with coins and whatever was available. After The Ramones walked off stage, I left, and the next day got a call from Alex apologizing for "wasting my time" and asking me to come by and pick up a check whenever it was convenient.

Alex was a rare human. Of all the promoters, club owners, and managers I've met, Alex stands head and shoulders above everyone else. When he passed, many of us in the music community understood we'd lost a great friend.

After disbanding the group, I remained in touch with Joel Dorn, who occasionally suggested different projects for me, including my writing songs for the artists he was working with. The most amusing was being asked to write a song for Michael Winslow of *Police Academy* movie fame.

Michael was a skilled comedian and actor with an uncanny ability to reproduce sounds ranging from Jimmy Page's guitar to a fighter jet. Joel was tasked with producing his newest album, and I was asked to write a song highlighting Michael's skills.

My friend Mike Orlin came over to my house to work on a demo, and we came up with a Barry White parody with a Star Wars theme. Using various machines to simulate sound effects, such as a variable speed drill to sound like a lightsaber, the song was funny, and Joel liked it. I knew Joel was working on the album, but after we hadn't talked for a couple of months, he called to explain that he and Michael were incompatable in the studio. Joel was my friend and a great guy, but I sensed he could be a little tough on anyone unequipped to handle his brutal frankness. I didn't know Michael then, but I also learned something similar had happened between Joel and Robert Palmer. Joel left or was removed from that project, and claimed Palmer didn't appreciate his approach.

About ten years later, while performing standup in Charleston, South Carolina, I came face to face with the other act on the bill, Michael Winslow. After reminding him about our connection, he filled in the blanks about his "road to almost" with Joel and making of his album.

I'm not big on clichés like "whatever happens is meant to be" but I have come to understand that success is subjective. I wasn't done walking the road to almost. I had many projects planned for the future and none involved me recording a version of "Sometimes When We Touch."

Dekalb court case forcing Jesse Sasser to get a haircut, 1969.

478-6175   478-9044   766-5821

Bow & Arrow Restaurant
8630 South Expressway — Jonesboro, Ga.

Yate's Hillbilly Steak House
Arrowhead Shopping Center
South Expressway at Old 41 Hwy.
Jonesboro, Georgia

Terrace Restaurant
Adjoining Atlanta Terrace Motel
South Freeway — Hapeville, Georgia

Grady C. Minter   Owner and Manager

If you want to help your Government "stamp out Segregation, then take a Nigger to lunch or dinner, but please don't come to our locations. And we don't want any Nigger business, and if it's forced on us, we sho can't help it. And we hope you white folks wont hold it against us.

P.S. I Didn't Vote For Johnson—

Jonesboro, Georgia, restaurant racist business card, 1964.

Right Wingnut journalism "Breaking the Hippie Code," 1967.

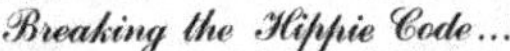

Breaking the Hippie Code...

Authorities in Santa Cruz County, Calif., have broken the new hippie code—symbols which are scrawled on sidewalks, fences, gate posts, and which advise transient hippies where to find a "crash pad" (one night's lodgings), warn of dangers, suggest methods of begging. Simple code is similar to the hobo signs found around railroad communities in Depression years. Police and residents had noticed rash of graffiti in recent months; amateur cryptologists couldn't break the symbols' meanings. Then police on narcotics raid picked up hippie type with poor memory—his notebook was a Rosetta Stone, giving symbols and their meanings in plain language. Markings usually found in crossroads communities, in this case, halfway between Haight-Ashbury district (San Francisco) and Big Sur (south of Monterey), both big hippie centers. Symbols now in nationwide use.

This way to...

Safe Camp

Be Good (religious)

If sick will Care for you

Police Uptight

Man with Gun

You will be beaten

Fink

House under surveillance

woman

Kindhearted woman

Tell pitiful story

Don't Give Up

Courtesy: THE NATIONAL EAGLE.

Their Peace Symbol - "The Broken Cross"

The Communists are winning their battle for men's minds. They make a special effort to capture the minds of our youth. And to destroy the will of all who resist their takeover.

Many Americans are familiar with the peace symbol shown here. Some are even willing to wear it. But, what most of them do not know, is that it is "the Broken Cross" of the anti-Christ.

The Communists won another victory when TIME magazine, on its cover of June 7, 1968, carried a picture of a bearded youth as the 1968 graduate. For all the world to see, he wore the Broken Cross!

The Communists have infiltrated the garment industry and you find the Broken Cross embroidered on jackets and other garments for the casual American to wear. The Broken Cross is also manufactured as a metal trinket, to be worn on a chain. And many of the younger set wear it thoughtlessly or as a peace symbol knowingly. But seldom do they realize that they are supporting the emblem of the anti-Christ, the Broken Cross.

Today many men's stores and ladies' ready-to-wear stores advertise this symbol of the atheists and sell it openly, perhaps even ignorantly to thoughtless people who do not know what they are buying or planning to wear. But every symbol of the Broken Cross that is publicly displayed is noted gleefully by the godless Communists, who can see how thoughtless and vulnerable the Americans really are.

THE "PEACE ACTION" SYMBOL AND HOW IT GREW

"The symbol of the Communist PEACE is a very well known symbol. It was called the Witch's Foot in the middle ages, and it was a common symbol of the Devil, with the cross reversed and broken."
—Michael Wurmbrand, formerly of Roumania

* THE BOOK OF SIGNS, by Rudolph Koch. (Symbols used from earliest times to the Mid-

* The Crow's foot, or witch's foot

"Beautify America" billboard, 1968.

The Catacombs, July, 1968.

Atlanta Municipal Auditorium with the Royal Guardsmen, 1968.

Atlanta Municipal Auditorium Christmas Concert, 1969.

The Bag at the Catacombs, 1967.
L-R: Monty Sasser (drums), Michael Brown (bass),
Bruce Lowe (guitar), Rick Simpson (guitar).

Banana promo shot at Piedmont Park, 1968.
L-R: Gary Lewis, Gary Dockery, Tom Raybon, Darryl Rhoades.

Lakeside High School Biafra Charity Dance, 1970.
L-R: Joe Neil (organ), Gary Lewis (guitar), Darryl Rhoades (drums).

Lakewood Fairgrounds concert, August 24, 1975.

Early promo shot in graveyard, 1975.
Back Row, L-R: Susan Kirkpatrick, Debbie Thompson, Jocy Dukes, Jimmy Royals, Marvin Jackson, Keith Christopher (kneeling), Jimmy Walker, David Irwin. Front Row: Jonny Hibbert, Darryl Rhoades.

Hahavishnu Orchestra. Bistro, Atlanta, Georgia, 1975.
Background: Debbie Thompson, Jimmy Royals, Susan Kirkpatrick,
Edward Tanner, Keith Christopher, Marvin Jackson.
Foreground: Gena Grant, Darryl Rhoades.

Early Hahavishnu promo, 1976.
Back Row, L-R: David Irwin, Jonny Hibbert, Jimmy Walker, Joey Dukes, Darryl Rhoades, Keith Christopher, Steve May, Marvin Jackson.
Front Row, L-R: Sue Schell, Susan Kirkpatrick, Jimmy Royals, Debbie Thompson, Gena Grant.

On the streets of Philadelphia, 1977.
Standing, L-R: Jerry Pece, Robert Estes, Jimmy Royals, Ronnie Chambley, Debbie Thompson, Susan Kirkpatrick, Joey Dukes, Darryl Rhoades, Keith Everett, Mary Lehman. Sitting, L-R: Tim Bernard, some guy playing accordion on the street, Marvin Jackson.

Iggy Pop (James Newell Osterberg, Jr.) and Darryl Rhoades
on stage in New York City at The Other End.
Hahavishnu appearance, 1977.

The Great Southeast Music Hall, with The Nighthawks,
Atlanta, Georgia, July 4, 1977.
L-R: Michael Colford, Jimmy Thackery, Mark Wenner, Marvin Jackson.

Sex Pistols' American debut, January 5, 1978.
The Great Southeast Music Hall, Atlanta, Georgia.
Darryl Rhoades, Robert Schmid, Rex Patton.

Rock 'n' Bowl NARAS event, August 15, 1981.
Bruce Hampton, Darryl Rhoades.

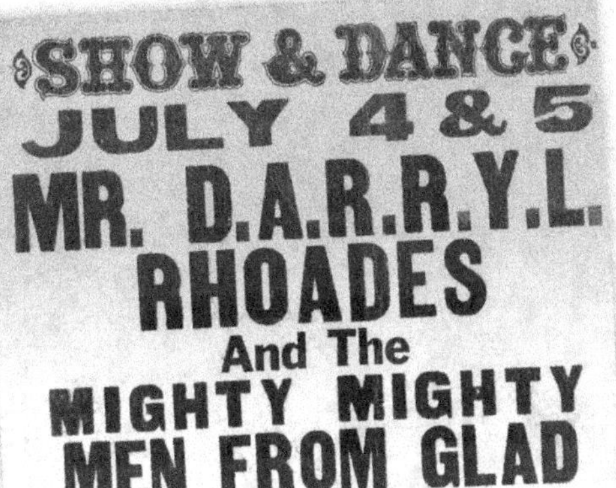

Various posters, 1985–1986.

Frontin' the Men from Glad at 688, Atlanta, Georgia, c. 1986.

L-R: Rick Hubbard, Bo Messina, Rick Kurtz c. 1986.

The Great Southeast Music Hall, Atlanta, Georgia. December 31, 1976.

Appearance on Nickelodeon, New York City, 1980. L-R: Darryl Rhoades, Jeff Calder, Peter Jarkunas, Mike Orlin, Jimmy Royals.

With Negro League Hall of Famer, Buck Leonard, 1992.

With my childhood idol, New York Yankees legend, Moose Skowron, 1993.

Hangin' with New York Yankees great, Hank Bauer, 1993.

Partying in New Orleans with Tommy Lasorda and Brendan O'Brien, 1984.

Midnight in the Garden of Evel Knievel promo poster, c. 1999.

Darryl jamming with The Dude and Lil' Dude.
Crazy Heart cast party Santa Fe, New Mexico, August, 2008.

Crazy Heart cast party, Santa Fe, New Mexico, August, 2008.
L-R: Maggie Gyllenhaal, Darryl, Jeff Bridges.

The Men from Glad with non-English speaking Cuban family,
Sloppy Joe's, Key West, Florida, date?.
Standing L-R: Bo Messina, Cuban mom, Danny Bigay, C. C. Sax (Carl
Crabtree), Cuban daughter, Cuban dad, Cuban son.
Sitting: Darryl Rhoades, Corky Hughes.

CHAPTER TEN

Burgers from Heaven

Without you in my world I have no place
With every burger that I eat I see your face
I can't believe you've left me I'm still in a daze
It's not the same I hear your name ooze out of the mayonnaise
Burgers from heaven sent from up above
Burgers from heaven . . . those burgers meant love

BURGERS FROM HEAVEN ©1975 DARRYL RHOADES

With no band to tour, I decided to record a solo album in the latter part of 1979. Several tracks had already been recorded, including "Burgers from Heaven," a sappy 1950s doo-wop parody released on my first single several years earlier. The 45 was the only recording released under "Darryl Rhoades & The Hahavishnu Orchestra." The record received considerable regional airplay and national exposure on the syndicated Dr. Demento Show. Since the 45 single was financed by our first acting manager, Jimmy Ginn, I had to buy back the publishing rights to re-release my song on the LP.

Once again, I was recording with my high school friend, David Michael, who had been instrumental in helping me record my bedroom tapes that received airplay on WIIN before the band's formation.

With no record company backing, I used some of the royalties from the Outlaws covering my song, "The Lights Are On (But Nobody's Home)," to finance the project. I made plans to record the album at Stone Mountain Studio, a 16-track facility, and work with engineer Bruce Baxter. I started putting together the musicians best suited for the different genres.

The LP contained 13 songs, nine from the Hahavishnu days, and included 28 performers. I was fortunate to have so many friends who were incredible players. Seemingly, everyone wanted to pitch in, and we completed the album in a month. I'd never worked with Bruce Baxter and only knew him from playing with Thermos Greenwood and the Colored People. He understood how to get the best out of everyone while keeping the energy positive. I called on former Hahavishnu band members and friends from The Dixie Dregs and The Nighthawks. Even the legendary bass player Harvey Brooks made an appearance on several songs.

The cover art was the work of Austin artist Rick Turner. Rick had been dating one of the Hahavishnu Orchestra dancers and followed us around the country, often painting amazing works on the dressing room walls. The artwork I used on the LP cover was from some of his posters to promote our appearance at the World Armadillo Headquarters, with hamburgers floating in the clouds over the Texas Capitol in Austin. The back cover was a takeoff of James Brown's "Don't Be a Dropout" picture with Vice President Hubert Humphrey. In my version, I was wearing my high school graduation gown with the tassel on the hat and holding a diploma with a blurb while shaking hands with wrestler Austin Idol. Austin's head was replaced in the picture with Hubert Humphrey's smiling face, and Austin's body made Hubert appear pumped up. Yes, those darn kids needed to stay in school. Putting the entire presentation together required a lot of skill and knowledge.

I wasn't educated enough on completing an album to be intimidated, so I didn't understand how many steps there were until I faced each one. I'd done recording in the studio, but packaging was a completely different issue. The most noted and respected album designer in the South was Michael McCarty. His history is tied to iconic Southern record releases like The Atlanta Rhythm Section, Beaverteeth, and many groups affiliated with noted publisher Bill Lowery. Michael would go on to work with me on more than half of my albums and was responsible for pulling all the artwork and text together. That was a lot of work for an album as varied as *Burgers from Heaven.*

A New York heart surgeon, Phil Levitan, was courting the Hahavishnu toward the end to manage them, and while I had disbanded the group, Phil and I remained in contact. He was talking to labels, hoping I would put a touring group together if he could land a record deal. One day, he called my home for a conference call with the A&R guy from RCA, who began to pick my brain about the material I was working on. I didn't feel a connection but was given $500 to record some tracks for them to listen to. I may have been shortsighted, but it never felt real to me, so I recorded songs I wanted to put on my LP regardless of the possibility that RCA might reject them. I recorded "She's a Mortician's Dream Come True" (about necrophilia), "I'm In With the Zen Crowd," "Critics Choice" (unreleased), and "I'll Do It My Way" (a rockabilly song about wanting other rockers to die so I could be No. 1). I believe this is called a self-fulfilling prophecy. RCA passed, and now I had four songs recorded, three of which were put on the album. For a time, I had a temporary recording studio set up in my garage, and the Hahavishnu's ex-sound man, Steve May, would engineer the recordings that yielded the demo of "The Lights Are On" and a couple of other songs which ended up later on other LPs. By bouncing the tracks on a 4-track recorder, I was able to sing 12 different vocals on the a cappella song, "Road Food."

The album's initial pressing sold out quickly thanks to the ads from Peaches Records and Tapes and the relentless guerrilla marketing used to promote the album. I had friends in record stores donating unused cardboard standup figures of Barbara Streisand, Dolly Parton, and Superman and replacing the faces with mine, with little blurbs coming out of my mouth to advertise the record. The cardboard Dolly Parton received a lot of attention with the caption, "Take Two; They're Small." I had almost no recording budget and even less for advertising, but had ideas and a lot of friends helping me execute them.

I put together several bizarre TV ads produced by friends that ran on local TV stations and satirized other cheesy record ads. One ad featured me with my hair combed over my face like Cousin Itt on the *Addams*

Family and a voiceover about my untimely demise: "He may be gone, but his music lives on," followed by short excerpts of several songs. In another ad, I introduced myself as Dick Clark while a beautiful woman in an evening gown sat at a table behind me, stuffing hamburger buns down her throat like she was starving.

From these marketing gimmicks, a write-up appeared in *Billboard* magazine, which caught the eye of a Nickelodeon producer who invited me to appear on the kids' talk show "Livewire." Their production company paid for the airline tickets to New York and hotels for me, Jimmy Royals, Mike Orlin, Jeff Calder, and Pete Jarkunas for a few nights. That particular show was titled "You Are What You Eat," and featured interviews from various nutritionists and people in the food industry. The show was shot on April 14, 1981, and aired on April 22. We performed "Road Food" live while all wearing paper hats from The Varsity (represent). We also lip-synched "Burgers from Heaven" dressed as 1950s greasers, and in "I Wanna Be Normal," Jimmy wore his girlfriend's robe and swept the stage after giving me a brown paper bag lunch with "Tom" written on it. I did the robot dance convincingly while wearing a lime green leisure suit and white patent leather shoes. We be stylin'!

I received a lot of support from college radio stations, leading to several appearances on WREK and WRAS in Atlanta and larger record company stores like Turtle's and Peaches. Peaches on Peachtree had a version of Grauman's Chinese Theater where performers placed their hands in cement. I was bestowed that honor with a small ceremony of having my handprint cemented. I'll always assume I was a quick substitution when the original honoree couldn't make the shoot, and they didn't want the concrete to go to waste.

Getting exposure and a lot of airplay on the nationally syndicated Dr. Demento show didn't hurt either. Dr. D. had a considerable fanbase and debuted the LP by playing the entire Side 1 when it came out. The LP release was in 1980, one year before the launch of MTV, a medium built on visual programming. The exposure on Dr. Demento, along with clever videos on MTV, was responsible for unleashing Weird Al Yankovic on the world.

On April 25, 1981, I participated in the Rock & Bowl contest against Col. Bruce Hampton as part of a NARAS/96 Rock promotion. A couple of attractive women in tights walked me in, wearing a shiny fake wrestling robe and blond streaks in my hair. I started talking rasslin' smack when I got the crowd's attention, and Bruce played it up on his end. I always viewed every event appearance as a performance possibility, and I attribute much of that schooling to people like Bruce.

I sent a couple of songs from the *Burgers* LP to producer Richard Gottehrer in New York on Doc Pomus's advice. Doc knew of my love for rockabilly and told me Richard was working with a new artist, Robert Gordon. If The Outlaws could record one of my songs, maybe I had a future placing my material with other artists.

Richard knew of me but considered me a "Southern artist." While I had just had a song covered by a Southern group and was a Southern guy, I never pigeonholed myself as a Southern artist. I was heavily inspired by Southern music and authors, but I didn't limit my influences to the South.

I sent two songs, "I'll Be Watching You" and "From the Heart," and about a week later, received a call. Robert Gordon really liked "I'll Be Watching You" and was thinking of cutting it, but then suddenly his attitude and voice changed as he blurted out, "That other song, 'From the Heart,' did you write that about me?" I was caught off guard. The song wasn't about anyone in particular, but I got the idea when I saw the newest Syl Sylvain album cover. "From the Heart" was about a musician who became a chameleon adapting to whatever new fad he thought would get him noticed.

> *There you stand, on the cover with your band*
> *Doing your Gene Vincent pose*
> *You used to be glitter but now you're young and bitter*
> *And what you're gonna be tomorrow nobody knows*

FROM THE HEART ©1975 DARRYL RHOADES

I wasn't even familiar with Syl Slyvain other than knowing he rebranded himself as a roots rocker after being in the New York Dolls, but I'm still wondering why Robert thought it was about him. Our conversation ended shortly after that, with Robert saying I would be hearing from Gottehrer, and I was excited. Sure enough, I got a call the next day, and Richard asked me who owned the publishing. I was familiar with the stories about artists who were ripped off because they didn't know how the game was played. I understood that record companies, record producers, managers, or any number of people would attempt to stick their hand in the pot whenever possible. When Gottehrer asked me, I told him that he could contact my music attorney and work it out. I wasn't doing a dodge but figured my interest would be better served by someone looking out for me with a better understanding of how the game was played.

But Richard backed off, and I took another step further to "almost." Robert went on to record some decent versions of a couple of Billy Lee Riley songs and tour with Link Wray as his guitarist. The thought that Link Wray might play on a song I wrote is exciting, and is another reason that this near-miss is one of my biggest disappointments.

The *Burgers* LP was released on August 1, 1980. I performed an abbreviated show on August 16 at the Agora Ballroom in Atlanta with Cruise-O-Matic. Then came several appearances on the WTBS variety show *Tush*, which showcased bands, comedians, and actors, giving me considerable exposure across the country in places I had never performed. I think I appeared on three episodes, shows lip-syncing "Burgers from Heaven" and "I'm In With the Zen Crowd," and playing drums behind Jan Hooks, who sang the parody of "I Am Woman" that we used to perform in the Hahavishnu Orchestra. I wore a wig, gold chains, and leisure suits to look as close to Ed Shaughnessy, the drummer on *The Tonight Show*, as possible. The entire episode was a takeoff on *The Tonight Show*, with the highlight being Jan satirizing a pretentious star singing a fan favorite. The show served as a jumpstart to Jan's career as a cast member of *Saturday Night Live*. The two main writers of *Tush*, Bonnie and Terry Turner, became sought-after screenwriters in Hollywood.

I was fortunate to have worked with so many talented people and happy for their careers taking off, but I felt like I was jogging in place.

I'll Be Watching You

I'll be watching you
No matter where you run to
There's nothing you can do
I'll be watching you

You said that you were leavin'
You told me I was blind
You laughed and called me jealous
And made me lose my mind
And so now you think we're through
But I'll be watching you

I believed what you told me
And you took me for a ride
You left my insides twisted
And something snapped inside
Now I can't be blamed for what I do
And I'll be watching you

This is not the first time
And it won't be the last
Soon the fear will vanish
And your pain will die out fast
You laughed and called me a fool
Now whose hurting who

You feel the desperation
You hear footsteps from behind
As you stand convicted
You slowly lose your mind
It's too late, you know it's true
Now I'm watching you
I am watching you
I am watching you
I am watching you

I'LL BE WATCHING YOU ©1980 DARRYL RHOADES

CHAPTER ELEVEN

Egg Suckin' Dogs and Pencil Neck Geeks

Heart Throb . . . You got that Vegas leg lock
You don't need no drop kick . . . to beat an escaped convict
Heart Throb with the body of Apollo and the mind of Einstein
Heart Throb . . . yeah he's the hero and you're the zero

HEART THROB ©1980 DARRYL RHOADES

Following the footsteps of several Hahavishnu alums, I hit the road in 1980, playing drums with the classic rock band Cruise-O-Matic for about a year. The band wasn't breaking new ground, but it was probably one of the best times I ever had on the road playing in bars and fraternity gigs. Not worrying about anything beyond showing up, playing drums, and having a good time with the Tanner brothers was a welcomed experience.

Edward and I shared a passion for wrestling, music, and comedy since his early days with the Hahavishnu Orchestra. In the 1970s to 1980s, Georgia Championship Wrestling was hugely popular on TV, and live matches were primarily held at the Atlanta Municipal Auditorium. The Auditorium had a special place in my heart. I had performed there several times and experienced some of my favorite concerts there in the 1960s. Wrestling fans would pack that place after watching the matches on WTBS, which to a degree served as an infomercial. There would be feuds not settled within the time constraints of TV, and for the price of a ticket, you could see this thing played out in the squared circle in the Auditorium.

The 1970s was a transformative time to be living in Atlanta. Ted Turner was changing the landscape of Atlanta sports by buying the Braves and Hawks and boosting his network's viewership with a national wrestling broadcast every Friday night. I attended several matches when they were filmed in a small studio in Midtown Atlanta before the entire operation moved close to Georgia Tech as it became WTBS, home of CNN. Turner's SuperStation played no small part in the growth of wrestling, as it was being rebranded from Georgia Championship Wrestling to World Championship Wrestling. I was inspired and adopted some of the wrestlers' rap in my shows while pointing at an audience member and proclaiming that "I'm flyin' all over the world, gettin' paid and gettin' laid, Japan on Monday, Australia on Tuesday, and if you're lucky baby, your house on Wednesday . . . You can't be first, but you can be next." Even when I didn't know what it meant, it just sounded damn good.

Wrestling took me back to when I was a boy in Kentucky and would watch it on TV with my dad. I always enjoyed the "heels," who were the bad guys with a talent for berating their opponents with superior name-calling like "egg-suckin' dog" and "ham and eggers." I found the "heels" more interesting than the "faces" or good guys. Wrestlers who held part-time jobs as teachers, firefighters, and nightclub bouncers could be transformed into German supervillains goosestepping in the ring, Arab butchers, and Middle Eastern madmen taunting the crowds and pissing off ring rats all across America.

In the 1950s and 1960s, guys like Dick the Bruiser, Lou Thesz, Gorgeous George, and Sputnik Monroe were rock stars before I had a clue what a rock star was. I stayed glued to the TV, watching these guys work the crowd and revving them up with name-calling and harassing the good guys. My absolute favorite, and the very best of all of them, was "Classy" Freddie Blassie. Blassie's signature phrase was calling someone a "Pencil Neck Geek," which would eventually become the title song of his 1975 cult hit single. Blassie was a king among men whom many unsuccessfully tried to imitate, but as we know, there was only one Blassie.

I'm not sure why Cruise-O-Matic adopted wrestling's golden boy, Austin "The Universal Heart Throb" Idol. With oratory excellence, Austin dubbed himself "the women's pet and the men's regret." He became the band's favorite wrestler, and we started attending his matches, but it didn't stop there.

We printed a fake newspaper, which we placed on the windows of cars parked in shopping centers and nightclubs to perpetuate the legend of Idolmania. We even made a giant green fake highway department road sign that read "Idol Mountain." We took it out to Stone Mountain, Georgia's most popular tourist attraction, to fool people into believing the big rock had a name change in honor of Austin Idol.

"Austin Idol for President" pins and bumper stickers were printed and ended up on the cars of people we didn't know. The owners had unknowingly parked their vehicles in a place begging for a bumper sticker on it, and we obliged. We took our campaign to motel parking lots, malls, and churches. No one was spared as the great wrestling spirits summoned us to do what needed to be done. There was an imperative to spread the word, and we were the messengers. Yes, many are called, but few are chosen.

The idea of Idol becoming President doesn't sound so crazy or impossible when considering the "Bedtime for Bonzo" chimpanzee's co-star, Ronald Reagan, was elected President a year later. Twenty years after that, WWF icon Jesse Ventura became governor of Minnesota, and a decade later, former reality TV star and occasional guest on the WWE, Donald Trump, was elected President. Politics makes strange bedfellows indeed!!! We should have viewed the Presidential push for the Universal Heart Throb's candidacy as groundbreaking and ahead of its time. One of the two dominant political parties should still consider drafting him. I see it as a no-lose proposition.

Religion, politics, and wrestling are similar. All three use name-calling, make-up, and outrageous rhetoric while attacking their opponents. When they were younger, I would have paid big bucks to step into the squared circle with Pat Robertson, Oral Roberts, or Jerry Falwell. They only needed to get into the ring to complete the trilogy.

Idolmania was taking hold, culminating with Cruise-O-Matic going into a small studio and recording a parody song of "Wild Thing" titled "Heart Throb." We appeared on WTBS with Bill Tush, lip-synching the song under the name The Idolators, and gave Austin a video copy. After delivering that video off stage before his next appearance on Georgia Championship Wrestling, Austin acted surprised when the host, Freddie Miller, played it during the interview.

This thing was catching fire with the right amount of stupid and dumb. When producer Sonny Limbo heard about it, he came up with the idea of re-recording it in a larger studio and releasing it. We struck a deal to bring Austin into the studio to do a voiceover on the song. Then we recorded the B side titled "Austin Idol for President," which touted his wisdom, strength, and promises to make the country a heavyweight champion once again. Limbo made a deal with a guy to press the records, and we were to be paid when the recording was finished. I didn't know if the record company guy had a side hustle, but I had never heard of him or his company before or since. He may have been one of Sonny Limbo's drinking buddies.

The songs were recorded and mixed within a week, but I knew how this would play out. After you've dealt with enough club owners, car dealers, and flaky people, you have a sixth sense when the deal you've made is on shaky ground, and this one felt like quicksand. We never saw anything from it, and I considered it a missed opportunity after the video had been replayed and watched by thousands.

Since we recorded it in the same studio where I was currently recording my first album, I found the master tape and snuck it out one night, then went to the guy who pressed the 45s and bought them all up. I still have a couple of boxes, but they have never been released to the public other than the few offered and sold on eBay.

Meanwhile, I started hanging out with Austin and attending a few of his matches while becoming enlightened to how wacky the fan base could be. I particularly enjoyed the feud between Austin and Baron von Raschke (James Donald Raschke). Raschke claimed to be from Germany and would goosestep into the ring. He had a great gimmick; he sold well, considering he was a substitute teacher born in Omaha, Nebraska, and was known for his signature hold, "The Claw." Most wrestlers had a signature hold. Austin had the "Vegas Leg Lock," Stan "The Man" Stasiak has the "Heart Punch," and Fritz Von Erich was credited with originating "the claw" featured in the popular 2023 film, *The Iron Claw.*

Austin taunted Raschke on TV appearances, calling him "Onion-head" because of his bald head. Taking it a step further, he encouraged people to bring onions to the ring. BIG MISTAKE. Never arm the lunatics. The night of the match, Austin got in the ring and had the crowd yelling, "Onionhead! Onionhead!" When Raschke started goose-stepping into the ring, a shower of onions rained down on him and anyone nearby. It took about five minutes to get the crowd under control before Austin made America safe again against German wrestlers from Omaha who also doubled as substitute teachers.

The emotions from the arena carried out into the real world. There were stories of wrestlers discovering their cars had been vandalized after a match. Slashed tires, broken windshields, or a scratched paint job would be the retribution for beating a crowd favorite in that night's match. Wrestling fans were protective of those they supported, some-times to the point of violence, as in the case of Blackjack Mulligan.

In a famed 1971 match between Blackjack Mulligan and Pedro Morales at the Boston Garden, the lights were all down except for one light hanging over the mat. Morales had Mulligan pinned near the ropes when a fan attacked Mulligan with a hawkbill knife, inflict-ing life-threatening injuries. The referee that night, Gorilla Monsoon, grabbed the fan and threw him to the police, who thought he was part of the show and promptly let him go. Matches now are always held under stadium lighting and more security.

Several times, I would use over-the-top language I learned from wrestlers in a bit I'd do while introducing a song. Usually, the crowds recognized my fake wrestling persona, but there were a few occasions when an audience member didn't appreciate being called a demeaning name, even if it was funny. I also took to challenging some journalists to wrestling matches. I often pestered Russell Shaw, probably the most influential music critic in Atlanta at the time, to wrestle me at The Agora with the proceeds going to charity, but it never happened because he wanted to "play wrestle," and I was dead serious. I enjoyed using my wrestling voice on the radio, challenging bands; I even printed music posters made to look like wrestling posters, where my band would be meeting the other band in the squared circle surrounded by barbed wire, with no time limits.

One Saturday morning, I rode down to WTBS studios with Austin and experienced the magic up close. The wrestling shows were shot early in the morning and aired later that day. The gang was there: Freddy, Gordon Solie, Olie Anderson, and the rest. The show needed a lot of energy and noise when the cameras started rolling, so I was asked to pump up the crowd, which was mainly kids and a few parents. At that time, Austin was a heel, so it behooved me to taunt the audience.

On a chalkboard, I drew a horizontal line through the middle of the board. At the top, I drew a giant stick figure, and at the bottom, a cluster of small stick figures. I told the audience they were the tiny figures, at the bottom where they belonged, and Austin was at the top, where he would remain, laughing at them because he was superior and they were nothing. The countdown for the cameras could barely be heard over the "fuck yous" from the little kids. Even as I write this, the tears of joy mist my eyes. I was then, as I am now, armed with a skill to piss off a multitude of people with only a few words. I have perfected and employed this technique many times over the years, and if you ever want to learn how to get a bunch of kids screaming and cussing at you, feel free to contact me.

I never heard another word from Sonny about the wrestling record. We stayed in touch and several times, Sonny would call me at predawn hours, suggesting we go to an all-night soul kitchen for breakfast. The invitation usually coincided with Sonny's partying the night before, which left him jacked up and wide awake, looking for someone who would listen to his stories, which often had no ending.

Sonny produced several successful acts, including Alabama and Bertie Higgins, who had a hit with "Key Largo." I had heard stories about Sonny sharing writer credits on songs where he changed a word or two. When I recorded my first LP, I wrote in the liner notes, "Thanks to Sonny Limbo, who didn't do anything, but requested his name to be on my album." When Bertie's second LP came out, Sonny wrote something similar about me in the liner notes. I hadn't requested it, but I thought it was funny. Everyone loved Sonny. He was easygoing, and when not in the studio, he could be found at his office across Buford Highway from a bar called The Rusty Nail. He lived a fast life, so I wasn't surprised but very saddened when he died of a heart attack in 1992. You know how people at a funeral sometimes say, "You can feel his presence?" Well, Sonny's funeral wasn't like that at all. It felt colorless and empty, and even more so when the minister got up to speak. Apparently, his approach was "one size fits all," as if he pulled out a standard form and filled in the blanks. Right off the bat, the minister's words made the moment awkward as he tried to sum up the life of a person they didn't know: "He was loved by his family and friends and worked in the entertainment field."

None of this got him good reviews, so Bertie Higgins walked up, took the mic out of the minister's hand, and talked about the Sonny we all knew. The mood drastically changed. There was laughter because the stories were honest and funny. Sonny had a big life with outrageous stories and louder laughs.

I don't spend much time thinking about my demise, but when the time comes, I hope someone will get up and make me sound more interesting. Something like, "He was a lunatic who made the world uncertain. His mind was always spinning plates while horrified crowds waited for the crash."

Most people are far more interesting than their obituaries. I've often considered setting up a business to write people's obituaries. I know it's how many journalists began their career, but when someone writes, "He loved his family, attended church, survived by a wife, and they had kids who had kids," I wonder if the guy had a sense of humor. Did he hold a grudge or have opinions? Did he ever do anything stupid and then laugh about it later? Did he have dreams?

Several years later, I mentioned the Idolators' recording experience to Joel Dorn, which sparked a discussion about recording a wrestling LP. Joel floated this idea to Cyndi Lauper's manager, Dave Wolff, who was affiliated with wrestling promoter Vince McMahon. I was asked to write a song for Hulk Hogan, so I went into the studio with Brendan O'Brien, and we started laying down tracks for a demo, addressing all the specifics they described. "Hulkamania" had a hook of a crowd chanting "Hulkamania! Hulk! Hulk!" and we layered about 30 voices, and then Brendan recorded that many tracks backward, and blended them with the forward tracks; it sounded huge.

We finished the song and sent it off to Joel, who thought it was perfect and forwarded it to the guys calling the shots. They did not share his enthusiasm, so our first attempt was rejected. Our second attempt was recorded in Philadelphia, with much less enthusiasm on my end. Other than it being my original idea, my contribution wasn't included in the 1985 LP *The Wrestling Album*, which peaked at No. 84 on the *Billboard* sales chart, and I quickly soured on the idea of being a songwriter "for hire."

I became friends with Brad Armstrong, one of the sons following in the footsteps of their legendary wrestling father, Bob Armstrong. Brad passed away in 2012, and at his service, I sat in the back and listened while he was being memorialized by friends who he had worked with. As several guys hobbled up to the podium, I recognized most of them from wrestling shows on TV when they were bouncing off the ropes and doing high dives. Most were years my junior, but now looked many years older, and some could barely stand. I was reminded of Icarus and wondered if that level of pain was the price that wrestlers often pay for overreaching, which wrestling demands. Maybe pain of one kind or another is too often the price for trying to be the hero. For at least 30 years in my life and music, I've often wrestled with that.

Canvas of Pain

They say he flew too close to the sun
And when the smoke finally cleared the damage was done
But you won't find a trace when they go down in flames
But the ashes scattered on the canvas of pain

Years ago on the road to fame
Where the winner takes all and the losers left the remains
Well he reached out too slowly to stake his claim
And instead found himself on the canvas of pain

Canvas of Pain
Where the sorrow cuts deep and the tears fall like rain
The memories fade leaving only a stain
Like the colors that run on the canvas of pain

She had a face just like Mona Lisa
Drawing on an inside straight
He couldn't read her . . . so he believed her
Until he found out too late
And he left himself wide open
Like Achilles in reverse
With his heart on his sleeve
He still couldn't leave her
Which made the pain only worse

Canvas of Pain
Where the innocence dies and love has been drained
When the heart is all gone and there only remains
A shell left standing on the canvas of pain

Canvas of Pain
Where the sorrow cuts deep and the tears fall like rain
The memories fade leaving only a stain
Like the colors that run on the canvas of pain

CHAPTER TWELVE

Throwing Darts at the Sun

Last night I dreamed I died and went to country music heaven
I wasn't there for a couple of minutes
Till I picked a fight with Brooks & Dunn
Well I sucker punched Garth Brooks with an empty whiskey bottle
And kicked Billy Ray Cyrus in his Achy Breaky nuts

COUNTRY MUSIC HEAVEN ©2005 DARRYL RHOADES

The running joke about most of the honky-tonks on Stewart Avenue in Atlanta was that they'd ask you at the door if you were carrying a weapon, and if the answer was no, they'd offer you one.

Along with Cleveland Avenue, Stewart was a pretty rough area known for its numerous bars that employed many musicians. I figured working those clubs was a character builder, if my character lived long enough to get built. Gunfire, muggings, and stabbings could, and did, often happen. I saw it all while I did my time in the honky-tonks.

Between the Palomino Club, West Texas, and Country Roads, I worked seven hours a night, six nights a week for months. In the early 1980s, clubs stayed busy, and the success of movies like *Urban Cowboy* made them more popular. Country music legends often came by to sit in after they performed their concerts in larger venues in Atlanta. Business was good.

Walt Page, the owner of West Texas, was a tough guy with a good sense of humor and always treated me well. Like myself, he was a Southside Atlanta guy, which usually meant several things. People on the Southside were generally a lot more blue-collar and sometimes a little less refined, or at least that would be the impression anyone would have if they came to Walt's bar. Walt once confided in me that his grandfather was one of the people in the mob that hung Leo Frank in Marietta back in 1913. Frank was accused of murdering Mary Phagan, a 13-year-old girl who worked at the pencil factory he managed. Frank had two strikes against him. He was Jewish and from the North, and it's believed he was an innocent victim of the mob lynching.

I was glad for the work, but it was like throwing darts at the sun. I felt I was spinning my wheels and isolated from everything around me, but it was my choice, and it was far better to be a working musician than an unemployed one. Occasionally, I'd go outside on breaks to escape the crying in my beer songs on the jukebox, to sit in my car or walk up to Popeye's Chicken for biscuits and jalapenos. Even doing that was taking a chance because you never knew who would throw what at you from a moving car. Guitarist Ken Kinsey got mugged one night by a hungry guy who pulled out a knife. Ken handed over his wallet, but apparently the guy went to his mugging job without making dinner plans, so he insisted on Ken giving up his box of chicken as well. Stealing money was bad enough, but taking a man's chicken, well, that was just damn cold.

Ken hired me to play drums for The Ken Kinsey Band after the previous drummer was too difficult to get along with. Apparently, the guy was a great drummer but had a challenging personality. The parting shot when he left was being told that it wasn't business; it was just personal.

One night, while on break, I was out front talking to one of the bouncers named Pee Wee. Pee Wee and Pat were brothers who were longtime bouncers at West Texas, and they were about as wide as they were tall. Both practiced an economy of words but were skilled at conveying their points nonverbally.

After about two minutes, a drunk approached and started running his mouth. Pee Wee said, "One more word, and I'm gonna lay you out." The drunk managed to get out "Well, I . . ." before Pat made good on his promise by picking up one of those big, heavy black flashlights that cops use and slammed it upside the drunk's head. I don't think it killed him, but a couple of the drunk's friends jumped out of a pickup, threw his limp body in the back of a truck bed, and drove away. Later that night, a small car sped through the parking lot and fired off a few rounds as they circled the club. Within seconds, several of the bouncers and a few of the bar patrons came out of the club shooting. Hot damn!!! Another night filled with fun, excitement, depressing songs, and the possibility of ending up in a box.

On occasion, country stars like Vern Gosdin or Buck Owens would swing by and join us on stage. Buck had attended a concert by Emmylou Harris at the Fox Theatre but got pissed off and stomped out because she didn't acknowledge him on stage. He left the show, went down to West Texas, and sat in with the band. I don't know if he saw any of us or even knew what planet he was on. Buck was lit!

My mind would wander most nights as I would be thinking about everything but where I was at the moment. I was playing with some skilled players armed with a good sense of humor that often helped to salvage the evening. The band often came up with different games to make the time go by. My specialty was "Let's Hide the Beat." We would enjoy this exercise when we would have locals sitting in to sing, or we were backing a "talent" contest for people who had none.

One of my favorites was Kay, another Southside resident. She was hard on the eyes and preferred to be introduced as "Fonda Peters." Each time she got on stage, she would proceed to do the same thing by bending over, pointing her large bulbous ass at the audience, and saying, "Let me take a picture with my brownie." I looked forward to her "comedy" the same way I always looked forward to someone hitting me in the balls with a sledgehammer. Then, like clockwork, she would introduce her take on "Apartment Number Nine" by George Jones, which she called "Apartment Sixty Nine." When Kay started to "sing," the band would pull any number of stunts to crack each other up. At the place of my choosing, I would go from laying down the beat on two and four to one and three and then back to two and four so Kay was appropriately thrown off. The trick would be for the bass player to stay with me and not laugh to the point that he had to stop playing.

I worked at West Texas with two bands, The Ken Kinsey Band and The Johnny Carlton Band. Ken was the son of Curly Kinsey, one of the original Oak Ridge Boys when they were a gospel group under Wally Fowler from Knoxville and named after the nearby town of Oak Ridge. Curly was a songwriter and recording artist who appeared on the first radio broadcast of *Louisiana Hayride*, and in 1949, Hank Williams recorded his song "I Just Told Mama Goodbye." Curly was killed in a car crash very early in Ken's life, and I always got the feeling it was something that affected Ken in many of his life decisions. He was funny, but the blues seemed to hover over him with a darkness that would occasionally make itself known.

Ken grew up in the north Georgia town of Summerville, as did Rodney, our fiddle player who played out of tune and looked like a frog but I never got his last name. They both told great stories about some of the characters there, like folk artist Howard Finster and Rick Camp, who pitched for the Atlanta Braves. One time Camp got drunk, climbed on the roof of the police department, and took a piss, and alcohol would usually be at the root of most of these stories. Ken was well-versed in all things spirit.

Ken introduced me to Paul Peek, who would join the band a couple of nights a week wearing an eye patch and a bad wig. He could sing and play guitar but was also a great character everyone loved. One night, in a conversation with Ken, I was educated about the fact that I was sharing the stage with a rock 'n' roll legend. Paul had joined Gene Vincent's Blue Caps in 1956, playing rhythm guitar behind legendary Cliff Gallup, who's credited as being a major influence on guitarists like Jeff Beck, Jimmy Page, Eric Clapton, and others. I was always chomping at the bit to find out more about my favorite early rock heroes, and after I learned this, I made it my mission to ask Paul as many questions and hear as many stories as possible.

Paul had some incredible tales about the early days of rock. He didn't play on the hit "Be-Bop-A-Lula," but he toured nonstop with the Blue Caps while the song climbed the charts. Both Lennon and McCartney have credited the Blue Caps' music as one of their inspirations. The surviving members of the Blue Caps were still doing occasional gigs in the 1980s, and in England, they were still rock gods. Paul took a temporary leave from the West Texas club to tour England with the Blue Caps and returned with stories of grown men weeping in the audience.

Paul joined the Blue Caps in time to appear in the 1956 Jayne Mansfield movie, *The Girl Can't Help It*, which I had seen as a six year old and thought was so cool. With cameo appearances from Little Richard, Eddie Cochran, Alan Freed, and others, it's often called one of the "greatest early rock movies of all time." In the scene with the Blue Caps, Paul stole the spotlight when he shook his head and his hat came off. The director loved how it looked and reshot the scene with the other band members following Paul's lead and shaking theirs off. Now I was sitting on drums behind this guy and watching him sing George Jones songs in a redneck honky-tonk on Cleveland Avenue.

If you want to see something cool, check out Gene Vincent and the Blue Caps' appearance in the lesser-known movie *Hot Rod Gang*, which came out in 1958. Paul was chewing gum, smiling, and looking hip while singing "Baby Blue" next to Gene. If I had never asked Paul all my questions, I would have never known the wealth of stories, and I still regret not sitting down with a recorder and taping everything Paul told me. However, I have been given a gift of several CDs of Paul's storytelling to his sisters shortly before he passed away in 2001.

Gene Vincent is intertwined with my favorite rocker of all time, Eddie Cochran. In 1960, Eddie and Gene were touring in England and were on their way to their next gig with songwriter Sharon Seeley, who was also Eddie's fiancée and manager. Their private taxi had an accident at high speed and Cochran, who was only 21, was thrown from the vehicle and died. Gene had severely injured his leg in a motorcycle crash five years before and refused to have it amputated, so going into the taxi crash, the leg was held together with pins and a metal sheath. After the crash, Gene had a permanent limp.

When I asked Paul what Eddie Cochran was like, he said he was just a regular guy who liked to go to the drive-in, drink beer, and make out with girls. I loved it. He sounded exactly like I had hoped, but Paul's follow-up comment about Eddie was even better. He told me that he was a good-looking guy and the girls all loved him, so Eddie was always making moves, but one day, he was dealing with a little distraction named Paul Anka. Anka was about 12 years old and was also performing on the tour. He idolized Eddie and followed him around like a puppy. Finally, Eddie grew tired of this kid bugging him and threatened to beat his ass if he didn't go away. There are so many reasons why this story excites me, but one big one is imagining that if Eddie Cochran had beaten Paul Anka's ass in the 1950s, maybe 20 years later we would all have been spared from Anka writing crap like "You're Having My Baby." To this day, I think Paul Anka should have his ass beaten daily, and I'm basing that on more than just one horrible song.

When Paul would talk about some of the rock legends he shared the stage with, it felt like he was right back there in time, and it also felt that way when one of them died. He reflected on his time with Buddy Knox, Danny Rapp of Danny & The Juniors, and many others, but I always saw him as a survivor. But the years of alcohol and late-night bars finally caught up with him when he developed liver disease and wasn't able to work in the latter part of the 1990s.

Around 1999, I bought an Esquerita CD online and discovered in the liner notes that Paul Peek was responsible for signing him to a record deal. Esquerita (Eskew Reeder Jr., aka Steven Quincy Reeder Jr.) was one of early rock's most flamboyant characters and is credited for being a major influence on Little Richard. Richard heard Esquerita, and it changed the style of how he played and performed. Esquerita was quite the showman who sometimes wore two wigs, sunglasses, and often a pompadour piled high on his head. Both "Rita" and Paul came out of Greenville, South Carolina, about two hours north of Atlanta.

I called Paul and told him about the CD, and he became excited. He commented he hadn't heard those songs in over 30 years, including several he had co-written with Rita, and I could feel Paul drifting in his memory. The next day, I visited Paul with a CD player. Not having seen Paul, he didn't look good. Even though I knew he had been ill, I wasn't ready to see a guy who looked like he'd aged 20 years since our previous time together less than a year before. Paul and I spoke only for a few minutes before I put the CD on. I caught a tear in the corner of his eye, but it was joyful. He was in a good place right then, and after listening to a few songs, he pointed at a guitar case on the floor and asked me to pull out the guitar signed by Jeff Beck.

Jeff had recently visited Atlanta, met with Paul, and gave him the guitar as a present. Paul loved that guitar, and having someone like Jeff Beck look him up and show such respect for his contributions did a lot to lift his spirits. Paul and I sat and talked for a while, and then he gave me a recently released compilation CD of his solo work. He autographed it for me, and it's a gift that I'll always treasure. He hugged me as I left and I figured I'd return to see him as soon as possible.

I played the CD when I got home and it was emotional. All those nights I had played with Paul, I never knew what an incredible singer he had been. "I'm Not Your Fool Anymore" still puts chills down my spine. He recorded with many of the great session guys in Atlanta at the time, including Joe South, Jerry Reed, and Ray Stevens, and lived this big life. For 20 years, I was lucky to call Paul a friend.

On April 3, 2001, I was checking out of my Montana hotel room when I got a call from Johnny Carlton informing me that Paul had passed away that morning. After hearing the details, I felt like I'd been sucker punched with even more force. Paul was scheduled to make an appearance with Brenda Lee, D. J. Fontana, and others for the Rocka-billy Music Foundation, and a driver who arrived to take Paul to Nash-ville found his body. Paul had lived his entire life as a musician until he couldn't anymore. In 2012, he was posthumously inducted into the Rock & Roll Hall of Fame with The Blue Caps, and in my mind, no one deserves that honor more. The history of rock music was written by guys like Paul who worked the road in the shadows while support-ing performers like Gene Vincent, Elvis, and Jerry Lee. Knowing that Paul was alive long enough to be acknowledged by the H.O.F. doesn't diminish his loss but I know it meant a great deal to him.

Right around the corner from West Texas, where I had played with Paul so many nights, was the Palomino Club on Stewart Avenue. On some nights, The Palomino Club made West Texas look like upscale Vegas. The band included some of the best players I'd ever worked with. Playing shitty songs was a little less depressing with Mike Holbrook on bass, Gary Hayes and Mike Garrich on guitars, and Jeff Stivers, who played piano like he was on speed and getting paid by the note, but he had chops.

Occasionally, Buddy Fowles would sing with the band. He had a knack for country music, crying-in-your-beer songs, and alcohol. The band would play four or five songs and then back up a guy named Sammy, which was no small feat. Sammy had the personality of sausage and looked almost life-like, but somehow he could rock a lime green leisure suit while wearing a wig that could have used a chin strap. As far as singing, he couldn't, but he was the "leader," which meant he called the shots and got paid several times more than the other players. In that role, Sammy also had to deal with the club owner, who was a special brand of crazy.

One night, the club owner told the band he wanted nothing but slow songs all night. Yeah, eight hours of George Jones's "He Stopped Loving Her Today" drinking songs. I have to assume that his insanity drove me to push the limits even further. I recognized the feeling bubbling under and it was just a matter of time. I had no control over the ideas bouncing around in my head. Boredom was making me its bitch.

An older guy, Jimmy, who played sax, would sit in the green room and only come out when we started into one of the several songs he played. Like ringing a feed bell for a hamster, it was comical and Pavlovian. Since the door to the greenroom was right by the drum riser, and it also had a padlock hasp on it, I decided one night to let my "inner asshole" come out and play. The door to the green room was closed, and I pulled the hasp together and stuck a drumstick in it so the door wouldn't open. As the band went into "Tequila," a big sax song, Jimmy went to open the door but couldn't, and started yelling, banging, and beating on it.

When the band looked back to see why he wasn't on stage, each player started laughing, and as they lost their place, the song fell apart. Yeah, it was a dick move, but I did eventually unlock the door after a couple of songs. Jimmy looked at me and said, "Why would you do that to me?" I guess answering with the truth and explaining, "It's nothing personal; I'm just a dick when I get bored," probably wouldn't have been much of a consolation.

I can't believe I didn't get fired from that gig. I stayed away from the owner and got along with Sammy. Even though he thought I was weird, he always treated me well.

I loved playing with the guys in that band because they were fun and great players. If you have to play songs you're not into, it's nice to play with guys who can make it enjoyable. Whenever possible, we would play some Bobby Bland or other cool stuff that got the band going, and then Sammy would treat everyone with his rousing version of "Tight Fittin' Jeans" by Conway Twitty while I planned my next dick move. And this mindset pointed me in the direction of a club called Country Roads, where I was hired to play drums for the Johnny Carlton Band.

Johnny was a guy who had been around Atlanta for many years and likely has at least a book or two in him. He worked in all the popular Atlanta clubs in the early 1960s, including The Playroom, one of the city's first upscale country music clubs.

Country Roads featured artists on their way up or down, and after a rehearsal with the band on Wednesday afternoon, we'd all play a show that night and every night through Saturday. Occasionally, we would get to work with someone with some serious talent like Tony Booth or Darrell McCall. Darrell McCall stands out because I love Texas swing, and he was a powerful singer who had worked with all the country greats.

My absolute favorite memory of playing at Country Roads was working with Bruce Mullen. At our rehearsal, I pretended to be blind, and bass player Gary Land led me on and offstage. When I was introduced to Bruce, I stuck my hand out as if trying to find his hand to shake it. After rehearsal, Bruce went back to his hotel, and we all laughed and looked forward to seeing this thing play out. I planned on having a fun night! When Bruce returned, I shook his hand as if I hadn't pulled the blind thing earlier in the day and he didn't budge one bit! He didn't even ask a question or acknowledge the shenanigans, so I was the one left scratching my head. Of course, another possibility could be that he had been dimmed out by playing with so many pickup bands that he never gave a thought about any of us after he clocked in and clocked back out. After playing six to eight straight hours of "drinking in my truck and looking for a fight on a Saturday night" songs, I can attest to that mindset

From August 13–15, we backed up Mack Vickery, who had written a song called "The Meat Man," a big hit for Jerry Lee Lewis. Mack looked like a wrestler, with a big body and a pile of slicked-back blond hair. He was a large presence on stage, hollering and raising hell. He could rock but was chemically fueled, and his tank was always full with the throttle wide open.

On Saturday night, he mentioned that Jerry Lee might drop in, and I figured it was just one more guy name-dropping and boasting to no avail, but sure enough, Jerry Lee Lewis showed up and was ready to jam. Incredibly, Gary Land had a cassette player, and we recorded the entire thing.

Jerry and Mack must have fueled up at the same place because he was primed and ready to go. Any musician who has played with Jerry Lee will tell you that tempo and meter are set and reset every ten seconds. A drummer will watch, listen, and hang on for dear life as Jerry takes everyone on a roller coaster ride. He became excited during one song, made everyone stop but me, and yelled, "Go, drummer, go! Rock and roll ain't dead!" then kicked the floor monitors off the stage, sat back down on the piano, and started pounding. I'd heard so many wild stories about Jerry Lee over the years and figured at 46 he had probably slowed down a bit, but on this night, he was what rock was all about: pure energy gone awry.

After the set, Jerry Lee sat down while a young guy traveling with him attempted to keep people at bay as they asked for autographs.

"Lady, get your tits out of his face so he can breathe," the young guy yelled, which made me laugh, and then I saw our piano player take an extinguished cigar Jerry had been smoking and put it in a baggy. I'm not sure what became of the cigar, but I suspect that it was used for cloning, which would explain the existence of pianist Jason D. Williams. Years later, I jammed with Jason, and the resemblance to Jerry Lee (no relation) was uncanny. Both possessed timing that would change without notice to anyone else on the bandstand.

The funniest thing about working Country Roads was backing the relatives of stars. No, I never backed up JOHNNY CASH, but I did play behind his brother, Tommy Cash. I never played with CONWAY TWITTY, but I backed up his son, Michael Twitty. No, I never played with WAYLON JENNINGS, but I did play with his brother, Tommy Jennings. In 1989, I was reminded of this phenomenon when a few seconds of my song, "Burgers from Heaven," was used in the movie *Fast Food*. This movie featured Melanie Griffith's sister, Tracy, and Bruce Springsteen's sister, Pamela.

It's difficult to pick the weirdest of the honky-tonks because they all had characters with different peculiarities and levels of danger. I pride myself in making the best of any situation, but that was tough when it came to working at Mr. J's in Smyrna, on the other side of Atlanta.

Mr. J's featured bouncers who wore smocks to conceal the .357s they all carried. The club was right down the street from several trailer parks occupied by many who received government allotments to get them through the month. The T.P.P. (Trailer Park People) would often frequent Mr. J's on the weekend while bringing their financial support from the government, which they would use to procure alcohol. Massive amounts of alcohol.

Every waitress was equipped with a cattle prod, and things would get pretty crazy but no crazier than the owner, Mr. J. himself, who would often grab the mic and, if the band was even 30 seconds late on getting back on the bandstand, yell, "Band time!" It was a 40-minute set with 20-minute breaks, and if you got off early or came back late, he kept a record and would tell you sometime in the night how much time you owed him. I was tempted to tell him I already had played a couple of hours at home and would be leaving early that night.

At the time, WTBS was replaying Atlanta Braves games overnight, and I was always focused on getting home quickly to watch. At 3 a.m. on a Sunday morning, I pulled into the driveway of my house on quiet, dead-end Loring Drive. I should have picked up on the signs in front of me, but I was so caught up with my obsession with watching the late night game I wasn't paying attention.

Why would my stage clothes, which were stored in the attic, be on my driveway? If my sensors had been on alert, I would have shoved the car in reverse and called the cops, but that thought never occurred.

It was pitch black as I walked up the steps and met someone carrying a box, and I still wasn't processing it. When I left for work, the lights had been on, so why was it so dark? "What's happenin'?" I asked the figure walking down the steps, almost brushing me.

What was happenin' was his buddy stepping out from the side of the house, crouching down, and pointing his pistol at me. He grabbed my ponytail, and I froze as he marched me into the house. I started talking, and I don't think I ever spoke as fast or chose my words more carefully. I probably sounded like the disclaimer in a drug ad when they're rapidly describing flatulence, acne, loose bowels, or other side effects. I just figured if the burglars saw me as a guy who wasn't resisting, had very little, and didn't want to die, they might take what they wanted and let me live.

"I can't see your face, don't let me see you, and there's nothing I have worth dying for," I said. "Take anything you want."

Every minute felt like an hour. I understood that this could quickly go sideways with the wrong word or movement.

"There's no need to hurt me, I can't see you, and you can take everything I have," I said.

I mean, I was a guy just like them, except I had never put a gun to somebody's head and threatened to kill them. Come to think of it, I wasn't anything like these guys. But in that moment, I was doing whatever I could to make some human connection with a guy who wanted me to know I was his bitch.

"Oh yeah, don't worry about that," this lowlife replied. "We're gonna take what we want."

With a pistol pressed against my head, I was led to the back bedroom, pushed face down on the bed, and soon felt a pillow on my head. Surely my last breath was coming soon. Both guys blindfolded and gagged me and then pulled a phone cord out of the wall and tied my hands and feet, then asked where my money, guns, and cocaine were. So now the lowlife wanted to carry on a conversation, after he gagged me. I was reminded of the dentist playing 20 questions with his fist in my mouth.

From their questions, I surmised the thieves didn't know me. They asked for drugs, money and guns. As best I could, I let them know I didn't do drugs and had no guns. When the lowlife looked in my wallet, the $5 he found let him know I also had no money. Yes, I was a drummer, what did he expect?

"Buddy, you're broker than me," he said. NO SHIT!!!! But I had to give him this: The lowlife demonstrated mad mathematical skills and no concerns about hurting my feelings while describing the poor state of my financial affairs. An impressive economy of words too.

The robbers parted with a warning that I shouldn't try to look at them, or they would do what they had to do to take care of me. I didn't need any specifics; by this point in the evening, I was a quick study. I burrowed my head into the pillow, and my mind went to many places simultaneously, but I never talked to Jesus, Buddha, or the Maharishi. I just knew I would not be seeing the Braves replay, or at least not in the pants I was wearing.

"Turn out the lights," one burglar said to the other, which I took to mean the end was near. To my surprise and relief, he actually meant "turn out the lights."

Still, I was far from sure of seeing daylight. As I heard them on the other side of the house pulling out drawers, I tried to stretch and loosen the phone cord tying my hands and feet. If I could free my feet, I could jump out the window and hopefully roll till I could get on my feet to run. Occasionally, I could hear one of the men walking back to check on me, and I would try to conceal that I had loosened the cord.

But then reality set in. The window was quite a distance from the ground, so I would likely land on my head and break my neck. I heard them crank up my car, rather, the Grand Prix rental that I called my car.

After a brief silence, I spit out the gag, forced the cord off my legs, ran across the street, and kicked the neighbor's door. I hadn't met any neighbors, so I wasn't surprised when this one came to the door with a pistol. After I quickly explained what had happened, he untied my hands and called the cops. The entire episode seemed like hours but it was now only around 4 a.m.

When the cops finally arrived, the night didn't get better. They wrongly inferred, probably from my appearance, that it was likely a drug burn, and all but accused me of being a drug dealer. They never bothered even taking prints, which stoked my intuition that no investigation would happen, and fueled my "wish I could find these rednecks" vengeance.

For at least a week, I couldn't get a grip on reality. After playing in all those honky-tonks where guns had been pulled, and fights started at the drop of a hat, I almost lost my life at the one place I considered to be my safety zone, my home on a sleepy, dead-end street surrounded by neighbors I'd never met.

As bad as this was, it could have been much worse. My girlfriend was in New York buying inventory for her vintage clothing store. She was safe, but my watch, class ring, and the Grand Prix were gone.

The Grand Prix was an insurance company rental after my head-on collision the week before. Seems I was on a roll. To this day, I believe this was all a message from the Universe saying, "Lube up, dude, this isn't going to be good, and it's not going to be good for a long time." (The Universe always spoke to me in a loud, thick Southern accent while calling me "dude.") The Universe wanted me to know that the 1980s would become my least favorite decade for many reasons, most of which will be evident soon.

The cops did call a few days later to let me know the Grand Prix was found about 40 miles south of Atlanta with the rear end torn out. At that point, the "investigation" concluded. Later, I attempted to find someone who could figure out a way to locate the burglars and take away their breathing privileges. I now realize I was lucky this plan didn't come to fruition, but it wasn't for lack of trying.

I couldn't shake the feeling of being detached from friends. I was quiet and distant for a week or two, and lumps began appearing in various parts of my body, especially my neck. I imagined these were physical manifestation of stress, anger, and a few other emotions, but I held onto them much longer than I should have.

One of the last honky-tonks I played regularly was a club called Nashville Sound in Acworth, further north of Mr. J's. I played with my buddies Johnny Carlton, Donna Brown, Al Cleghorn, Gary Land, and Randy Sorrells. I only found out a couple of years later why Nashville Sound fired the band. As the club owner, R. L. inherited the long-standing tradition of treating musicians like shit, he took this obligation very seriously.

R. L. figured he could pay the band less if I was removed and Donna was put on drums. Johnny Carlton, being the guy he is, stood up to R. L. and stated that I had done nothing worthy of being fired. They argued every week when it came time to get paid, until finally R. L. grew tired of it and fired the entire band.

A few years later at the same club, I was hired to play with Ken Kinsey from my West Texas club days, but this time we would back up a guy who had wormed himself into being directly employed by the club. We were playing five sets a night, including backing up Mr. Vocal Hack for the first 20 minutes of each set. His large physique housed a small amount of talent, which towered over his diminutive sense of humor. He wasn't much of a performer, but he was politically astute when it came to working the room.

At the end of playing a Beatles song one night, several of us were laughing and parodying the "I buried Paul" chant, but substituted the hack singer's name. Nothing was said that night, but at the end of the following night, Mr. Vocal Hack called me into the green room to let me know he didn't appreciate it, and I was fired. I could only laugh about it then, and still strikes me as stupidly funny even now. Even more amusing was finding out that the hack was screwing one of the band member's wives in the same room I was fired while her husband was playing on stage. I lost total respect for the wife for having such bad taste.

Forty years later, a concrete slab sits where the West Texas club was once located, with a dry cleaning service next door. The Palomino Club is now a strip club called The Gold Rush Show Bar, and Stewart Avenue has been renamed Metropolitan Parkway. Nashville Sounds, Mr. J's, and Country Roads are gone, as are so many I worked with or met in those clubs. The last honky-tonk in Atlanta was Southern Comfort, where I worked on some scenes in the 2018 Jennifer Aniston movie *Dumplin'*. The bar barely got by on the business at night but did well with rental income from movie production companies. Still, it could not sustain itself and closed down several years ago.

I don't fondly look back at most of the 1980s, but I did appreciate being a working musician, and I miss some of the people I worked with in honky-tonks. Ken Kinsey and Mike Garrich both committed suicide. I guess many of us react to that kind of news similarly: anger, many questions, and heartbreak. Buddy Fowles and Paul Peek both died from liver diseases, as did quite a few others who worked in those bars. Walt Page died of cancer, and I can't imagine that many of the people I knew from his West Texas club are still around. The incredibly talented pedal steel guitarist Randy Sorrells, who I worked with at West Texas and Nashville Sound, went on to play with the country group Montgomery Gentry before being taken by cancer. Some musicians from that era are still playing gigs at retirement homes, Mexican restaurants, occasional bar gigs, or recording

The days of the honky-tonks are long gone, like drive-in movies. There is one remaining drive-in movie in the Atlanta area, and it's on the Southside. The Starlight Theatre on Moreland Avenue shows films, hosts weekend flea markets, and occasionally features concert events as they did years back with the frontman from the 13th Floor Elevators, Roky Erickson.

I have mixed emotions and memories of enjoying my time playing in the honky-tonks. I felt my share of depression while playing songs about some loser sitting in a bar and drinking away the blues. I choose to cling to the memories of locking musicians in a dressing room, playing offbeat during the talent shows, and making up stupid words to songs I didn't know to crack up the band. Even during the times I was fired, I had fun getting there. I wasn't going to be stressed out when making fun of the situation was much more enjoyable.

Years later, I sat around with several old buddies who served in Vietnam and were trading war stories. They would talk about fighting in the rice patties of Hanoi and Saigon, and I would talk about playing bars on Stewart and Moreland Avenue. The conversation would always end with them shaking my hand and saying, "Welcome home, brother." I didn't think the honky-tonks were hell, especially after the robbers tied me up, but things were about to get a lot worse.

There's gonna be a bar room fight tonight in country music heaven
With my boot up the ass of the pretty boys and their tight fittin' jeans
And Patsy Cline will be singin' with them Honkey-tonk Angels
I just dropped by to remind them, Hank Williams is still the king

COUNTRY MUSIC HEAVEN ©2005 DARRYL RHOADES

CHAPTER THIRTEEN

Outrunning the Blues

When the house that you've built surely tumbles to the ground
Cause things you said in anger will one day come back around
And your words will seem hollow once this truth is known
Like birds on a wire when your love has flown

BIRDS ON A WIRE ©2008 DARRYL RHOADES AND TOMMY STRAIN

I was a fan of the blues, but now it was too relatable. The lyrics were jagged and the pain sharp and I took it all personally.

I had the heartbreak that wouldn't let go. After the end of a six-and-a-half-year relationship tied to too many shared friends and memories, I felt like wherever I was, I needed to be somewhere else. The split and everything following it put me in a deep funk. I had no stereo; my car was totaled on the way to a rehearsal for a gig I didn't enjoy so I could pay for the house I no longer wanted to live in.

I was becoming the guy I couldn't stand. I wasn't earth-friendly by a long shot.

Uncharacteristically unfocused with every aspect of my life slowly draining me, at 32 I'd had my fill of being empty. I felt overwhelmed and needed clarity and decided to write down every obstacle to overcome and kept analyzing my list and imagining how to resolve each issue.

I got an offer from The Dixie Dregs to move into their rehearsal house a few blocks away. They thought it would be a good idea to have someone onsite as security for all their band equipment and gave me half the band house with a promise that the guys would always contact me in advance when rehearsing. They even broached needing a road manager, but the conversation didn't go far. The quickest way to end multiple friendships with that band would be to accept a job as their road manager because they were on the road a great deal. The rent was more than reasonable, so it was the perfect set-up for me. I rented my house in Little Five Points, which resolved my unhappy living situation, the first issue on the list.

I played bars from 8 p.m. till 4 a.m. every night with little time for a social life, which worked out perfectly since I didn't feel sociable. Spinning my wheels, doing whatever I could to fill up a day, I came up with a plan to go to Europe and reconnect with my friends Michael Brown and Frank Moates, with the hope of putting a band together and gigging in England.

On January 27, 1985, I left Atlanta in my 1964 Chevy Impala, which had a heater and fan my dad had rigged together, controlled by a toggle switch under the dash. Braving a few blizzards, I headed to Philly, where I stayed with friends, rode horses on their ranch, and attended several concerts. I met Joel Dorn in a studio in Philadelphia to rework a song I had written for Hulk Hogan.

On February 2, I flew from Philly to London's Gatwick Airport. I checked into the hotel where Michael and Frank stayed, and the following morning got the news that they were running out of money and would soon be leaving. I couldn't help but feel abandoned. I'd made my plans based on their urging, and now my follow-through was met with their leaving.

I did some touristy stuff while dropping tapes off at Island, Arista, and Phonogram Records with zero expectations, which proved right on the money. Rejection letters from other countries were essential to proving my versatility. Anyone can be turned down nationally, but I was going for international rejection—go big or go home.

After checking the local papers for concert info, I would ride the Tube to hear incredible music all over London. When I saw one of my heroes, Neil Innes, at a London pub, I should have introduced myself but instead left after a set. No matter where I was, even if I was enjoying myself, it always felt like the meter was running.

In one packed pub, I saw Frankie Miller with Simon Kirke on drums. I loved Simon's work with Free and Bad Company, and Frankie was one of my favorite singers. I was feelin' it, and it was doing the job. Jonesing to get behind a set, I built up the nerve to ask bands if I could sit in and even managed to play with several groups. But I made no lasting connections that would keep me in any one place for very long.

After 10 days in London, I headed to Amsterdam and loved the vibe there. I felt like such a rube walking through the red-light district, seeing prostitutes in windows, wearing garter belts and casually reading while waiting for customers, and I tried not to stare. I befriended the hotel manager Miro, who was from Malta and joined me to see an American blues guitarist that he wasn't familiar with, Roy Buchanan. I assured Miro that Roy would be excellent, and he was. Roy mostly performed surf songs and 1950s instrumentals and was backed up by musicians who were likely a pickup band. Even though I was the farthest I had ever been from home, the music and the way that it was played felt familiar and comforting. Maybe hearing the songs of my youth didn't heal the savage beast, but it went a long way toward treating the pain.

I rarely knew where I was going until the night before when I would study my Frommer's travel guide. The trip was all about instincts and acting on my gut before heading to Hamburg, Frankfort, Berlin, Paris, Brussels, and eventually back to London. I had no plan, and that was the plan.

I jammed with musicians in Hamburg, stayed at Hotel Kuntz in Paris, and stole a monogrammed towel because I loved the hotel's name. I always heard how romantic Paris was, but now, I felt like a chump, a mark, a patsy, a soft touch, a fall guy—like I was a sucker stuck in a 1940s movie with Edmond O'Brien, only walking solo down the Champs-Elysées. Still, describing the experience this way allows me to use phrases unfairly discarded by the American public and, at the same time, include the name of one of my favorite actors.

I should go back one day and give the Louvre another shot. Standing in front of Hieronymus Bosch's *Ship of Fools* and the real *Mona Lisa* likely won't feel so hollow next time. But there were moments when I did feel like myself again. I was never intimidated and kept a sense of humor while dealing with obstacles, like whenever I got lost walking around in Paris. The locals always showed little interest in helping me. When I approached a security guard at a bank and told him I was lost, he said he didn't speak English, so I pulled out the one phrase I knew in French: "Je suis du fromage." He smiled and said in perfect English, "I am cheese?" I figured if I could make him laugh at the original American idiot, I stood a chance, and it worked. In perfect English he explained where I was and how to get to where I needed to be.

In East Berlin, making my way into West Berlin was still a little scary. My brother, Billy, had been an MP at Checkpoint Charlie in the late 1960s, and I was curious but not ready for what I was about to experience in 1985, four years before the Berlin Wall fell. I had read a lot of history about the wall and had to see this monument of man-made suffering.

At the Wall Museum, I saw many pictures of people being shot while trying to escape East Germany, with their mangled bodies hanging on the barbed wire. I took pictures of so many heartbreaking images, like a painting by a child, that I can't forget. It shows two children waving at each other from opposite sides of the wall, where a spider lives in a web. "On the Wall, Nothing Can Live But Spiders," the child artist captioned it.

Walking around took me to a place I wasn't prepared for: the paintings on the buildings around the wall. One showed witches stirring a caldron filled with children. My attempts to take pictures of the guards in the towers would piss them off, and they would always quickly turn their backs.

It was now March and I was thinking about coming home. I knew the trip had a purpose, but I was still unsure if I'd found it. Making my way back to London, I went to a small club, and on my way in, I met Austin's Fabulous Thunderbirds on their way out. I knew the bassist, Preston Hubbard, who told me they were running late to the studio where they were working on their first album with Dave Edmunds. We talked for a few minutes before I saw one of the best shows of my life, Billy Bremner, years before I would hear of Rockpile. A guy was standing next to me who looked like a ghost, the palest dude I'd ever brushed up against. We started talking, and he told me he was a musician and writer and then introduced himself. Years later, I understood Jim Carroll as the author of the hit "People Who Died" and the autobiographical book *The Basketball Diaries*, which became a 1995 movie featuring Leonardo DiCaprio.

There was no one event that made me want to form another band, but after seeing and hearing all the music in these six weeks, I felt the fire was lit again. I headed back to Atlanta with the idea of putting together a band, recording some new songs, and performing them live. Seven years after disbanding the Hahavishnu Orchestra, I felt I had something to prove. I knew that if I was going to shake the blues, I would have to surround myself with the things and people I loved and mattered to me.

Eighteen musicians would play on The Mighty Mighty Men from Glad's first LP *Better Dead Than Mellow*. The Hahavishnu Orchestra had received so much press for its outrageousness and musicianship that attempting to replicate that would be a mistake. My *Burgers* LP had sold well, my songwriting had become stronger, and while I wanted to incorporate satire, I also wanted to branch out. I expected comparisons from fans of the old band but chose to focus on putting together a tight live band that could make the new songs pop. Performing a show unlike anything anyone else was doing at the time was still a priority as well.

I had worked with producer Brendan O'Brien a good bit and knew him to be a quick study in the studio. He understood me and knew how to capture energy, which is no small feat, which is why I wanted to work with him on this new project. Unfortunately, I had lost touch with him. I started asking around and learned he'd taken some time off from working in the studio and was a little reclusive. I had no idea where he was until a mutual friend got word to him that I was looking for him. He called a few days later and agreed to work with me on the LP.

My immediate plan after the LP was to assemble a group to play live, and tour in support of the record. I knew that most of the band members I had assembled for the initial studio group wouldn't be into touring as much as I knew it would take, and they considered the project as a work in progress. My intentional approach in putting this touring group together was a complete break from how The Hahavishnu Orchestra organically came together. Keeping a band together was always challenging, and at the height of the Orchestra's popularity, we kept chasing the elusive record contract with no success. Waiting for someone to offer a contract wasn't a consideration.

The new band came together with an energy that was new to me, and the recording of this LP was much more relaxed. Friends would drop by and contribute their playing on a cut or two. Having two of Atlanta's best rock guitarists, Rick Richards and Brendan O'Brien, playing a few songs didn't suck either. The LP also featured members of The Dregs, Swimming Pool Qs, and The Glenn Phillips Band. The initial band included only two ex-Hahavishnu players, my friend Jimmy Royals (keyboards and trombone) and drummer Joey Dukes, and it was refreshing to record newer songs not associated with our old group. The album had a fresh sound and feeling about it, with 11 songs, some hilarious and some were great pop songs, but one of the most popular ones was our big band lounge version of "Born To Be Wild." We played our version during a soundcheck at the Center Stage Theatre in Atlanta when we were opening for Steppenwolf, and after their band stopped laughing, they warned us not to do that when frontman John Kay showed up. For the sake of peace, I left it out that night, which I now regret. Performing it in front of Mr. Kay could have made an incredible story.

The LP was therapeutic on several levels. I was confronting the anger and lingering issues by writing songs with lyrics like "Trust Me." For all the miles and time I had put in attempting to create distance from the blues, I hadn't learned how to let 'em go so they became fuel for the fire.

TRUST ME ©1985 DARRYL RHOADES

Even before touring, *Better Dead than Mellow* garnered much press and airplay. The cover was shot by Rick Diamond, and the album layout was by Michael McCarty. All the players wore white clothes and put white powder in their hair or wore wigs after spraying the hair white. In contrast, I wore all black and, at that time, had black hair. The photo on the back cover is special to me because it's the one time my dad was involved in any of my music projects. He's seen holding a bottle of root beer, with smudges like a hobo, along with Paul Peek and album designer Mike McCarty leaning over him, looking like they were nursing a five-day drunk. Record company guy Marshall Madden is lying on the floor with garbage piled all over him.

I would have loved for The MMMFG to be on a major label, but even that doesn't guarantee decent distribution, accurate record sales accounting, or tour support. I'd witnessed several friends with major record deals who never saw a dime from their record company. I knew bands so anxious to sign a record deal that they gave away control and their publishing rights. For me, it was never about the money as much as the exposure. I wanted people to hear the songs and check out the band.

One issue was constant: how to make touring financially viable. The MMMFG would eventually become a steady working band with entirely different personnel than on the album, because of my conscientious decision to assemble a smaller touring group. I couldn't go through what I had with The Hahavishnu, the record companies complaining about the cost of breaking a large group and the day-to-day expenses of maintaining a tour schedule.

The MMMFG metamorphosis pared us down to Bo Messina (bass), Rick Kurtz (guitar), Danny Bigay (drums), and Carl "C.C. Sax" Crabtree (sax and keys). It was an incredibly tight band, and because it was smaller, all the players had to be mindful of filling up the sound and their presence on stage. Energy was key, and we had plenty of it. Great bands are all about chemistry and audience connection, and most of the time, that was never an issue with The MMMFG. It rocked with hipper songs and raw energy, but the glitz and variety were replaced with more emotion, and the humor seemed to have more jagged edges.

I don't know if there were fewer challenges than with the Orchestra, maybe just different ones. We didn't tour as much as we should have. We did travel up and down the eastern seaboard but mostly played the clubs in Atlanta, Birmingham, and Nashville. If someone was coming to hear a rehash of the band I had the decade before, they were undoubtedly surprised. On some levels, the new band was vastly superior, but when great musicians have little to show for their work, personnel changes were to be expected. When Rick Kurtz left to play with Delbert McClinton, I was happy for him but had no idea how he could be replaced. He was a monster player, but equally important, he possessed an insane sense of humor and had become a good friend to all of us. Rick took pride in his playing, and anyone sitting in beside him better be on their game because you can be sure he was.

After Rick gave notice, we started holding auditions and running a few ads in the local music paper and the word got out. Auditioning new players was a pain in my ass. I found it more efficient if I sent cassettes of several original songs of varying genres that I expected the musician to learn, along with audition time and location info. The process included time for the band to talk with the player to see if they felt a connection, but sometimes the audition wouldn't last that long. I wasn't attempting to be a hard-ass, but if a player showed up incredibly late or didn't bother to learn the songs for an audition, I knew I couldn't expect different behavior from them down the road. Be on time, come prepared, and bring your personality, i.e., don't be a dick.

Several players came unprepared. After setting up their rig, they'd apologize because they hadn't gotten around to learning the songs. I would thank them for their time and end the audition on the spot. The audition was more than showing me they could play their instrument. I assumed they knew how to do that.

Then, THAT guy came in who blew us all away.

Corky Hughes was from Mobile and played slide guitar as well as anyone I'd heard. With Rick Kurtz being from Birmingham, I figured there was something in the Alabama water. There was no comparing them; both guys had their distinct approach to guitar and equally different personalities. Playing with either one of them made you a better musician.

Corky was coming off a stint with Black Oak Arkansas, and his playing was transformative. He gave every song he played a different personality. Over the years, he's played on several of my recordings, giving other guitarists fits when they attempted to reproduce his sound live. Like Rick, Corky brought a professional attitude and a strong sense of humor that The MMMFG quickly put to use.

Our show could be very quirky, and we would often come out and open the show as a different band. My favorite was dressing up and covering rock songs as a country band. We went a little out of our way one week at the Harvest Moon in Atlanta when we put on tons of makeup and dresses and opened the show as The Paper Dudes (satirizing a popular all-female regional band, The Paper Dolls), singing mostly country versions of rock songs and occasional standards like "Stand By Your Man." I wore my hair in a tall beehive, and a killer yellow dress to die for (I had to use that phrase just because it never made sense but sounded like something a guy would say if he wore a beehive 'do and yellow dress). We were one band of the ugliest women in rock other than The New York Dolls.

The MMMFG always strived to make the show bigger and hopefully different, incorporating some of the show aspects of the Orchestra, as well as adding new ones. At the beginning of shows, I got attention by stripping the sound from a video clip and inserting our narrative. I wrote a song titled "Jesus is Screaming on My TV," so it was only natural that we would use a clip of Jim and Tammy Faye Bakker challenging Jerry Falwell to a Texas Death Match after Tammy proclaimed that Jerry allegedly attacked Jim outside after a sermon. Anytime we could attach wrestling, religion, and music, I considered it the holy trinity, and we did it often. I was never concerned about irreverence. The religious con was always in my sights, and I could never figure out how they kept fostering a new flock to fleece (big fan of alliteration). I didn't mind pissing off people but enjoyed a headstart whenever needed and possible.

There were a few gigs that required a swift departure. I don't know what some club owners were thinking when they booked us, but that wasn't new territory either. If we had played boogie music, we would have been heralded as a great drinking band, but instead, on several occasions when the videos started playing to set up a song, napkins, straws, and whatever the Neanderthals could pick up came raining down on the band. We would turn it up and leave out most of the pauses in between songs until last call, and it was time to settle. We were a good band with a great show but often found ourselves to be the wrong band for the wrong venue.

I got the Devil in my pants, I got the Devil in my pants
Makin' me say things that I don't mean . . .
I'm talkin' crude and actin' obscene
I'm just a victim of circumstance and every time it happens
It's the Devil in my pants
Some blame it on whiskey some blame it on pills . . .
I just can't stop it breaks down my will
I gotta one track mind and I'm in a trance . . .
I'll blame it on the Devil in my pants

I'VE GOT THE DEVIL IN MY PANTS ©1987 DARRYL RHOADES

When The MMMFG would perform in Atlanta, I forked out my own money for promotions. I had rasslin'-type posters printed, or beautiful colorful cardboard signs like those advertising great R&B acts at the legendary Royal Peacock Lounge. To create an event that shouldn't be missed, I was going for that retro look and feel.

We performed our final Atlanta show at a club located on Peachtree Street on Memorial Day weekend, May 28, 1988. Billed as our last

Atlanta appearance of that year that shouldn't be missed, it turned into an event many people felt comfortable missing. When I went to collect our guarantee, the club manager said he had instructions to give us less from the absent club owner, whom I had made a deal with and had left the manager to do his dirty work. The explanation for that evening's reaming was that the band had recently drawn a better turnout at another local club, so we shouldn't be paid for this turnout that was less than expected. I didn't remember ever getting a raise or extra pay when we packed his room previously, but when it came to coming up short, musicians were expected to bear the brunt of a slow night. I promptly marched the entire band into the office and made the club manager repeat the explanation to everyone as to why we were being violated without the aid of a lubricant.

After paying the rest of the band, my share didn't even cover the cost of the posters. The same club owner has allegedly pulled that scam on other bands and is still in the business in Atlanta. Being bitter about some business dealings doesn't serve anyone, but I have been able to joke about it by saying, "Every time I hear a criminal has been arrested, I try to find out what club he's booking."

That final Atlanta appearance in the summer of 1988 preceded the last big road trip, which opened with a show in Columbia, South Carolina. We were working a door deal but only found out when we arrived that it was $1 night, women got in free, and beer was half price. We played for almost no money to a packed room of really drunk people. After the gig, we drove to Philadelphia, where we had a short tour of five dates booked. Like magic, all fell through except one, which wasn't promoted. After that depressing part of the tour, we headed to NYC for a showcase for invited industry people who didn't show up at the iconic Lone Star Cafe.

Iconic is another word for "you're not going to make any money, but it could help your career, but likely not." When it was all said and not done, it costs us to have no one see us. The MMMFG was entertaining, but again, there was no manager or plan for where we were going or how to get there. You hang on by a thread held together with promises, but the signs couldn't have been more obvious: It was time to make another change. Surely there are better ways to not make enough money to live on while doing what you love in life. That's when I heard the Universe whisper in my ear, "Dude, I ain't done yet. Keep the K-Y handy. I got plans."

Rain & Stone

There's only so much your heart can take
So much bend before you break
It's the storms that wither our soul
Like the rain against the stone

I watched the shoreline disappear
So slowly over the years
I never noticed until it was gone
Just like the rain against the stone

Earthquakes will rumble
And mountains will crumble
There's some things that we can't control
But the heartache and pain
Just like the rain
Will slowly wear down your soul
There was a time long ago
When the anger tore at my soul
I carried it around and it wore me down
Just like the rain against the stone

And maybe it's all the years
Of seeing all of the tears
Bear down on those left alone
Like the rain against the stone

So now I set aside
All the anger, guilt and pride
Freed of sins I atone
Like the rain against the stone

RAIN & STONE ©2017 DARRYL RHOADES

CHAPTER FOURTEEN

I Just Wanted to Be the Drummer

I remember long ago when I was very young
Pretending to be Keith Moon while I played my drums
Lay in bed at night and listened to my radio
Where I figured I'd learn everything I need to know
In my room I listened to the Beatles and the Stones
A teenage rebel but I never felt alone
From coast to coast I listened to the friends I'd never met
Which makes it harder now since I can't forget
My Radio Sucks

MY RADIO SUCKS ©2003 DARRYL RHOADES

In 1982, I got a call from Eddie Hinton, the legendary Muscle Shoals session guitarist, on the recommendation of The Nighthawks' drummer, Pete Ragusa. Eddie was about to hit the road for a few dates playing college bars and blues clubs and urgently needed a drummer. I had never met him but was very impressed with the stories about the guy who had written hit songs for the Box Tops, Dusty Springfield, and others. I felt lucky for the opportunity to play with a well-seasoned studio musician who had recorded with so many of my favorite artists.

He invited me to his house in Macon several days later. I met his wife, Sandra, and we rehearsed for a few hours before calling it a night with plans on hitting it again early the following day.

In the guest bedroom, I started listening to the rehearsal cassette we had just recorded. While lying on top of the bed, I noticed a roach, then another roach, and I started counting the roaches on the wall, ceiling, and floors. After a couple of hundred, I quit counting and decided I needed to sleep in my car. I packed my clothes, drove to an all-night store for coffee, and then returned to the driveway, where I slept. I set an alarm and woke up early but never mentioned it to Eddie. I didn't want to hurt his feelings, but I had to strategize a discreet way to bring up "bugapalooza" the following morning.

Eddie explained that he no longer used insecticide because the brother of his large English sheepdog had recently died from eating poisoned roaches on the floor. So now the bugs flourished. I wondered how many poisoned insects a large English sheepdog could eat before being poisoned to death. While that might be a sad thought, it would be a kickass trivia question on *Jeopardy*.

Hey, what's a few roaches, give or take a hundred or two? I was playing with Eddie Hinton, who had recorded with Aretha Franklin, Wilson Pickett, Joe Tex, Otis Redding, and too many other legends to mention. Reportedly, Duane Allman had offered him a spot when he formed the Allman Brothers, but Eddie turned it down to write and record in Muscle Shoals. Many regarded Eddie as one of our generation's greatest blue-eyed soul singers, so roaches weren't gonna be the reason I didn't want to play with him. Other reasons came along shortly.

After rehearsal the following morning, I loaded up and headed back to Atlanta, where Eddie and the rest of the band picked me up for our first gig out of town. The bass player, Calvin Arline, had played with Aretha, Marvin Gaye, Mavis Staples, and many other R&B greats. He was a big guy and a solid player with a great feel. The sax player, Sonny Brown, had just toured with Little Richard and had that great tone I love, like Arthur Prysock and King Curtis. The band was called The Rocking Horses, consisting of guitar, bass, sax, and drums, but when Eddie started singing, we could have just as well stopped playing because it was his voice selling the song. He had the power, and you felt it behind him.

His 1978 debut album, *Very Extremely Dangerous*, remains one of my favorites. Eddie's voice was soulful, and I believe his picture was intentionally left off the LP cover so listeners might think he was Black. This album should have made some serious noise, but the lack of touring, and little promo by his record label, Capricorn Records, didn't help. There were tales of drugs and money problems blamed in part for the label folding in 1979, but not before putting their stamp on the legacy of Southern rock.

Eddie was a monster talent in need of management and guidance, and infamous for his limited dietary habits. When we would stop to eat on the road, he and his wife would stay in the van and make bologna or peanut butter sandwiches while the rest of us would go into the restaurants for a hot meal. I don't remember him eating with the rest of the band; he always pulled out a loaf of bread and put something in between two slices, which would consistently be Eddie and Sandra's roadside dining experience. Years later, I discovered the Drive-By Truckers had recorded a song about Eddie and his meal habits, titled "Sandwiches for the Road."

I can generally read most people, but Eddie wasn't most people. He could be volatile. You could be laughing with him one minute, and the next, he'd give you a look like there was about to be a problem. I saw it several times when he argued with Sonny and a few times with myself. When our tour came back to Atlanta, I invited Eddie and Sandra to stay the night at the house I shared with my girlfriend. I wish I had recorded my nighttime conversations with Eddie; he traveled the cosmos.

I have a cassette of one of our sets from the first night I played with Eddie at a club called The Cat's Cradle in Chapel Hill, North Carolina. We played to less than 20 people, which was how most of the dates went down. On one of the earlier dates, the club owner invited us to stay at his house after the gig, where he gave Eddie a small portion of the money they agreed to and promised to send the rest later. "Later" is a term many club owners use to mean "never." "Later" happened on several gigs we did on this tour, which would be why I turned down the following tour dates when Eddie called a month later. By then I was involved in other projects.

When he hit the road again, Eddie didn't seem to have his act together, but that was Eddie. He toured for a while with several new members but hit a rough patch and became homeless and in bad health. Several friends tried to help, and during the next few years, he recorded a few CDs, one in the back of a furniture store. I would occasionally hear of him making appearances over the years, but sadly, he died of a heart attack in 1995.

One of Eddie's friends, John Wyker of the group Sailcat, contacted me a few years later and sent a VHS tape of him and Eddie in a basement doing an interview and playing. The tape could have been better recorded, and they seemed scattered. They put the video together to sell, and I can't imagine it generated much interest. Over the years, I've had several journalists contact me to discuss Eddie in hopes of producing a book or documentary, and I gave them as much info as I could. During the writing of this book, I learned of the recent release of *Everybody Needs Love*, a book about Eddie where I was quoted along with many others who knew and worked with him. I've watched YouTube videos of Eddie performing in concerts and small clubs overseas, but they don't come close to the feeling of being on drums behind him and hearing that voice come out of the mouth.

Eddie Hinton is another story similar to many who should have experienced more success. He was a great singer, musician, and writer whose songs were covered by several prominent artists. He made a small fortune recording with everyone from Elvis to Dylan, but died like so many musicians have in the past, broke and homeless.

Later that year I got a call to play drums for a one-nighter behind Tommy Roe, whom I had never met. I was familiar with much of his music and thought of it as bubble gum except for his hit "Everybody," which reminded me a little of one of my rockabilly heroes, Eddie Cochran. Since Tommy rarely performed in Atlanta I knew there would be a large audience for his homecoming.

Acting band leader Johnny Carlton set up a rehearsal for the day before the show in a club on Peachtree Street called Animal Crackers. The night before rehearsal, I was watching a TV show featuring rock and roll stars singing oldies and, in particular, one of my favorites, Bobby Vee. Bobby's hits, "The Night Has a Thousand Eyes," "Rubber Ball," and "Take Good Care of My Baby" were well produced, with him doing most of the harmonies. When he performed on TV, he wore a jumpsuit similar to those Elvis and Neil Diamond wore. It struck me so weird I wondered why everyone was wearing jumpsuits, looking like the Pillsbury Doughboy after a binge with his bedazzler.

The next day at rehearsal, I spoke with Tommy about seeing Bobby Vee, and we both laughed about the jumpsuit phenomena. The rehearsal lasted for a few hours and we ran through most of Tommy's hits. He was in good voice and we were all looking forward to the show. I liked Tommy; he had a great sense of humor, and the band sounded great.

The following day, we all got to the club early for a sound check and then Tommy showed us the pictures from when he toured England in 1963 with the Beatles as his opening act. He had some great stories, including the time on the bus when he and John Lennon got into an ugly disagreement over a comment Lennon made to singer Chris Montez.

When it came time for us to hit the stage at Animal Crackers, the band was to perform a few songs and then bring Tommy out. The place was packed, and the energy was high. When it came time for Tommy to make his grand entrance, I started playing the drum roll to "Sheila," as Johnny announced, "Now, ladies and gentlemen, the man you all came to see, Tommy Roe!" When I looked up, here comes Tommy briskly approaching the stage as if he were "poppin' fresh from the oven" with sparkly little stones glistening in the spotlight. YES, HE WAS WEARIN' A DAMN JUMPSUIT WITH RHINESTONES!!!! I couldn't contain myself when our eyes met, and he gave me the biggest shit-eatin' grin I've ever seen. I managed to keep playing, but it wasn't easy. The story is funny but also a reminder that I'd been better served one more time by keeping my mouth shut.

I was excited when I got a call asking if I was interested in doing a date with Chuck Berry. I was interested in seeing how it would pan out for me because I'd heard so many stories from people playing with him, including several friends.

Rick Hinkle, for one, dropped some acid before his gig with Chuck. Suddenly moved to make a trip to the bathroom, Rick was late making his way to the stage, where Chuck and the band were already playing. Mr. Berry sidelined Rick for a few songs and later brought him on stage, but it didn't sit well with Rick. Unable to contain himself in the middle of a slow blues song Chuck and his daughter were singing, Rick ran up to the front of the stage and slid on his knees, playing a loud lick that couldn't be ignored. Without looking up at Chuck, Rick turned, unplugged his guitar, walked down the steps, and left Chuck uttering some profanities.

My gig with Chuck was set for the iconic Chastain Amphitheatre with Rex Patton on bass and Dean Daughtry from the Atlanta Rhythm Section on piano. Dean had played on several of my albums and was a personal hero of mine, dating back to his days with the Candymen. Rex had worked with Chuck before and gave us the layout of what to expect. There would be no rehearsal or heads-up on what we would be playing, so don't even ask. If you were playing and Chuck lifted his foot and came down, you stopped playing, and if you weren't playing and he raised his foot, you started. Figuring we all were familiar with Chuck's work, none of this should be a problem, and as a drummer I didn't have to try like the other players to figure out what key the songs were in. Asking Chuck what songs you would be playing usually ended with the response, "We're playin' Chuck Berry music," so you might as well sit back and enjoy the ride, bumps and all. I wasn't intimidated because Chuck's music was in my wheelhouse, or at least most of it. I was looking forward to it.

Chuck had a reputation and could be prickly. I'd heard firsthand from a guy who was in the audience for the taping of the film *Hail! Hail! Rock 'n' Roll* about Linda Ronstadt asking Chuck to lower the key for the song she was singing, "Living in the U.S.A." He promised he would and then ignored her request on stage, so she sang it and stormed off afterward into her limo waiting outside.

Chuck was another genius with issues. Rightfully suspicious when it came to business, he demanded cash before taking the stage and usually put it in a bag inside his guitar case, which never left his line of sight while he played. Some shows never happened because Chuck wouldn't budge on the cash. Knowing Chuck was all about control, I approached him when he first came down the hallway backstage and introduced myself: "Hello, Mr. Berry, I'm Darryl Rhoades, and I'll be working for you tonight on drums." He gave me a big grin, shook my hand, and said, "Let's rock," to which I responded, "Yes, sir, I fully intend to."

The three of us had done a sound check earlier in the day, before Chuck's arrival, but you never know how much good the sound check will do when you're the last act on the bill. Once you're on stage, the only thing you can control is your playing; everything else is in the hands of the sound person. A good one marks the levels and settings and can make a monumental difference in the band's sound.

The opening act, Little Richard, had two drummers, both showmen and in sync. Being a huge fan of Richard, I walked out into the audience to check the sound but also to listen to him as a fan. I always considered him to be the real king of rock 'n' roll. He gave everything he had, even if his energy had diminished over the years. The band kicked ass and the sound was as perfect as it could be for an outside venue. Mixing a band in any outside gig can be a challenge but Richard was in good voice. The only thing we could control was how we did our job on stage behind Chuck and leave everything else up to Chuck and the production crew.

On the first song, Chuck started with the groove of swingin' on four like "Johnny B. Goode," which I love. I'm not trying to be disrespectful when I say he sounded like he hadn't tuned his guitar since the middle of the 1960s. About 15 seconds into the song, he stopped the band, looked at us, and then started stomping his feet, which would usually indicate we were rushing the tempo. I laughed because I knew better. He was pissing on us and marking his territory; a point he made again a month later when Rex saw him do the same thing to his backup band in Las Vegas. Yes, Chuck was a control guy.

Rex understood what the bass player played on every Chuck Berry record, but on the gig that night at Chastain Park Amphitheatre, Chuck wouldn't allow Rex to walk on the bass; he was instructed to play the bottom with eighth notes. Most guys like Chuck had been playing their songs for decades and knew what they wanted, or maybe they had played with many musicians who couldn't cop the groove, so they just wanted to get through the night. Drummers who played what they thought was the "Bo Diddley rhythm" behind Mr. Diddley usually got a quick lesson on playing 2/4 against the guitar, actually doing the rhythm and not the other way around. The artist always makes the call; it's his name on the ticket.

Our set included a big hit that truly sucks ass. Knowing "My Ding-a-Ling" is Chuck's only No. 1 hit speaks volumes about the public's taste, and to me, it's in the vein of "Shaving Cream" by Benny Bell. Chuck, a founding father of rock, wrote songs likely outliving us all, and few songwriters can come anywhere close to his lyrical brilliance. When Chuck went into "My Ding-a-Ling," I laid out and wouldn't look up, and it didn't matter to him; he had the audience singing along with the enthusiasm of "99 Bottles of Beer on the Wall."

A week later, I was performing standup in Rochester, and appeared on a local morning radio show along with several other artists, including Southside Johnny from the Asbury Jukes. The DJ opened by mentioning a new *Rolling Stone* ranking of the top 100 guitarists, and hinted that one of guest had just performed with someone on the list. In my interview, the DJ mentioned Chuck, and we spoke for several minutes, then during the break, Southside Johnny asked me how I got along with Chuck. I told him it was a pleasant experience but figured I'd caught Chuck on a good day. Johnny then laughed and began to tell me how excited his friend, Bruce Springsteen, was to back up Chuck early in his career but unknowingly did something that aggravated Chuck, who began to cuss Bruce out in front of his hometown crowd. Hail! Hail! Rock 'n' Roll!

I figure it this way, I played drums behind a guy who wrote songs influencing some of the greatest artists of my lifetime. Listening to Chuck Berry, Little Richard, and the early R&B music was the reason why I became a drummer and I never questioned it. I learned the difference between the manic passionate artists and the posers. When it came to "Tutti Frutti" it was always Little Richard . . . never Pat Boone.

You Beat Me to the Paunch

Although my teeth are all but gone, I got my guitar out of pawn
Gonna reform the old band, and we're gonna make it big as my prostate gland
Well uh huh uh huh oh yeah

Well our first gig is in Oklahoma, I can't drive cause I got glaucoma
And Jimmy is on keys and he really smokes,
But just with one hand now after the stroke
Well uh huh uh huh oh yeah

Well rock & roll will never die, but when you hear us play you'll wonder why
We used to party all night and scream and shout
But now we're talkin' ruffage when we blow it on out

Well that's Freddie rockin' out on the Fender,
Playin' the only song that he can remember
His pants are tight but his stomach sags, he's gotta leave room for his colostomy bag
Well uh huh uh huh oh yeah

Well rock & roll is here to stay, It's not dead it just smells that way
There's always plenty groupies hangin' around
But now we can't get it up enough to even get down

Yeah, I used to be an angry young man, now I got liver spots all over my hand
Yeah we used to hit the stage and play long shows,
But now we cut 'em short because of bladder control
Well uh huh uh huh oh yeah

Well arthritis, bursitis, lumbago,
My blood pressure's high and my butt's hangin' low
This indigestion is killin' me, it's hard to sing when you gotta (burp)

And Buddy is still beatin' the skins, but his hemorrhoids are back again
So he stands up when he plays cause he's got bad knees
But all I wanna know is "who cut the cheese"
Well uh huh uh huh oh yeah

YOU BEAT ME TO THE PAUNCH ©2000 DARRYL RHOADES

CHAPTER FIFTEEN

Hell's Half Wise Acre

I'm staying where the band stayed
Sleeping where the drummer got laid
Where the juices are still flowing
And I got no way of knowing
What's crawling up my leg
I'm in the house where the band stays
Don't eat the open jar of mayonnaise
There's pubic hair on my soap
And I feel like I've been groped
Yeah, I'm an entertainer

THE BAND HOUSE (I'M AN ENTERTAINER) ©2014 DARRYL RHOADES

only considered doing stand-up comedy after being encouraged by a few professional comedians who told me they had performed some of my songs in their shows. I constantly resisted the term "comedy music" to describe my bands, but now I had to rethink how to market myself in a way to make a living and continue performing. I didn't have the passion I'd heard so many describe about stand-up, but it had to be preferable to continually ramming my head against the wall to keep a band together. I started doing stand-up in 1988, a few years after the major boom in comedy; it was all over TV, and clubs were opening like Waffle Houses on the interstate. Comedians were the new rock stars, with some getting tons of TV exposure, which helped pack the clubs.

Standing on stage without a band seemed foreign and a little scary. I had watched Kelly Monteith, Tom Parks, and other comedians open shows for the Hahavishnu and never thought about trying it. Now I began to see that all those setups for songs, crowd interaction, and much of my material as stand-up, only with props and music. What I had been doing most of my life as a performer was stand-up in mostly music venues.

When I started entertaining the idea of trying stand-up comedy, I went to several shows to get a handle on how it worked with my eye on entering one of comedy contests being held at the Punchline Comedy Club in Atlanta. I hadn't worked any comedy shows yet and would be competing with comedians who had been working the road for years. I began writing and reworking material I'd done on stage with bands. Even after all the years of performing for thousands of people, I would fight the urge to throw up while I waited behind the curtain to be introduced on stage. Getting that first laugh was key, and so was remembering to breathe.

I understood that my approach would be a little unorthodox, playing backing music tracks from a boombox while singing songs like "Think of Me When You're Under Him" as a character named "Vinnie Martel" who wore a wig that looked like something I scraped off the highway. Performing character pieces instantly grabbed the audience, especially when I tapped into my redneck roots as "Buck Nekkid" and sang "Meet My Wife (She's My Sister)." Loudly preaching to the audience about how they would be going to hell for frequenting the comedy den of iniquity would set me apart from the other acts, kill in the competitions, and become an issue as part of my set when I started working the clubs.

I placed second in the first stand-up competition I entered. The next day, I got a call from Ronnie Bullard, who was headlining the club that week. Being a novice, I had yet to learn the common practice many comics or wannabe comedians employ, but Ronnie informed me that the guy who came in first did so while cherry-picking tried and true tested material from other comics. It never crossed my mind to perform any material that I didn't write. Ronnie was complimentary, and true to his word, he followed up by connecting me with Creative Talent out of Charlotte. Creative, also known as The Comedy Zone, was a growing agency booking 30 to 40 weeks of one-nighters and full-time clubs. They were always looking for entertainers to fill the slots; my timing couldn't have been better. I won the next comedy competition, used the videotape to get work from other agencies, and soon began working 45 to 50 weeks a year. It was essential to work for as many clubs and agencies as possible, as many found out when they depended on any one club or booking agency.

The standard comedy show generally consisted of three performers: emcee, feature, and headliner. I emceed for a few weeks without understanding that emcees are expected to prepare the audience for the show and make the transitions for the comedians as smooth as possible. Instead, I'd hit the stage and start spewing my material at breakneck speeds, often to the point that the audience couldn't understand me. Because I was different, I was promoted quickly as a feature, probably before I was ready. I didn't know what I didn't know: the art of writing jokes, how to be a part of the show rather than be the show, and navigating around the massive egos of those jaded comics who felt their careers should have progressed further.

Until the comedy boom in the early 1980s, most comedians worked in strip bars, supper clubs, and anywhere else they could perform for money and stage time. Way before I ever considered doing stand-up, because I wanted to improve my comic timing in my music act, I would study the old masters like Jonathan Winters, Lenny Bruce, or George Carlin. I had been exposed to strip club comedians a few times when I played drums backing the "exotic dancers" from exciting faraway lands like Waycross, Georgia, and Heflin, Alabama, and was curious. A couple of times, I went to a local strip club on Peachtree Street in Atlanta, where I saw Gene "Truckstop" Tracy perform his act.

Gene's act was tits and ass jokes during the breaks between the girls dancing. I was intrigued that a man could go up and tell old jokes and make a living. I introduced myself to Gene after his set and made a plan to have lunch the next day. I wanted to pick his brain about what he did for a living, and he was curious about my material, hoping I might sell him some jokes or songs he could use. Nothing I had would work for him, but still, I looked forward to hanging out with him.

During lunch the next day, he told me a great story about meeting "a Black guy" in Macon, Georgia, where he appeared at a strip club. The Black guy liked Gene's act and invited him to have lunch with him and his wife the next day. Gene told me he felt a little ambivalent about going because he assumed the couple was likely poor and didn't want to take the food out of their mouths, but drove to the address he was given. When he arrived, he pulled up to some big iron gates, which automatically opened, and went a little distance, making his way to the house where he met the couple for lunch. Gene had never heard of Jaimoe (drummer and percussionist John Lee Johnson) or The Allman Brothers, and laughed as he told me the ending of that story. Years later, I met Jaimoe and retold Gene's story. Jaimoe broke out laughing and then confirmed it was all true.

On the comedy circuit, I would run into others with solid musical backgrounds trying to adapt their talent into a comedy act, some with more success than others. The trick was balancing the two. There's a long history of brilliant comedians who have used their musical skills and instruments as props to set up their jokes. I grew up watching Jack Benny playing violin, The Smothers Brothers on guitars, and even Victor Borge, classically trained on piano. Many comics frowned on those who played instruments in their show, which always seemed a little shortsighted to me. I believe you should use whatever you have in your arsenal. I appreciated all approaches to comedy and performed with ventriloquists, impressionists, mimes, and political humorists. A few billed themselves as improv comedians, often doing the same "improv" from gig to gig.

I never worried about working with an act that was similar to mine. I didn't usually work with comics who played music in their show, but since I didn't take a guitar on stage, bookers occasionally paired me with guys who were considered music acts. There were successful comedy duos performing music like Pinkard and Bowden, and

Malone & Nootcheez, but I wanted to try something different. Most music acts performed parodies, and some were brilliant, but I always felt they were taking the easy way out. Half the work was already done since the music was being copied and the lyrics rewritten. Performing any of my songs on stage required a lot of editing to make the songs shorter, while using the funniest lines and without repeating a chorus. Some comics were better at this than others. Writing a humorous song to record or perform with a band could be much different than writing for the comedy club stage.

I was more comfortable referring to myself as an entertainer. I came to admire the art form and many of those I worked with who were very helpful and inspiring. Success wasn't a fluke and required effort with a degree of luck and timing. As in music, originality in stand-up comedy often attracted some copycats looking for shortcuts. I worked with Mitch Hedberg when he was a young kid and saw how much he believed in himself and his approach and how much work he put in. When he finally gained notoriety, some tried to emulate his cadence and delivery without having the chops or work ethic. Even with Mitch's success, his brand of comedy wasn't for everyone. At one Funny Bone comedy club, he was asked to trade places with a local high-energy feature act, and he wouldn't, so that cut short his week-long gig.

One of my favorites, comedian and country singer Tim Wilson, worked as hard at his craft as anyone I'd known. He scored great success from his many appearances on nationally syndicated radio shows that played his songs. I could make a long list of names of comics I worked with who went on to be cast members on *Saturday Night Live*, successful screenwriters who had their own TV shows or wrote for other TV shows, and none of that success happened by accident.

I was working with Darrell Hammond at Charlie Goodnights in Raleigh. The show was billed as a triple headliner week, and since I performed music, the other two acts alternated the feature position, and I was asked to close. After we worked a couple of shows together, I began to dread following Darrell every other night because he was so talented; at the same time, I became a fan and started hanging out with him, even though he constantly demeaned himself. I got the impression that he never knew how good he was, even though we were in Raleigh when he got a call to audition for *SNL*. When Darrell said, "I'd give anything if I were naturally funny like you," I went off on him a little. He wasn't faking it or fishing for compliments. He genuinely didn't understand why audiences were crazy about him. His gift for uncanny spot-on impressions became his trademark for 14 seasons on *SNL*.

I was 38 when I started doing stand-up, a little older than most of the comics I worked with but I started getting work quickly. I had all those years of fronting bands and playing drums on stage, so being in front of a large crowd wasn't as intimidating. Most of the comics were cool, but occasionally, you'd meet some who were insecure, especially if they had difficulty following you like I was with Darrell. I was very high energy, so I saw that a few times. Some comics let their insecurities get the better of them, and they'd wind up complaining to bookers or club owners. I would watch some headliners pacing, looking at their watches, and complaining the preceding act had gone over their time. Usually, it wasn't the case; these comics were bitching because they just knew they'd have to work harder after a great set by someone else. I experienced both sides of it and grew to understand you put the praise in the same box as the criticism and never allow yourself to get too high or too low. Other comics worried about being the best on the bill and viewed the rest of us as competition. Those guys had no groove. Comedians with twisted mindsets never enjoyed the ride, which was my big payoff.

When I started, the comedy scene reminded me a lot of what I imagined vaudeville was like. There was a lot of diversity in the clubs, from magicians to ventriloquists, hypnotists, monologists, and music acts. Audiences were more open-minded as long as you could entertain them.

Occasionally, I'd work with someone completely unique. I've always put a high priority on authentic characters, free thinkers, and originality. I relished being around that kind of energy. I saw that when I worked with Bill Sacra from Louisville. He was such a throwback that his promo picture was shot in sepia. He wore a suit and looked like he walked on stage from the 1940s with a W. C. Fields thing going on, and he was the most unique character I've ever worked with. He performed a ventriloquism bit he called "Answer Baby," where he put a doll on his lap, and the audience would ask it questions. He was spontaneously hilarious.

Some performers were over-the-top outrageous, and I appreciated their fire. Otto Peterson had an act with a dummy called "Otto & George." They started in the streets before becoming an X-rated act in the clubs. Most of the time, Otto slayed the audience, with one notable exception. He was working a show one evening when the dummy called an audience member a name, and the angry man lashed out with a knife and stabbed the puppet.

Over the years of performing, I understood what it meant to be a professional and the importance of being reliable and showing up on time. Even though I was meticulous, I understood some would never treat comedy as a business. I kept my distance from them and focused on what I needed to do.

I once booked a gig in Germany through an agency based in Houston. Several friends had worked for these people and never had any issues. Then again, they weren't me. I always showed up when and where I was supposed to be. I flew out of Atlanta when I was supposed to, and I landed in Frankfort, Germany, when I was supposed to, and no one was waiting to meet me. I was supposed to be taken to Ramstein Air Force Base to do a show that night. I had wrongly assumed someone would be holding a sign with my name on it and figured they might be running late, so I waited. Then I waited a while longer. After about eight hours, I called Houston (yes, we have a problem) and was told someone would be there ASAP. After 18 hours of no one showing up, I got back on a plane and flew home. I had received a 50% deposit before I left, and that would be my pay for sitting at the airport eating shitty food without sleep. I never got an apology or an explanation.

Most of the time, it was fun working the road, but I saw many who flamed out quickly with the help of cocaine and alcohol abuse. Even though I abstained from using drugs, I knew they were always present in my band days, but nothing like what I saw when I started stand-up. Cocaine was everywhere, and some comics would ask for an advance and ended up spending their entire pay before they were halfway through the week. There were a few club owners who would often take the comics out to party and do coke with them and then, at the end of the week, deduct the drug cost from their salary. Most of the time, you could predict how long a club would stay in business by how much coke the owner was doing, but money was good, the clubs were busy, and business was solid.

I settled into working regularly and being paid weekly, which was unfamiliar territory. So was traveling alone. I loved the camaraderie of playing in bands, but I wasn't used to consistently making money when working with bands. I adjusted quickly to checking into a clean hotel paid for by someone else. Most comedy clubs then were open on Tuesdays to Sundays, and you'd usually travel on Mondays to the next club and stay in "comedy condos," similar to the "band houses" I had stayed in while climbing the ropes of disrespect. I knew the layout of the real estate a little too well because I couldn't forget where I had first learned about scabies, crabs, and waitresses who "partied with the band last week." A club in Akron, Ohio, housed the comedians in a basement under the club. When I worked there, I instantly understood how circus rats feel when they're let out of the cage, only to be put back in after they performed their dinner show.

Staying in comedy condos required common sense and a hipness to the unwritten rules like "don't eat the open jar of mayonnaise." There were tales of comics who allegedly had a reputation for masturbating into the mayonnaise, and most seasoned road comics were familiar with the stories even if they didn't know the veracity of that story. Experience taught me years ago that it was always a good policy to check under the bed for used condoms or pubic hair on the sheets. I'm surprised there was never an outbreak of dysentery given how dirty and disgusting many condos were. Usually, your shoes would stick to the carpet like flies on fly paper. I don't know if it was glue, but I remember it sometimes smelled like mayonnaise.

I learned some comics would travel with shower curtains, bed linens, towels, and disinfectants. Many "event comedians" (comics with TV shows or credits that gave them drawing power) would always demand a hotel because they'd done their time in comedy hell. For the rest of us working the road, you're always spending money, so it was always about bringing home as much of your pay as possible. Clubs offering free food were a plus, and since I didn't drink alcohol or use drugs, living was easy. Comics would travel between gigs and look for inexpensive lodging, although I preferred to camp in a tent whenever possible, like after a three-nighter in Lincoln, Nebraska. My provisions were in a gym bag lined with a plastic bag, which I had taken into an all-you-can-eat pizza buffet and methodically filled up with slices.

Speaking of food, I first worked with Carrot Top at a hotel gig in Lafayette, Louisiana. I have to give him "props." Years before he became a millionaire with a house gig in Vegas, his act was killing in all the bars, hotels, and colleges that we were all working to make a living and polish our acts. After we finished a show in Lafayette, Louisiana, a guy approached us; he looked both of us in the eye and said, "I lost my wife six months ago in a car wreck and never thought I'd ever laugh again . . . thank you both so much." I remember getting a little teary-eyed and thinking that in a short time, I would forget where I spent the money I earned that night, but I'll never forget how I felt when that man spoke his heart to us. Money comes and goes, but that experience is why comics do what they do. Well, that and the free pizza, but still, it touched me deeply.

Comedians were a close-knit group, and word spread quickly about broken-down condos and club owners who tended to be shady. I also enjoyed having my own room on the road; I didn't miss corralling five to 10 other people to reach our next destination, and looked forward to driving across the country alone with my thoughts. I wrote some of my best songs and comedy ideas while frequently putting over 50,000 miles a year on my Honda Accord.

Occasionally, several performers would ride together to keep expenses down, and time would pass more quickly. One memorable exception was the comic I barely knew who was on the same bill in Marshall, Texas, and caught a ride with me from Atlanta. About 20 minutes into the trip, I realized I had hooked up with the man who never met a word he didn't use. I knew he was wordy on stage, but now he was relentless without commas and periods. So, I told him I hadn't been on stage for a couple of weeks and needed to refresh my memory, and I had to listen to a tape of my act on my cassette player (remember, this was the early 1990s) and put the headphones on and never hit play. I drove almost the entire distance to Texas without hearing one more damn thing about his girlfriend and her parents.

Comics sometimes could be irritating. After a show started in Memphis, I was sitting in the lobby talking with the club owner when the door guy came out and said, "There's an obnoxious guy in the club talkin' loud and pissing off everybody." The club owner said, "Kick him out," and the door guy replied, "I can't; he's on stage."

Randy Howard was a laid-back guy who I became friends with the first time I worked with him on a college gig in Tennessee. He liked to keep a bottle of whiskey behind his amp, a practice most bookers and club owners generally frown on. I was unaware he had a reputation until I got a call from the booker the next day, dancing around the question before finally asking if Randy was drinking. Hey, I was barely getting paid enough to perform a comedy show, and damned if I was going to double as a rat, along with the fact that it wasn't my style. The same agency had previously asked me to rat out other comics, so I quickly understood they were likely calling comics I worked with to rat me out. I wasn't aware of any possible infractions, but I did once lose a booking because the club owner confused me with another long-haired comic who used the n-word in a comedy bit on stage. Most comics were hip, but some punks were always willing to do whatever they thought would help them curry favor with club owners or bookers.

Randy had written songs for other artists, and I enjoyed our conversations about songwriting and sharing road stories. He invited me several times to visit him at his cabin in Lynchburg, Tennessee, to do some songwriting, and I always meant to but seemed to be working nonstop in those days. I knew Randy wasn't working the comedy clubs as much and spent most of his time at home focusing on music, but I was unaware of his struggles with the bottle and the law. The last time I saw him, he was performing at the wedding of Jack Tarver, former owner of the Great Southeast Music Hall. I enjoyed catching up with

Randy, and we once again discussed finding time to get together and do some songwriting. I learned not long afterward that he had missed a court date for DUI and drug charges, so the bail bond agents hired a bounty hunter to pick up Randy at his house. On June 9, 2015, the bounty hunter kicked in the door to Randy's cabin and caught him off guard; Randy assumed it was a home invasion and reached for his pistol and got off a shot, injuring the bounty hunter, who returned fire and mortally wounded Randy. Under Tennessee law, bounty hunters had the legal authority to break in, and even though Randy was in the act of defending himself, the intruder was never charged with his murder. Bounty hunters seem to be afforded more latitude than cops in Tennessee when forcefully entering someone's home.

In comedy, marketing often trumps talent, even if not in the long run. A comedian who has tons of exposure with a guarantee of asses in seats will be working for the clubs that some comedic geniuses can't even get on the phone. I began to create my work by cold-calling bars and nightclubs and introducing the possibility of the club promoting a comedy show. It was certainly more lucrative making my deals and taking control of the promotion with my own posters and special tickets. Usually, it was a pleasant experience, although I once booked myself into a club in LaFontaine, Indiana, which proved otherwise.

My contract said cash, and when I finished the show with a packed club, I was told I would have to take a check because "the tickets were paid for by credit cards, and there wasn't enough cash." I had no recourse, and when I returned home and deposited the check, it bounced because of insufficient funds. After calling and being stalled several times, I finally got the club owner on the phone, who promised to take care of it, and then the circus began.

After a week of no return calls, I left word that this would not end well and set about a plan to post on social media about what happened. Then I listed the phone number of the club and asked everyone to call, be courteous, and ask, "Why are you not paying Darryl Rhoades?" By most accounts, there were over 1,000 calls in two days, which tied up the phone and made taking credit cards virtually impossible. I received phone threats from guys I didn't know, and after stating I wouldn't back down or off, a friend picked up a certified check for me. I tell this story only because you come to a point where you've had enough, and that's always been a thing with me. After a while, you tire of bullies and people trying to take advantage of you with threats, which won't work when you draw a line.

I had done a lot of interviews to promote bands while touring, and in comedy, it was a weekly thing. Radio interviews were something I looked forward to or dreaded, depending on the interviewer. Interviews are commercials to draw a potential audience in, so I would outline my topics and figure out a way to make the conversation flow so it doesn't sound forced. I always familiarized myself with the show by listening on the way to the station, and referencing an earlier topic or person would ingratiate me to the interviewers. The best advice about radio interviews that I ever heard but didn't need came from Jerry Seinfeld, who recommended that once you start talking, don't give up the reins. This was because you had to get your best-prepared material out before some DJs would step on it in their effort to show off their comedic genius. When I quit worrying about radio interviews, I started enjoying them a lot more, and never made the mistake of thinking anyone would remember my name 15 minutes after it was over. This point was made when an over-complimenting interviewer, who had been treating me like an old friend, ended an interview with "I would like to thank Daman Rose for coming in today."

My favorite on-air personality was the Rochester, New York radio legend Brother Wease (Alan Levin). His studio was huge, and he would often have various entertainers and authors hawking their new books. I was on a show once with Neil Innes (Bonzo Dog Band, The Rutles), Southside Johnny (Asbury Jukes), and a young band from Japan who couldn't speak English. It sounds like a ridiculous lineup, but Wease always pulled it off. Brother Wease was so popular that being on the air with him could make a massive difference in the crowd size that night. My most memorable interview with him was one morning on location at a popular restaurant. Wease did his show from a table while the guests had breakfast. Appearing with me was comic Eric Kirkland, who I was working with that week, plus blues singer Shemekia Copeland, daughter of famed blues guitarist Johnny Copeland. Shemekia was promoting her new CD, produced by renowned guitarist Steve Cropper. Eric and I, being friendly, attempted to speak with Shemekia during the commercials, and she couldn't have been colder. Got nothin', gave nothin', etc. When her segment was over, there was a commercial break. Then Wease introduced me by saying, "Our next guest is a poet, songwriter, comedian, actor, drummer . . ." and it was about this time Shemekia yelled out, "Yeah, he done found a bunch a stuff to do that he can't make no money doin'!" I've told that story several times and often I'm asked if it made me mad, and my answer then and now is, "Hell no, it was funny! And even more to the point, all true."

The first time I worked the room in Rochester, I learned students from a school for deaf students attended a show every week. They would sit at a table by the stage and watch the signer close to me translate the jokes. It was too tempting; I couldn't act like this wasn't a thing. I went into my act and saw the signer doing her job and I began to speak gibberish. The audience erupted in laughter, not so much at my nonsense but the signer's response to it. She continued to sign but only used one finger for my benefit.

The more media-savvy comics flourished even when they might not have the comedy chops of more talented road warriors. Some worked all day in their rooms writing, putting together mailing lists, and establishing contacts with their sites set for higher goals. Being funny was critical, but it was always about putting asses in seats. The following post on social media by a former club owner and currently successful manager put it all in perspective for me:

"I want to apologize to all the comics in the country, on behalf of most Comedy Club owners. We know you have been working on your craft for more than ten years. Working shit rooms and making people laugh all over America. Sleeping in bad hotels and shitty condos. You've made sacrifices that most people will never understand. You wonder why you're not getting bookings. We really want to book funny people. But if we have to choose between you and someone with a million hits on YouTube. You lose! We are Comedy Club Owners. It's just our nature!"

I forged many friendships on the road with comics; some I ran across more often than others, but it was a fraternity. Occasionally, there'd be a message at the club condo from the comic who worked the club the week before, and they'd leave passes for movies or other activities. Sometimes they just left suggestions like "Stay away from the redheaded waitress; she's screwing the club owner." That advice was helpful for those who possessed restraint and not so much for those who didn't. As a club owner once told me, "If comics only understood the reasons many aren't rehired have little to do with their performance on stage." I got his point, but many didn't, and I don't have the time or inclination to list some of the stupid infractions many couldn't help themselves from committing.

While most of the comics were a good hang, I occasionally encountered the misunderstood tortured souls. I think that's how you describe some people, although it was just easier for me to refer to them as assholes. For me, comedy was a joyous experience when hanging out with creatively funny people and a pain in the ass when I worked with whiny bitchy people pissed off because they thought they should be in a better place in their career.

Open micers want to emcee, emcees want to feature, features want to headline, and headliners want their own TV shows. Working with as many comics as I did, there would always be the misfits with insecurities. There were the joke thieves, guys who constantly accused others of stealing the jokes they had stolen from someone else, and guys who would use your name without asking your permission to get into a club they weren't working. If they sucked, you had to be honest when the club owner called you for a reference, even if you liked the comic personally. I never set about bad-mouthing another act; it was a bad practice some didn't mind engaging in, but I never saw the benefit.

The same rule applies to club owners. Some would be a dick for no other reason than they could. One club owner with such a reputation was a guy I became friends with. In those days, comics would submit VCR tapes of their acts to secure a booking in a new club. The club owner told me about getting several calls from a guy before he decided to take his call. When the comic asked, "Did you get a chance to look at my tape yet?" the club owner replied, "No, there was something on TV I wanted to record, so I taped over your act," and he was serious. I laughed. It was funny, and while laughing, I understood one day I would likely be one of his stories. It would be arrogant to assume you're immune from the person's pettiness. When you're hangin' with someone who is bad-mouthing everyone else, you're just standing in line.

So many comics I worked with retained their smart-ass immaturity, which I found appealing. My most memorable gig with Charles Vericola was on New Year's Eve, in a club booked by one of the largest comedy booking agencies in the country. The club was located in the hotel where we were staying. We learned the agency's owner was coming in that night to catch the show while also meeting a woman other than the one he was currently married to. The wheels were set in motion. We had a plan.

I can't remember who came up with the idea of going to a porn store, buying tons of gay porn and several rubber dildos, but money exchanged hands. We convinced the hotel front desk clerk of our appreciation for the work and support we received from the agency and wanted to leave some gifts in the room reserved for the CEO of the comedy chain. After the clerk commented about how nice we were, she gave us the key, and we did what any 12-year-old boy would do if left to his own devices. We hid dildos under the pillows, in the showers, and between the couch cushions. There were pictures of masked men dressed in leather fit to be lubed, grooved, and tattooed in the magazines left on the nightstands by the bed for some leisurely nighttime reading. We threw in several tubes of K-Y lube and Preparation H for good measure. There was no particular reason for the Prep H, but it was a nice touch to round out the party plans, and it looked good in the gift basket.

Some of the most forgettable gigs resulted in some of the best stories. I never could have predicted meeting legendary comedian/civil rights activist Dick Gregory at a Ramada Inn gig in Winston-Salem on a Wednesday night.

I was working with comedy veteran Lance Montalto when I spotted Mr. Gregory in the audience before the show. I went over and introduced myself, and we spoke for a few minutes. As a child, I remember seeing him on TV doing stand-up and later as a civil rights activist. He also received notoriety for his Bahamian diet and attempts to help people, most notably Walter Hudson, get on track with their health issues. Hudson was a man Mr. Gregory described as 1,200 pounds and hadn't been outside his bedroom for 27 years. Hudson was down to 875 when he died of a heart attack a couple of years before I met Mr. Gregory.

I invited Mr. Gregory to do a guest set, and it never dawned on me that I would have to follow a legend; I was ecstatic he was at the show, and now I was going to watch him work. He told a joke I still remember today: "Columbus Day: when Columbus discovered America, which surprised the hell out of the Indians who had been living there for years. That's like me going to the parking lot and discovering your car."

I followed him and remembered doing a joke I'd written about J. Edgar Hoover, the FBI director who kept files on people like Dick Gregory. After the show, Mr. Gregory complimented that specific joke (one I can't remember) and invited me to breakfast.

I was eating an omelet and we were talking about his Bahamian diet when he told me he didn't eat anything that didn't fall out of a tree. My only response was that I only ate things that fell out of a chicken's butt. He brought up the Hoover joke again while addressing the file that the FBI kept on him. I've always been interested in that part of history; he had much to say about it. Volunteering his views on several conspiracy theories, Mr. Gregory proposed space stations were being built because man was destroying this planet. He observed that politicians like the Kennedys and Bushes weren't families as much as dynasties, and his following comment stayed with me all these years later: "They're building a better world, and you're not invited."

We talked about the early days of stand-up, where he offered his opinion on his favorite three humorists, whom he called geniuses—Mark Twain, Lenny Bruce, and Richard Pryor. His advice was to try to write comedy that would say something important to people and make the world better. Great advice that I rarely remember when I'm in a bar where people are playing pool in the back and only stop if they hear a great dick joke.

I'd heard all the accusations about joke thieves going back to the 1940s and 1950s, including prominent performers like Jackie Gleason and Milton Berle. I learned quickly that this practice still existed at every level. I've witnessed comics sitting in the back of the room with a pen and paper, writing down the comic's material being performed so they could rewrite it and perform it as their own later on the road. I'd heard the stories about a well-known author in Atlanta who would sit in the back of The Punchline and cop comics' lines for his newspaper column. When you make your living from delivering the material you wrote, it feels like someone broke into your house when someone steals that material. When you labor over the correct wording, reworking a piece after trying various approaches on stage, I understand being angry when someone wants to take the shortcut and credit after stealing someone else's work. I saw it no differently than stealing song lyrics or melodies.

So many stories about lifting jokes have been attributed to one guy that his name became a synonym for joke thievery. There were jokes written about his supposed joke thievery, including his obituary in an industry paper, which commented: "When Ollie Joe died, a little bit of other comics died with him."

Ollie Joe weighed over 400 pounds and had a knack for hearing someone else's joke and doing it better in his act, or at least that was the compliment given to him by some who had shared the stage with him. Allegedly, before DVR and VHS recorders' popularity, Ollie would sit in the green room before his second show and watch Johnny Carson do his monologue. When he hit the stage, he'd perform Carson's monologue word for word, slay the audience, and no one knew he had lifted from the Carson show. I've heard variations on an old joke that if Ollie bought you a drink, he stole one of your jokes; if Ollie bought you a meal, he stole one of your bits; and if he invited you to party with him all night, you just killed in Pittsburgh.

In my comedy career, I got as much from the road experience as possible. I visited places I would have never seen, made friends, and took the opportunity to visit interesting people while feeding another one of my passions. Some comedians want to be musicians; some musicians would rather be comedians. I would have traded it all in to bat a career .300 average, hit 500 home runs, or pitch 300 wins.

I've been fascinated by the history of baseball since being a Little Leaguer in Kentucky and growing up as a Milwaukee Braves fan. The only thing I knew, or cared to know, about New York City was that it claimed three teams: The Brooklyn Dodgers, New York Giants, and New York Yankees. I chose Mathews, Aaron, and Adcock over Snyder, Hodges, Mantle, and Berra. I knew every trade made in the off-season, the starting lineup of all eight National League teams, and saved baseball cards from my childhood in the 1950s. When our family moved, my mom convinced me to give all my cards to one of my cousins instead of lugging them to Georgia. We all have those stories, and I grew tired of hearing them when I used to buy and sell cards at sports memorabilia shows. I was working steadily and buying cards as if cementing my financial future. I bought 'em by the case, sold some at shows, and then took that money to purchase more. Sure, I wasn't doing drugs, but who can afford crack when you're trying to put together a mint condition set of 1957 Topps?

As a kid, I became fascinated with the history of the Negro Leagues because I couldn't process the reality that there was an entirely different league where Robinson, Mays, Banks, and Aaron played before becoming Dodgers, Giants, Cubs, and Braves. I became a student of greats like Leon Day, Cool Papa Bell, and Buck Leonard, and as an adult, I started contacting them.

While working comedy clubs on the East Coast, I performed a one-nighter in Rocky Mount, North Carolina, and found that Negro League Hall of Famer, Buck Leonard, lived there. His name, Walter Fenner Leonard, was in the phone book (yes, it's a book with people's phone numbers) and when he picked up the phone, I introduced myself, and we spoke briefly before I told him I hoped to meet him in person one day. He quickly invited me over, so I made plans to follow up the next day.

Mr. Leonard couldn't have been more gracious. We settled into his memorabilia room, where he had me put on a left-handed first baseman's mitt and told me it was given to him by Cincinnati Reds star Ted

Kluszewski. I picked up a bat, swung it, and was told it was presented to him by Ted Williams. We spent most of the day talking about those he played with in his 17 years with the Homestead Grays, including his roommate, Josh Gibson. He showed me a Homestead Gray uniform on his wall, which I assumed was original. When he mentioned he was selling it for $5,000, I commented about how tough it must be for him to let it go, and he laughed then said, "It's ok, next week I'll have another one."

Buck was one of Josh's pallbearers, and while he didn't mind rehashing a conversation he'd probably had a thousand times, his eyes sparkled when I brought up names like Judy Johnson, Martin Dihigo, Double Duty Radcliffe, or Turkey Stearnes. When asked how I knew about those guys, I gave him references with names of videos, books, and conversations with other Negro League players I had contacted. I left Buck with a book he was prominently mentioned in but unaware of, *The Legacy of Jackie Robinson.*

Every baseball card show on the road or in Atlanta was an opportunity to get rid of some of the money I had worked so hard to keep. Autographed baseballs and cards were my addiction, and constant working on the road gave me access to feed that addiction.

As hard as comedians work to be funny, sometimes people show us up without trying. At the same strip club on Peachtree Street where I met Gene "Truckstop" Tracy, I also met Vern Dean. Vern physically resembled George Carlin and billed himself with the slogan, "VD is funny." His jokes were corny, blue, and prehistoric. On his promo picture, his bent index finger looked like it was halfway up his nose. Years later, I was asked to be a guest host for a local TV entertainment show and given permission to pick the guests I wanted, so I invited Vern along with the B-52's, former Georgia governor, Lester Maddox, and an African American comedian friend named Steve Smith (who pretended to be an Elvis impersonator). I also brought in Alan Thornton, who re-created his "Deaf Mute Toyota" commercial he had performed and won first prize in a *Gong Show* parody I hosted between two Hahavishnu shows at the Great Southeast Music Hall.

I was courteous to Lester Maddox since he was polite enough to respond to my invitation. During this interview, Lester unknowingly gave me a few of my favorite quotes I used on stage when performing my Preacher character. "The only trip I ever took was the trip to the altar, and the only pill I ever took was the gospill," Lester told me. I tell ya, the man was a poet.

Lester amused me with stories about walking out on Dick Cavett as well as Joe Pyne. Pyne was the guy who set the stage for over-the-top TV talk show hosts much the same way Rush Limbaugh spawned aggressive, loud right-wingers on talk radio. Pyne was a veteran WWII Marine with a wooden leg due to cancer in 1955. His specialty was treating guests obnoxiously and sometimes inspiring heated audience reactions. My favorite alleged story was when Frank Zappa appeared on the show. Pyne reportedly said, "I guess your long hair makes you a woman," to which Zappa responded, "So I guess your wooden leg makes you a table." I have been unable to confirm this 100 percent, but in my heart, I want it to be true just because it's so damn funny.

I had a friend chastise me for not going after Maddox, but I figured it would be wrong to invite someone into your home and then attack them. He was the last guest on that day, and after the show, he said, "I've been invited to do a lot of shows and turned them all down. I don't know why I accepted your invitation, but I'm glad I did," and then he shook my hand.

A couple of weeks later, I received some autographed recordings from him. I was not a fan of Maddox and never agreed with his racist politics; I can only say that he was a gentleman on this day, and I chose to be courteous and listen to him rather than play gotcha.

A couple of years before, Lester had appeared on the *Dick Cavett Show* along with football legend Jim Brown. After a few minutes of conversation, Brown said to Maddox, "You don't know who I am, do you?" Maddox replied, "Yeah, you're some soul singer."

OK, I don't care who you are. That was funny.

Occasionally, I would volunteer to perform for benefits to help a cause and catch up with other comedians. After Tropical Storm Alberto in 1994, a benefit was held for flood victims in Macon at the Uptown Comedy Club in Atlanta. The room was packed, and about a dozen comedians were waiting to perform, so we were asked to keep our sets to 10 to 15 minutes. Some are better than others about watching their time, and my friend, Ben Beall, was completely unaware that the light from the sound booth signaled his time was up around 12 minutes into his act. Ben kept going for another eight until the soundman walked up the back of the stage and placed a headlight from a 1954 Ford at Ben's feet. When Ben turned around, the soundman threw down a set of keys and said, "Lock up when you're done." Comics were falling out of their chairs.

Doing comedy, I never felt locked in and always understood a great response on Tuesday's show didn't guarantee the same the next night. I've bombed and watched comedians perform in front and after me bomb as well. Bad shows became a rarity, but they were always a possibility, and I quit questioning why, even when it would get to me later.

On several occasions, I worked at Bears in Bloomington, Indiana, advertised as one of the oldest one-nighter comedy venues in the country. Every time I performed there, I made it a point to read the local review framed and mounted on the wall years before. The yellow piece of paper told the story of a comedian who bombed, as we all have at one point. Still, instead of going into the green room and sulking until the room cleared, she stood at the exit door and thanked everyone for coming. I've never met Rosanne Barr, but I saw her on *The Tonight Show* and understood why college kids in a bar might not get her. But the point of that clipping about her is that we do our best to read the room and adjust, but there will always be nights when you don't make the connection.

You're out of luck when you fall out of favor, which could happen anytime for any reason. Getting fired didn't require logic or justification. You could be mistaken for another comic who crossed a line and then not get hired, perform material some found offensive, or be the wrong guy for the wrong room. I've experienced all of it, but not to excess. I knew guys who were fired for being drunk, late, no-shows, abusive to the crowd, or sometimes not even aware of their infractions.

At a hotel in Orlando, I was fired for performing material I'd done many times by a Bible-thumping general manager wearing a 50s Amy Winehouse beehive hairdo. Several days later, she was fired for being drunk and having sex in the hotel bathroom with the emcee of the show. I'm sure, once again, "Jesus wept."

As more clubs closed and work started drying up, many comics chose to work the cruise ships, which were lucrative and kept entertainers busy working from ship to ship. I have been tempted several times but always questioned if I would be a good fit. You could easily say something deemed offensive by anyone who would complain at any time, and it would be grounds for firing. Worrying about offending people never seemed that interesting.

After 2016, I witnessed firsthand how audiences became more outspoken and would yell during a comedian's joke about a politician the audience member likely supported. I get it. Freedom of speech until you disagree and then yell stupid shit from the audience instead of letting the comedian stand or fall on the strength of their writing. Then there are some comics that try to be edgy and political and make a statement. When they don't have the comedy chops, the statement they often make is that they're an asshole.

I still perform comedy over 30 years after taking the stage for the first time in a contest. Most of the "full-time" clubs have vanished, and the landscape has changed greatly; I'm not touring 48 weeks a year or traveling all over the country as I did, but I still enjoy performing with the same passion. I'm happiest when I'm busy while balancing my performances between stand-up and music.

I miss the camaraderie and quiet time while traveling, but it's always a trade-off. I now spend more time recording and writing music. To be sure, I don't miss driving in the winter weather in places like Edmonton, Canada, or Minot, North Dakota, where the windchill often bottomed out around -90°F. I've gone through my share of whiteouts, hurricanes, and being stranded on the side of the road waiting for AAA.

I never want to live my life with decisions full of regret. I've enjoyed every aspect of the process I could control, and with comedy just as with music, rolling the dice was just a part of the deal. When I hear comics who have transitioned into becoming movie stars praising the fact they no longer have to perform stand-up, I get it, but performing live has always been energizing for me, and I've heard comics say they'd do it for free. I'm not that guy, but I will likely be doing some form of live performance until it's physically impossible. I looked forward to taking the stage every time.

When I first started, I would hear stories about road comics who had been doing stand-up for a while. Hands down, without a doubt, the most notorious comedian with the craziest stories was Frankie Bastille. We worked together several times, traveled together, and became friends. They say everyone has a book in them, and if that's true, Frankie Bastille was probably a library. He was a gifted comedian, poet, and addict.

Over 25 years after his death, you can bring up his name to any old-time road comic, and they'll have Frankie Bastille stories. Some may have been embellished, but they needn't be; the truth was often funnier and more bizarre than most could fabricate. There are online clips of Frankie and stories about him by Marc Maron and other podcasters.

My favorite story was when he was working with my friend, Steve Arik, at a club in Cincinnati that put the comics up at a Ramada Inn that was also hosting a dog show. The dogs were barking and waking him up at 7 a.m. when he'd only gotten to bed an hour or two before, and Frankie complained, but the hotel was sold out and they couldn't move him to another room. He'd had enough, so he invested in a dog whistle, and after returning from his gig around 2 a.m., he walked the halls of the hotel blowing the dog whistle no human could hear. The dogs went crazy and woke their owners and everyone else in the hotel. Frankie then called the front desk and complained. Since the comedy club already comped his room and couldn't be moved, the hotel offered to comp any in-room movie charges and meals for him. Frankie being Frankie pushed to get the same comps for the other comics on the bill, who received complimentary porn and room service that week as a result of Frankie's brilliance.

I've always been drawn to characters, especially when they spark creativity. That was Frankie. I included a picture of him in a dedication on my 1997 CD, *Radio Daze . . . The Shroud of Tourin'*. Frankie passed on Jan. 18, 1997, after losing his father four days before. I still remember a poem, printed in the program at his funeral, that Frankie recited on stage at a gig we did together in Jacksonville. I related to the words which summed up his life.

THE EDGE ©1983 FRANKIE BASTILLE

CHAPTER SIXTEEN

Several Freaks and a Sideshow Geek

Well the years have come and the years have passed
And I pray everyday it'll be my last
Cause everyday seems just like a week
We got three kids in our family but now they're all workin' for me
Cause I own a circus and they're all sideshow geeks . . . and I mean freaks

UGLY ©2000 DARRYL RHOADES

Bennie Wade, a.k.a. Sideshow Bennie, had skills envied by most mortal men. He employed some of the standards, like lying on a bed of nails and letting audience members throw darts in his back, and the man had some seriously wicked chops when it came to horrifying the audience. Most of the crowd seemed stunned while attempting to process Sideshow Bennie's performance. His "Human Blockhead," where he would drive nails into his nose and nail his tongue to a 2x4, was a real sphincter tightener. Putting his hands in animal traps, fire-eating, and lifting weights with his nipple and earrings was not for the fainthearted. The man was nothing if not a role model for today's youth. My balls hurt just watching him.

Sideshow Bennie and I were part of a depraved comedy show birthed in 1999 when I reconnected with Rev. Billy Wirtz who, like myself, had been working steadily as a solo artist. We started talking about working together and offering a unique show that could be a draw in larger comedy venues and small theatres. Billy brought in Sideshow Bennie and a mutual friend, stand-up comic Mo Alexander.

I had worked with Mo before and was familiar with his comedy and depravity. His physical presence as a huge Black man who could connect with an audience made him the perfect choice to emcee and set up the show, which basically meant warning the audience about what they were about to experience. We had them going crazy after they'd witnessed some of the most bizarre moments on stage they'd likely ever see.

To prepare this level of degeneracy, we set about rehearsing in my home right outside of Atlanta, where I generally kept a low profile. Mo reminded me of one incident involving a guy who lived a couple of doors down and howled at the moon when he was drunk, which means when I was home, I often heard some serious howling going on. "I don't know if you remember me being at your place with Bennie and Billy about to leave, and one of your old ass racist neighbors was talking to you, then saw me get out of a car and said, 'Holy shit, you got a nigger over here. Let me go get my gun.' You and Billy shooed him away and told me to go inside." For the most part, I was almost always working out of town, so I only knew a few of my neighbors, but of course the one I did know was a racist asshole. I could have been the poster boy for a new revolutionary product, the "Ronco's Asshole Magnet."

We struggled to find a name that fit our group, considering several suggestions like Hoosier Daddy and Freaks to Men before settling on Midnight in the Garden of Evel Knievel, a play on the movie *Midnight in the Garden of Good and Evil*. Nothing could or did compare to this traveling comedy roadshow. Every time we took the stage, it was another opportunity to step over the line, and we never failed.

Mo usually had the audience as soon as he hit the stage, working for about 25 minutes, followed by Bennie performing the Lord's work for 30 to 40 minutes. Watching those two guys in front of Billy and me was inspirational. Wirtz was/is a masterful pianist with a sharp sense of humor, vast knowledge of the blues, and great songwriting chops. He'd worked in comedy clubs but was a favorite in blues bars and clubs where people could keep up with his quick-paced stage banter.

The show was nonstop and kept the audience on its toes. I brought to the project some of the techniques I used from my years with the Hahavishnu and from working in comedy clubs.

I used percussion buttons connected to a sampler, so when I hit my pockets, the drums sounded like John Bonham playing in a large concert hall.

We would alternate our original songs as I would do "interpretive dancing" during Billy's song "Inbred," and he would play lounge piano as I went into the crowd and performed my parody, "Think of Me When You're Under Him." The act was the perfect vehicle to showcase the skills of what we all had been doing separately for years.

As with the Mighty Mighty Men from Glad, I employed videos to set up a song. With video monitors set up on both sides of the stage, we would start our portion of the show by running a video of the infamous Robert Tilton Fart Tapes. If you are unfamiliar with this reference, the full impact can only be experienced by viewing the legendary video.

Tilton is one of those over-the-top televangelists with a decent head of hair, excellent dental work, and a face I'd love to punch. Like most in his line of work, he's always working on increasing his bank account in the name of God. Someone edited clips of Tilton doing his act and making faces and then inserting fart noises at the appropriate time, and every time seemed appropriate. I'm sure it may sound sophomoric to some, but I dare anyone reading this to watch it and not burst out laughing. I've heard various stories about the origin of this tape, but I'm just thankful it was released.

I had never seen a show like Bennie's before and loved his dedication to the art. He introduced us to one of his mentors, Melvin Burkhart, who came to see us perform in Tampa. Mr. Burkhart, in his early 90s, was the last survivor of America's great sideshow era, having spent his life performing in circuses and freak shows of every size and reputation.

We performed as a quartet for around eight dates before Billy and I started working as The Wirtz & Rhoades Show, which I guess could be viewed as a little more mainstream for comedy clubs. Local emcees opened before our part of the show, and we killed in every club, although there would be people in the community who still didn't get it.

Little Rock comes to mind, and the lame-ass radio DJ who would ask a question and then try to answer it before we could. Talking was something both Billy and I excelled at, and our radio interviews were unlike most acts. We would always attempt to crack each other up with one-upmanship. But this interviewer sucked all the funny out of every joke, so all we could do is keep talking and wonder why we were even there. Here's why so many wacky wake-up in the Morning Zoo crew radio teams use laugh tracks: they have to tell you exactly where the supposedly funny punchlines are. Otherwise, you'd never recognize them!

Most of our venues were listening rooms through Billy's connections. Our most bizarre gig resulted from Billy's strong following from his airplay on the off-the-wall *The Love Doctors* radio talk show in the West Palm Beach, Florida, area.

Radio station WZZR promoted "Freakfest" as a special two-show evening set in a beautiful old theatre in the small town of Stuart. The Lyric Theatre was packed out with an audience that had gotten in their week's allotment of alcohol a couple of hours before the show; from the beginning, we knew it was going to be a clusterfuck. When the first show went surprisingly well, we foolishly believed the second show would keep the clusterfuckery at bay.

In between shows was the perfect spot to give the crowd more time to drink while the radio guys brought people on stage. The intermission is where we gained more clarity about why the show was billed as "Freakfest." The DJs filled the stage with drunk, shirtless men in thongs wearing dog collars and being walked around by leather-wearing dominatrices and told to eat dog food out of a bowl on the floor.

The party didn't stop there. The drunks cheered them on, followed by a few transgender go-go dancers and various other freaks (it was called Freakfest, after all), making me feel as if I wasn't dressed for the occasion. Still, we readied ourselves for the second show to complete our contractual obligation. Mo took the stage, and within a few minutes, a couple of knuckledraggers started yelling racist slurs. Alcohol didn't make those idiots stupid; it just helped them advertise it. "I was hyped as hell after such a fun first show. I was ready," Mo told me later. "The intro music played, we clapped it up, and I ran on stage to the mic. Before I even started my first words, I heard the first 'nigger,' then heard it again and again, which became a chant. I stood there for a few seconds while it got louder and louder and walked off stage visibly shaken. I went somewhere to be private and somehow made out with the trans chick from the radio station. I still could hear the crowd chanting when someone found me and brought me back to the side of the stage. Billy walked out onstage, and the chanting turned to cheers. Billy stopped them and said something like, 'You motherfuckers just insulted my little brother, and fuck y'all,' and started kicking sections of the crowd out, then brought me back onstage and told me not to worry and do my thing. I did, but it was the most uncomfortable I've ever been onstage."

Next up was Sideshow Bennie, who was up for the challenge. He plowed through with his set to a decent response, which gave me hope that the Neanderthals were calming down. I remember talking fast, playing loudly, and looking for a clock on the wall. We had a good set, but our hearts weren't in it. In my head, I was back to singing "Yikes! Here Comes the Negroes" to some who not only missed the humor; they felt emboldened by words that were meant to be satire. "The whole ugly evening really soured me on the morning zoo crowd. That was a tough one," Billy said later. "However, the Double Door and what happened there damn near made up for it."

Located in Charlotte, The Double Door was part of my personal history. I had played it once with the Banana in the early 1970s and my first case of crabs resulted from spending the night at the club and sleeping on the floor with what's her name. "The Double Door was quite friendly to musicians," Billy agreed. "I don't know about you, but there was a time pre-AIDS when we got laid every single night on the road." I also worked The Double Door several times in the 1980s with the Mighty Mighty Men from Glad, sans crabs.

When Midnight in the Garden of Evel Knievel performed there, it was something most had never seen before, weren't braced for, and most likely caused nightmares some experienced later. I'll explain.

At the end of Bennie's crowd-pleasing act, he required someone to come up on the stage, throw darts at his back, and participate in various other audience activities. He would then move into his closer of lifting weights with his balls. With multiple piercings on his body, including some rings in his scrotum, he would attach chains to the rings and weights or bowling balls on the other end. After this was done, he would lift the weight of whatever was connected to the chain with his nuts. With a sheet drawn across the stage, you could only see the shadow unless the sheet came down, and then you saw a hairy guy exposing his scrotum to the audience with a weight tied to it.

The audience and club owner that night were treated to such a sight, as was whoever represented the liquor board. "We actually caused audiences to go from sobbing with helpless laughter to screaming in horror at the sight of a large hairy man swinging household irons connected by a chain attached to the ring in his scrotal region," Sideshow Bennie said later. "That bit was followed by a four-man version of 'Bread and Butter' for the finish. The crowd loved it; the Charlotte Liquor Board was not amused."

I later learned the club was fined more than $1,200, and the owner, Nick, the incredibly cool guy he was, never said a word to us about it, much less deduct it from our salary. He was one of the best club owners I've ever worked for. The Double Door closed in 2017 after 42 years of featuring all kinds of traveling acts, some of the most incredible blues acts in the country, and one cluster of misfits that cost the club an additional $1,200.

If we even had a lane, we sure as hell weren't good at staying in it. Billy summed it up perfectly: "The Midnight in the Garden act was terribly clever and pretty damn funny as well. Unfortunately, show biz tends to be uncomfortable with edgy acts that don't fit into an easy description. Too much music for comedy clubs and too much humor for the music rooms and too outrageous for either."

He and I eventually started performing as The Wirtz & Rhoades Show, and expanded our repertoire to include more music and a longer show. There was a lot of crowd interaction, and we often left the stage littered with props, keyboards, drums, guitars, and tripods with storyboards and lyrics for the audience to follow. Between the material and stage show, Wirtz & Rhoades was a can't-miss that sometimes did, like in Little Rock.

Our first appearance at The Looney Bin Comedy Club in Memphis drew big crowds and an incredible audience response and surpassed all our expectations. Several months later, the club brought us back for the big 1999 New Year's millennium celebration, infamous for more than Y2K. Most clubs took a beating that night, as did the one where we appeared.

We were always pushing, and I remain proud of that, even though some of the documentation was never fully realized. In Memphis, we hired a professional photographer and film crew to record a couple of shows there to beef up our promo and secure more work. I still have all the videos that were never edited. We performed several songs on our radio morning show appearances on WEGR Rock 103, and one of those, "My Duet with Natalie Wood," did make it on my CD, *Rhoades All Over the Map*. Midnight in the Garden of Evel Knievel really was well-named because we all had the daredevil showmanship and the attitude that Evel himself summed up this way: "All Elvis did was stand on a stage and play a guitar. He never fell off on that pavement at no 80 mph." Ours was a show I would have enjoyed watching if I hadn't been a part of it, and I never thought what we did was over anybody's head. I just figured they were too close to the ground.

You know after three packs of cigarettes and a ten dollar bill
I called that little girl mine
Now the warden tells me he says "Hey Darryl you gotta go"
But warden I can't leave her behind

In the background I can hear them David Allan Coe songs
While I stared into his bloodshot eyes
And the tattoo on his left arm read "Born To Lose"
But on the right one it just said "Momma Tried"
And you know, people can be so hard
Well, I guess it's true in my case
But I can't hold back these tears of sadness
When I stare into his pockmarked face
But people are so judgemental like many of you out there
You're pointing and goin' "that's sick, that's an unnatural act"
But I'll always have memories of holding you
With Kathy Lee Gifford's picture taped on your back

I'M GOIN' BACK TO THE WOMAN WHO USED TO BE MY MAN
©2000 DARRYL RHOADES

CHAPTER SEVENTEEN

The Glamorous Life of Hurry Up and Wait

It's a road that is littered with might ofs and should have beens
Where the players often roll the dice, but seldom ever win
And they all have their story, some are sad and some are mean
Like the concrete beneath the feet on the boulevard of broken dreams

THE BOULEVARD OF BROKEN DREAMS ©1994 DARRYL RHOADES

Acting was part of the end game for several comedians I knew, and some succeeded. I was never interested in portraying a wacky neighbor, becoming a game show host or reality star. But playing a drummer in a honky-tonk on an Oscar-nominated film was something that came up through an old friend and turned into a gig I'll never forget.

In August 2008, I was performing stand-up at the Hard Rock Cafe in Mobile, Aladamnbama, and felt like I was coming down with something. I struggled to talk, much less sing, while trying to get through the set. It was one of those nights that couldn't end fast enough. There was a bed in my room waiting for me; all I had to do was stagger through an hour without passing out.

I hadn't been in my room for more than a few minutes when my phone rang; it was my high school friend, Michael Simpson. Michael had moved to Los Angeles several years after getting established as a writer and director in the Atlanta film community. In 1989, he directed the movie *Fast Food*, featuring Jim Varney, and used a few seconds of my song, "Burgers from Heaven," in one of the movie scenes. Whenever I performed near locations of movie shoots that involved him, he would catch my act. Michael was a quick study and hard worker, and with his wife, Judy Cairo, made a formidable pair who understood the value of networking.

Now Michael was working on a movie called *Crazy Heart* with Jeff Bridges, and they needed a drummer backing up Jeff in some scenes. Michael called me after getting approval from director Scott Cooper, and asked if I was interested. After approximately three seconds of intense soul-searching, I responded with, "Hell yeah!"

I felt like death warmed over, but the longer we talked, the more I started feeling better. I had about a week to learn a few recorded tracks and would play in sync with the band behind Jeff Bridges. All I had to do was cancel a gig in Jackson, Tennessee, which guaranteed small crowds and shitty money, and then get myself out to Santa Fe.

When the limo picked me up at the airport, I was nervous but excited, especially when the driver told me he had picked up Robert Duvall the day before. Holy shit!!! Boo Radley may have farted in the very backseat I now occupied.

We were on track to start filming the next night with Jeff, so I expected a long rehearsal after meeting the band. The legendary producer, T Bone Burnett, was scheduled to work with us, but due to his work schedule in Los Angeles, his longtime friend, Stephen Bruton, was acting as the music director and making sure we all had our parts down.

I didn't know Stephen and only learned about his massive talent and musical history much later. I only knew that he was the guy I was listening to and the one I had to make happy. He seemed a bit standoffish, but I understood that I was new guy joining the other musicians who had previously met.

After rehearsing 45 minutes, Stephen called it a night. Admittedly, I was confused why the rehearsal was so short. While we were packing up, the bass player, Luis Guerra, pulled me aside and explained that before my arrival, Stephen had told the rest of the musicians he'd never met me and didn't know anything about me. I assumed he questioned if I had the chops and possibly gotten the gig because I knew someone. Luckily, I had come prepared and quickly allayed any of his fears. While I didn't feel a connection with Stephen, I found out later he was having some severe health issues.

I stayed with my friends, Michael and Judy, at the apartment they had rented for the duration of their film work in Santa Fe. Of course, I was a little nervous, but my old high school friend and his wife made me feel right at home. Even though I was still feeling under the weather, I settled in and was looking forward to working. I'd performed a few times in that area but never really took the time to check out the town. Santa Fe is beautiful and when I wasn't on the set, Michael showed me around, and took me to other shooting locations to watch Jeff and Maggie Gyllenhaal work.

I've since been on sets where there was tension, and the experience wasn't pleasant. As sure of ourselves as most performers seem, we all have our insecurities, and it's one of the reasons we became performers. Many of us need the adulation and a slap on the back to let us know our work is good enough. I guess a better way of saying it is we're just pussies in need of being reminded we don't suck. Fortunately the *Crazy Heart* film crew and everyone on the set were very accepting and easy to hang with.

The band consisted of pianist Rick Dial, accordionist Joel Guzman, bass player Luis Guerra, and a local pedal steel player named Rick McGrath. Rick McGrath was a local guy who I sensed was a decent player, but never heard play or rarely saw because he was always on the other side of the stage.

Rick Dial also had a speaking role as Maggie Gyllenhaal's uncle, Wesley Barnes. He may have been the most humble guy I've ever met. When I arrived on the set the first day of shooting, I was adjusting the drums when Robert Duvall walked in, went directly over to Rick, and hugged him. It was evident that they had worked together before, and I was looking forward to learning about one of my favorite actors.

Rick had played a significant role in the movie *Slingblade*, which I didn't remember until we sat down during a lunch break, and I asked him how he got involved in *Crazy Heart*. I learned he owned a furniture store in his hometown in Arkansas, but also was the local sports announcer for the Malvern Leopards high school football team when not being on the film sets with movie icons. Turns out that an old friend contacted him, which sounded familiar.

He told me he'd grown up with Billy Bob Thornton and got a call out of the blue one day from Billy Bob informing him about a movie he was shooting and wanted Rick to be in it. Rick responded with, "You're crazy as hell, Billy, I ain't no actor," and then continued with the story, "but he kept on, so I was in *Slingblade*, and then Bobby Duvall saw me and put me in his movie, *The Apostle*." Rick actually didn't act in any of the scenes; he became the person he portrayed. It was impossible to catch him acting.

Rick further amused me when I asked him what his plans were after he finished with *Crazy Heart*, and he replied, "I got to get back to Arkansas cause we've gotta Labor Day sale at the store on Monday." How's that for humility? His first movie role was in the blockbuster hit, *Slingblade*; he called Robert Duvall "Bobby," had some major speaking parts in scenes with Jeff Bridges, and now had to get back to Arkansas to sell couches and ottomans at the Labor Day sale in his furniture store in Little Rock!

In two days, we completed shooting the scenes that involved me, and both were around 12-hour work days. There's always a lot of stopping, starting, and shooting scenes that aren't used. I had heard all the stories about hours of edits on the cutting room floor. Occasionally, an actor's entire performance was edited out of a movie. I was surprised when one of the scenes I goofed my way through was left in.

In it, Jeff is being hit on by a barfly (hot girl in the bar), and the band is on stage in the background, and the director, Scott Cooper, instructed the band to act like we were taking a break. We were told not to speak, but to pantomime like you see extras do in background scenes. Being the smartass that I am, I figured I would try to crack up

the band without calling attention to myself. When Scott said "action,"
I put a root beer bottle to my mouth as if I were drinking beer and
under my breath just loud enough for Luis the bass player standing next
to me to hear, I uttered some of the most crude and disgusting things
I could think of. It was all Luis could do to keep from laughing. This
was noticed by the accordion player, Joel, who leaned in close enough
for me to follow up with a repetition of the comment with even more
disgusting words.

I didn't expect that scene to be in the movie and snickered when
I first saw it while sitting in the theatre audience. If you ever see this
scene, notice that I have a bottle up to my mouth, and it's shaking a little as I fight back the laughter. They shot the scene from an angle where
you can't see the rest of the band, so their response was not captured,
but I still know, and it's there for eternity.

On my second day of shooting, I showed up early and got behind
the drums, jamming with Luis the bass player and Joel on piano. Joel
was a great accordion player but was killing it on keys playing Latin
jazz. The film crew hadn't shown up yet, and closing my eyes playing, I
was digging the groove. About 15 minutes later, I opened my eyes and
the place was packed, and Robert Duvall was dancing.

When the rest of the crew showed up, we worked into the night to
wind up our part of the bar gig scenes. I gained a healthy respect for
the dedication required of actors and the enormous work and preparation they put into their performances. Shooting the most minor
scenes requires a talented crew. The cast and crew on *Crazy Heart* came
together and ran like a well-oiled machine. If there were complications,
I was unaware of them.

The next day, the musicians got invited to play at the cast party
hosted by Mr. Duvall, and as it turned out, I was the only band player
staying in town, so my wife flew in and we attended the party with
Michael and Judy. A party band was playing, and I couldn't resist when
Jeff called me up, and I got to play with him and Stephen. I realized
what a great musician Stephen Bruton was when we jammed, and even
more after I got back to Atlanta and researched him. Stephen had played

with Bonnie Raitt and Kris Kristofferson and was highly respected as an incredible guitarist and songwriter. Sadly, Stephen passed away from cancer in May 2009, before the movie was released, and Rick Dial died of a heart attack two years later.

Though my part was small, I took great pride in working with Jeff and was thrilled when he won the Academy Award for Best Actor in 2010. Sometimes, we're disappointed when we meet a star, but he turned out to be a real gentleman with class and treated everyone like he'd known them for years. The 2010 Oscar for best song went to Ryan Bingham and T Bone Burnett for "The Weary Kind (Theme from *Crazy Heart*)." I remember thinking it odd that T Bone gave the acceptance speech alone on stage. Later, I learned that Ryan was outside smoking a cigarette with a well-known actor and missed his chance to say a few words to a global TV audience.

Since I was playing the part of a drummer in a honky-tonk, it would be a stretch to refer to me as an actor. I never caught the bug, although when movie and TV production companies started moving into Atlanta, I did list myself with several casting companies. When I wasn't busy performing comedy shows or music projects, I would pick up some background film work to keep me busy.

I've had friends identify me in some background scenes and ask about that experience and how they could get into that kind of work. My answer to the first part of the question is that it was like any other job. Depending on the project and the people you dealt with, it could be a breeze or many hours waiting for directions while scenes were being set up. I've never fully resolved my relationship with boredom and working on movies has reminded me of this dislike. I never took any of my background movie work seriously, and as meaningful work goes, I thought it was a waste of my time and often felt irrelevant while being paid horribly. I likely will never do it again. It goes against one of my self-imposed rules, "never chase disrespect."

Many background actors that I've talked to agree there were better ways to spend their time. I was hired several times as a biker on TV series like *Ozark* and several movies, and paid extra for the use of my bike in some scenes. I believe my importance as an extra was captured in the words of a biker sitting with me on the set of *Dumplin'* when he said, "It's a hell of a thing to be working here all day while your bike is sitting out in the parking lot making more money than you."

CHAPTER EIGHTEEN

When Blue Was Just a Color

In the bottom of the ninth
With the bases loaded
We always hit the winning run
When blue was just a color
And the world was turning slower
While we played in the fire of the sun

WHEN BLUE WAS JUST A COLOR ©2017 DARRYL RHOADES

"When you're a writer, you write without ever knowing if what you do will make you a dime," Doc Pomus says in the opening scene of the 2012 documentary, *AKA Doc Pomus*. He had also said that to me on one of my earliest visits to his apartment. I hung onto every word and piece of advice Doc Pomus took the time to share, because he spoke to me as a writer, speaking to another writer. But I never viewed myself in that way. I never viewed writing as a career choice as much as a life choice.

Some live by design and credit their plan, luck, and faith for success. That's not me. I can't claim I would have had a more lucrative career if I had pursued songwriting more seriously early on. There was no end game or plan; it was always about following a passion, working hard, and having fun.

I've often written songs without understanding what they were about until they were finished. My response to loss, joy, depression, and heartbreak was writing. With words, I could create and control a world when the one I lived in made no sense. Songwriting to me was playing in the fire of the sun. I could look at the world through the eyes of my childhood when blue was a color rather than an emotion I had yet to feel.

Writing funny songs came easily; the payoff was immediate gratification through laughter. I've felt that way about stage performances, especially with stand-up comedy. Sure, it was and is a job, but by managing my own career, I can take or leave performing when it's not joyous.

Toward the end of the Hahavishnu Orchestra, I was already starting to write some non-comedic songs and experienced some success with songs being covered or used in films, but I intentionally didn't work the paths that were opening up, like when Doc Pomus suggested I move to NYC. He was responsible for my signing with the agencies that handled my business when my songs were covered. He set up appointments for interviews and helped me on many levels. We spoke regularly on the phone after the group disbanded, and he would offer advice about songs I was working on. Even though I made several trips there to meet and work briefly with Joel Dorn, I just couldn't see myself in New York. Atlanta was my home.

When I recorded my second LP, *Better Dead than Mellow*, it was my follow-up to *Burgers from Heaven*, which sold well. The only pressure on me to release records was my passion for doing it. I was never offered the deal by a major label that I couldn't refuse. I never signed a management deal, never trusted that my business would be better off in someone else's hands. Every recording project came together with a small budget, the help of friends, and the need to get it done.

I worked with Brendan O'Brien on *Better Dead* and my third release, *No Glove/No Love*. When I worked with him, he was just a talented friend I enjoyed hanging out with. We played some gigs and recorded together, and Brendan methodically kept his eyes on his prize too. He eventually moved to Los Angeles, began working with Rick Rubin, and became hugely successful producing Springsteen, Pearl Jam, Aerosmith, and many other prominent artists. In several phone conversations, Brendan encouraged me to move to LA and even offered to put me up. I chose to continue to work the comedy circuit because work was consistently providing a much-needed paycheck. I was happy performing stand-up at that time; it came easily. Even though I deeply respect both Doc and Brendan's friendship and suggestions about moving, I have no regrets about staying in the South.

I've worked with four different producers/engineers on my recordings, and every one of them brought something meaningful to the table. Patience was never my strong suit, and a good producer in the studio possesses an enormous amount of patience. I'm unsure how many albums I released before I started to settle down and quit wanting a sound or lick played before I explained what I wanted. We were playing in the fire of the sun, and these guys helped me focus for the best results, no matter where we recorded.

At LeFevre Studios, where I had recorded with the Celestial Voluptuous Banana, it was collaborative when we recorded the 45 of "Burgers from Heaven." At Stone Mountain Studios with Bruce Baxter, who I knew as a great guitarist with Thermos Greenwood and the Colored People, we recorded the *Burgers* LP. A small studio on Spring Street owned by Ricky Keller was where Brendan O'Brien and I mainly recorded the subsequent two LPs.

After the 1988 breakup of The Mighty Mighty Men from Glad, when I wanted to get back into the studio, I was still determining who to contact and how to make that happen. Since I was working the comedy circuit, I wasn't focused on writing songs for a band as much as bits for my comedy act. This was my fourth release, and a completely different experience, with advancing technology and working with someone I had no history with. Jim Boling had played on the road with Peabo Bryson and several R&B greats but now was settling into a recording routine with quite a few artists, including rockabilly legend Billy Lee Riley and doo-wop icon Len Barry. Jim was the most talented guy I'd worked with at that time, and I recorded seven albums with him.

Jim was a master in the studio when it came to editing. His work on the *Radio Daze. . . The Shroud of Tourin'* CD should be a template for studio interns. Along with working with many personalities and instruments, Jim shined on the trumpet but was proficient on multiple instruments. If a particular instrument was needed on a recording, Jim would often go to the pawn shop, buy it, learn the part, and lay it down himself rather than bring a new person into the session. On the 2005 CD release *Raparations*, we recorded a song titled "Arkansas the Musical," which included six movements and multiple time changes. Jim played French horn, flute, and trumpet, sang background vocals, and arranged the strings. The song was like a vignette, and Jim supplied the sound effects and orchestration.

I worked with Jim Boling from 1992 to 2008 and was amazed at some of the sounds we got in his basement studio, along with the sizable list of gifted musicians who worked on my recordings. At the same time I met Jim, I started working with my friend, Tommy Strain, an incredible guitarist with an uncanny ability to sit comfortably in any genre I threw at him. Like myself, he had played with copy bands coming up, and he could cop any lick or groove, but when he started playing on my recordings, he shined and elevated the quality of the composition.

Jim Boling was almost too intelligent. A two-hour recording session could go astray immediately when the shortest question could result in a 90-minute answer with diagrams, examples, and references. He knew things . . . lots of things. The last album Jim and I worked together was *Weapons of Mass Deception* in 2008. It remains one of my favorite releases. I was getting some excellent reviews and inspiration for the next big event. I saw this CD as a personal breakthrough, with my songs becoming more introspective and the rebellion that never stopped.

> *I got white line fever and I'm peggin' the meter*
> *with no fear of ever hittin' the wall*
> *Blue lights flashin' with Jesus on my dash*
> *and I'm one step ahead of the law*

ADDICTION TO FRICTION ©2008 DARRYL RHOADES

I'm generally not big on sentimentality, but 31 years after the last Hahavishnu Orchestra show, I was inspired to put together a massive "Hahavishnu Celebration Show." I attempted to recruit as many original band members as possible. I contacted my friend, Bill Tush, to emcee the evening, and he was more than a little hesitant about saying yes. I don't think he realized how beloved he was and how many people were longtime fans, but he was about to find out.

While some declined for various reasons, seven Hahavishnu family members plus a cast of characters and friends committed to the show, which meant being willing to put in the time to structure it. I've always been fanatical about details and long rehearsals; everyone knew the material when they hit the stage. We rehearsed for weeks to play that two-hour show. The band captured much of the same energy, with Gina coming to dance, Jerry Pece setting up special staging, and Farrell Roberts running the lights. (Farrell was the lighting guy for the Hahavishnu for years on the road and was now the house lighting director at the Variety Playhouse.)

We sold out the Variety on September 12, 2009, and performed nonstop for more than two hours along with several encores and standing ovations. It took a lot out of us, but it rivaled some of the best shows the original band did several decades earlier.

On that night I was reminded that we meant something to many people. Some flew in from Los Angeles, Canada, and New York to catch the show. I have some incredible memories from that night, but the one that grabbed my heart was when I was approached by a couple of young men who said their parents, no longer alive, were big fans and used to talk about me and the band. They had to come that night and were glad they did.

I was encouraged to keep it going, a pleasant thought that evaporated when I realized how difficult it was to maintain a large ensemble afloat in the 1970s. Now, 30 years later, nothing has changed other than fewer clubs, less money, and more challenges.

The show was recorded on a 24-track machine, and some videos from audience members exist online. I have videos from the concert, but they were never processed. The audio recording has yet to be mixed. Several skilled photographers took pictures that night. One of them was Mark Kocher, who shot the front and back cover photos of this book.

I went back to my own projects, but Jim Boling's health issues meant he didn't have the stamina to take on labor-intensive projects. As difficult as it was to consider finding someone new to work with, I started asking around. When I met with Martin Kearns to discuss recording a new CD, *Darryl Rhoades Presents Songs for Teenagers in Heat*, he got it in the first five minutes. He played a few recordings from projects he'd worked on, and I was impressed. He'd worked with some heavy hitters such as Gregg Allman, RuPaul, The Indigo Girls, and Shawn Mullins, along with jazz icons like Earl Klugh and Grant Green Jr. Martin played several instruments and had an incredible range of knowledge about studio work. To date, I've released two albums from working with him. The way songs are released has changed to the degree that the demand for physical products is almost obsolete, but that hasn't slowed down the output.

We recorded the *Teenagers in Heat* CD in 2014, which was the most fun I'd had in a while. Martin was quick and had it down. Working with him and Tommy Strain on every song was about as efficient as recording an album could be. A large cast of friends appeared on this CD, along with a few surprises, like Jimmy Cobb, a guy I knew from my days playing at The Catacombs. When I met Jimmy in the 1960s, he was the bass player for Radar and one of a few people I considered a genius. When he heard my song on the LP, "Torch Songs Burn a Hole in My Heart," he asked if I'd mind him putting a string arrangement on it that I could disregard if it didn't please me. The song already had an eerie quality, but his James Bond-like string arrangement was haunting and still puts shivers down my spine. I had envisioned a Julie London breathy vocal but could not find that person. Another longtime friend, Jimmy Royals, suggested his daughter, Jessica, would give it a shot, and when I heard her sing it, I couldn't hear it any other way.

Listening to playbacks of some of my songs, I've almost felt guilty for calling it "my song" after hearing it transformed into something I could never have imagined. I've often felt that while working with Martin Kearns, Tommy Strain, Martina Albino, and many musicians who play on my recordings.

Jimmy Cobb may have been one of the strongest human beings I ever knew. He struggled with health issues for years but still played Radar reunion shows and recorded his brilliant compositions. I'm so happy to have worked with him in the studio and alongside him at a live sold-out concert at the Red Clay Music Foundry in 2015. The Red Clay concert involved many characters and friends I'd known for years, and when the planned lineup changed a little before the date, Jimmy stepped up. I don't understand how he got through that show, but his masterful synthesizer skills rounded out the horn section with Jimmy Royals on trombone and Jeff Crompton on sax.

I have tons of pictures from that show, and a video somewhere in my archives. It was the last big band show I did before turning my energy to writing songs and performing songwriting appearances with Tommy Strain. During the COVID years of 2020–2021, when the pandemic claimed many lives weekly, I buckled down and wrote a song about every two to three days. When the threat was dialed down, I started recording, and in the last couple of years, I've recorded and released several albums worth of material on streaming platforms.

Most of this material is superior to earlier releases, even if it doesn't get the exposure it deserves since I'm not touring with a band.

I still live in Atlanta, but like most big cities, it's almost unrecognizable from the city I knew 40 years ago. I have a second home in Puerto Vallarta, Mexico, where I occasionally escape to write or get away from the constant noise in the U.S. I'll be performing until my last breath, not because I have to but because it's who I am. I still don't fear failure as much as unhappiness. I don't look back with regrets; it serves no purpose. Success is subjective, and I still have the fire and desire to write daily. There is much to learn, and I've been fortunate to have friends who inspire me on many levels.

There will always be subjects and people begging to be mocked, and some will be insulted. I want to be here for all those people for as long as possible. If I've never offended you, please be patient. There are only so many hours a day, and I'll get to you as soon as possible.

Guns

Some call him the Messiah . . . He's God's only son
Many follow him because he's the chosen one
They say one day he'll return and bring peace when he comes
Until that time, I think that I'm
Gonna fill my house with guns

There'll be guns in all the churches
Guns in schools and bars
Guns on planes, guns on trains
Guns in every car
Let's put guns in cereal boxes
Guns in Cracker Jacks
Let's arm everybody on the streets
Until Jesus comes back

We need Guns Guns Guns Guns Guns Guns Guns
Guns Guns Guns Guns Guns Guns Guns

Some believe in scripture and what bumper stickers say
So put your faith in Jesus but send your money to the NRA
Makes you feel bigger . . . with your hand on the trigger
Shoot your gun in the air cause you just don't care
Yes . . . Guns Guns Guns Guns Guns Guns Guns
Guns Guns Guns Guns Guns Guns Guns

Get all decked out on Saturday night
Wearing your best wife beater
You'll be the penis envy of all your friends
When you strap on your brand new heater
The longer the barrel the bigger the man
You feel ten feet tall when it's in your hand

When you have Guns Guns Guns Guns Guns Guns Guns
Guns Guns Guns Guns Guns Guns Guns

Guns for Christmas, guns for Easter, guns for Valentine's
Guns for Vegas and Sandy Hook and guns for Columbine
Meet the gang at the Waffle House they're open round the clock
Order smothered, covered, locked and loaded while fingering your glock

Cause we got Guns Guns Guns Guns Guns Guns Guns
Guns Guns Guns Guns Guns Guns Guns

Guns for the family . . . Guns for mom and dad
Guns for all the kids and guns in political ads
Make guns the national anthem, Before class has begun
Make 'em pledge allegiance to the flag
To God, Country, and Guns

Gun tattoos on people
Guns on front yard signs
Guns on bumper stickers
We got guns on our mind

We got gun clubs and gun shows
How many we need God only knows
We got open carry and conceal
Makes you hot when you feel

Guns Guns Guns Guns Guns Guns Guns
Guns Guns Guns Guns Guns Guns Guns
Guns Guns Guns Guns Guns Guns Guns
Guns Guns Guns Guns Guns Guns Guns

©2023 DARRYL RHOADES

music-comedy.com
darrylrhoades.bandcamp.com

DISCOGRAPHY

1. BURGERS FROM HEAVEN/SURFIN' SHARK (45 rpm); 1976;
Wonder Records
Darryl Rhoades & The Hahavishunu Orchestra
Recorded June 14, 1976, Lefevre Sound Studio (Atlanta, Georgia)
Engineers: Stan Dacus, Don Johnson
Executive Producer: Jimmy Ginn

CREDITS:
Burgers from Heaven (Side A)
Guitar: David Michaels
Bass: Keith Christopher
Piano: Jimmy Walker
Saxophone: Jonny Hibbert
Drums, lead vocal: Darryl Rhoades
Background vocals: David Michaels, Jimmy Royals, Darryl Rhoades

Surfin' Shark (Side B)
Guitar: David Michaels
Bass: Keith Christopher
Piano: Jimmy Walker
Drums, lead vocal: Darryl Rhoades
Background vocals: Susan Kirkpatrick, Debbie Thompson, Jimmy
Royals

2. HEART THROB/AUSTIN IDOL FOR PRESIDENT (45 rpm); 1980;
Atteiram Records
The Idolators
Recorded at Stone Mountain Music (Atlanta, Georgia)
Produced by Sonny Limbo
Engineer: Bruce Baxter

CREDITS:
    Heart Throb (Side A)
    Austin Idol for President (Side B)
    Guitar: Edward Tanner, Bob Cunningham
    Bass: Jason Keene
    Keyboards: Blair Tanner
    Drums, lead vocal: Darryl Rhoades
    Background vocals: Edward Tanner, Bob Cunningham, Jason Keene, Blair Tanner, Darryl Rhoades

3. BURGERS FROM HEAVEN (LP); Release date: October 1, 1980; No Big Deal Records
    The Darryl Rhoades Orchestra
    Recorded in Atlanta, Georgia, at Stone Mountain Studio, Lefevre Studio, Songbird Studio
    Produced by Bruce Baxter, Darryl Rhoades
    Engineer: Bruce Baxter

TRACKS:

Side One
1. I Wanna Be Normal
2. I'll Be Watching You
3. Road Food (Recorded at home on a Teac 3340 and engineered by Steve May)
4. (She's) A Mortician's Dream Come True
5. He Found Jesus (But He Lost His Head)
6. Burgers from Heaven (1976)

Side Two
1. Fresh Meat
2. I'm In With the Zen Crowd
3. This Song Is Boring
4. From the Heart
5. 876-5561
6. I'll Do It My Way
7. No Shoes, No Shirt, No Service

CD release 1985 with bonus tracks "Surfin' Shark," "Leprosy Queen," "Heart Throb"

CREDITS (LP AND CD):
Guitar: David Michaels, George Coats, Jimmy Thackery, Edward Tanner, Michael Colford, Bob Cunningham
Bass: Harvey Brooks, Ronnie Chambley, Andy West, David Compton, Keith Christopher, Jason Keene
Drums: Darryl Rhoades, except Pete Ragusa, "This Song Is Boring"
Keyboards: Bob Estes, Michael Brown, T Lavitz, Bennie Boynton, Blair Tanner
Saxophone: Jonny Hibbert
Harmonica: Tim Bernard
Violin: Allen Sloan, Deborah Spring
Cello: Andy West
Clarinet: Peter Mercure
Vibes, marimba: Tim Embry
Lead vocal: Darryl Rhoades
Background vocals: Jimmy Royals , David Michaels, Nancy Doe, Trudy Fair, Rick Dovi, Darryl Rhoades, Susan Kirkpatrick, Debbie Thompson
Percussion: Bruce Baxter, Tim Bernard, Darryl Rhoades
Narration: Peter Mercure, "I Wanna Be Normal"; Dana Moore, "876-5561"
Tympani: Jack Bell

4. **BETTER DEAD THAN MELLOW** (LP); Release date: February 1, 1986, (CD) Release date: 1991; No Big Deal Records
Darryl Rhoades & The Mighty Mighty Men from Glad
Recorded at Southern Living At It's Finest (Atlanta, Georgia)
Produced by Brendan O'Brien, Darryl Rhoades
Engineer: Brendan O'Brien

TRACKS:
Side One
1. You Say I'm Schizophrenic (But I Don't Think We Are)
2. It's About Time
3. Livin' in the Real World
4. Trust Me
5. The Lights Are On (But Nobody's Home)

Side Two
1. The Song of a Happy Man
2. When She Was Mine

3. Shaft on Welfare
4. Rock 'n' Roll Wasn't Made for Queers
5. Bunky Finds a Home (Whitebread)
6. Born to Be Wild

Credits:
Guitar: Brendan O'Brien, Billy Urick, Jimmy O'Neil, George Coats, Rick Richards, Dan Baird
Bass: Bob Glick, Tommy Vickery, Bill Rea
Keyboards: Hank Ruffin, Jeff Crompton, Bennie Boynton
Drums: Darryl Rhoades, Joey Dukes
Percussion: Rod Morganstein
Saxophone: Jeff Crompton, Joey Duclos
Trombone: Jimmy Royals, Tom Snyder
Lead vocal: Darryl Rhoades
Background vocals: Jimmy Royals, Brendan O'Brien, Darryl Rhoades, Ricky Keller, Jeff Calder, Bill Burton
Narration: Peggy Goodnight, "Trust Me"; Rex Patton, "Born to Be Wild"

5. NO GLOVE NO LOVE (CD) Recorded 1987–1988; Release date: October 7, 1991; No Big Deal Records; Enhanced with a video from a 1977 performance of The Hahavishnu Orchestra
Darryl Rhoades & The Mighty Mighty Men from Glad
Recorded at Southern Living at It's Finest (Atlanta, Georgia)
Produced by Brendan O'Brien, Darryl Rhoades
Engineer: Brendan O'Brien

Tracks:
1. Rebel Without a Clue
2. Murder on the American Express
3. The Devil in My Pants
4. We're Not Lovers
5. Meet My Wife (She's My Sister)
6. Fingernails on a Chalkboard
7. I'll Be Back
8. I Like Ugly White Girls
9. Girls, Can't Live with 'Em
10. She's Such a Man
11. Jesus Is Screamin' on My TV
12. It's Just a Matter of Timin'

Guitar: Corky Hughes, Rick Kurtz
Bass: Bo Messina, Tommy Vickery
Keyboards: Rick Hubbard, Bill Brandenburg
Drums: Danny Bigay, Darryl Rhoades
Saxophone: C.C. Sax (Carl Crabtree), Stutz Wimmer, Jeff Crompton
Trombone: Jimmy Royals, Tom Snyder
Lead vocal: Darryl Rhoades
Background vocals: Bo Messina, Brendan O'Brien
Narration: Corky Hughes, "Jesus Is Screamin' on My TV"
Laugh at the end of the CD: Missy from the Double Door

6. COWPOKIN' & UDDER LOVE SONGS (CD); Release date: May 18, 1992; No Big Deal Records

Darryl Rhoades
Recorded at Jim Boling's studio (Smyrna, Georgia)
Produced by Jim Boling, Darryl Rhoades
Engineer: Jim Boling

TRACKS:

1. Suicide
2. Hole in My Heart
3. I Hate Every Bone in Your Body But Mine
4. Ty
5. Think of Me (When You're Under Him)
6. How Can I Take You Seriously? (Recorded in 1980 on a Teac 3340 4-track)
7. I'm Anal Retentive
8. I Let the Little Head Do the Thinkin' For the Big Head
9. Cowpokin'
10. Je Suis Fromage
11. Yikes Here Come the Negroes
12. Jet Speaks
13. Helium Head
14. Dig This!!!
15. My Blow Up Doll's Gone Down on Me
16. No Shoes, No Shirt, No Service (Live)
17. A Plea for Jimmy

CREDITS:

Guitar: Tommy Strain, Edward Tanner, Johnny Carlton, Mike Orlin, Van Temple, Spencer Kirkpatrick

Keyboards: Jimmy Royals, George Martin, Wayne Famous (McNatt)
Bass: Jim Boling, Keith Christopher, Tommy Vickery
Drums: Darryl Rhoades
Saxophone: Nick Longo, Jonny Hibbert
Pedal steel: Gates Nichols
Mallet instruments: Tim Embry, Jim Boling
Harmonica: Jamie Russell
Narration: Rex Patton, "Suicide"
Narration: Edward Tanner, Leonard Sharing, "Dig This!!!"
Voice of Jet Goutier (president of No Big Deal Reocrds): Jimmy
   Royals
Impressionist: Alex Kothe
Burp: Debbie Montalto
Lead vocal: Darryl Rhoades
Background vocals: Rick Dovi, Debbie Thompson, Jimmy Royals
Reprimand: Hilda Rhoades (Mom)
Live band recording: Hahavishnu 1977, Live at The Great Southeast
   Music Hall (Atlanta, Georgia)

7. THE LEAN YEARS (1950–1994)(CD); Release date: September 12, 1994;
No Big Deal Records
   Darryl Rhoades
   Recorded at Jim Boling's studio (Smyrna, Ga.)
   Produced by Jim Boling, Darryl Rhoades
   Engineer: Jim Boling

TRACKS:
   1. I'm Livin' in the House of Jack Lord
   2. I Fell in Love While Pumpin' Ethyl
   3. My Duet with Natalie
   4. I Go Insane
   5. U Suck #1 (beer commercial)
   6. NPR/Trailer Trash
   7. Clueless
   8. I Don't Mind
   9. U Suck #2 (beer commercial)
   10. Nuclear Kids on the Block
   11. U Suck Rap (beer commercial)
   12. Givin' Back to the People
   13. I'm Having Trouble
   14. Canvas of Pain

15. U Suck #3 (beer commercial)
16. She Spoke French
17. On Track
18. U Suck #4 (beer commercial)
19. She's Not You
20. The Boulevard of Broken Dreams
21. Jet Speaks Boldly
22. U Suck (reprise)

CREDITS

Guitar: Tommy Strain, Brendan O'Brien, Rick Hinkle, Johnny Carlton

Bass: Rex Patton, Tim Smith, Jim Boling, Gary Land (upright)

Keyboards: Don Mcbroom, George Martin, Wayne Famous (McNatt), Jim Boling

Drums: Darryl Rhoades

Pedal steel: Tommy Dodd

Fiddle: Dan Taylor

Saxophone: Wally Tirado

Lead vocal: Darryl Rhoades, except Tim Smith, "I Don't Mind"

Background vocals: Jimmy Royals, Jan Nusekabel, Ken Kensey, Ben Beall, Darryl Rhoades

Impressionist: Mike Wilson

Announcer: Suzanne Deaton, NPR voice, "Trailer Trash"; French speaker, "She Spoke French"

8. RADIO DAZE (THE SHROUD OF TOURIN') (CD); Release date:
April 15, 1997; No Big Deal Records

Darryl Rhoades

Recorded at Jim Boling's studio (Smyrna, Georgia)

Produced by Jim Boling, Darryl Rhoades

Engineer: Jim Boling

TRACKS:

WOOD 108.2

1. Wood ID/Chazz the Spazz
2. UFO
3. Barney Fife Station ID
4. Chazz the Spazz
5. Twilight Zone
6. Hooked on Gangsta

WGOD

7. The Deacon Jenkins Show
8. White Gospel Music
9. Back with Deacon Jenkins
10. Testimoney
11. Lush Winbag

WANG 108.2

12. Station ID
13. Rock & Roll Hell
14. Chet the Jet/Station ID
15. Buster's R&B Classics
16. U Suck Tragedy (beer commercial)
17. Chet the Jet
18. At the Beach

KOTX

19. Woman Talk/Traffic Copter
20. Dr. Carla Show
21. Inspirational Message

WUUT 108.2

22. The Jim Ed Bob & Billy Boy Large Show
23. Cajun U Suck Beer (beer commercial)
24. A Closer Walk with Me
25. Jim Ed Bob & Billy Boy
26. She Won't Shut Up

WUNO

27. DJ/Pingaloca Peguenita
28. Lush Winbag II

KRUD 108.2

29. The Tin Man & Jerry Show
30. Buster for Aardvark
31. Buster's Gospel Session Outtakes
32. Tinman & Jerry
33. My Baby Likes Fishin'
34. 1-900-Bonefon

108 FX

35. Station ID
36. Almost Again
37. Station ID

WBOR 108.2

38. Station ID/Vic Morrow Trio
39. Battle of the Blands
40. Lush Winbag III

WELV

41. Station ID
42. Selling Elvis

WBRO

43. Don Cornelius
44. Just Us
45. Mom

CREDITS:

Guitar: Tommy Strain, Johnny Carlton, Jeremy Graf, Rick Kurtz
Keyboards: Jimmy Royals, Jim Boling, Dean Daughtry, Don
  McBroom, George Martin
Bass: Tommy Vickery, Rex Patton
Saxophone: Michael Hoskin
Drums: Darryl Rhoades
Steel guitar, fiddle samples: Jim Boling
Pedal steel: Randy Sorrells
Trumpet: Jim Boling
Impressionists: Mike Wilson (Barney Fife, Casey Kasem); Tim
  Wilkins (Don Cornelius)
Character voices: Kay Boling, Jim Boling "Hooked on Gangsta"
Background vocals: Jan Nusekabel, Jimmy Royals, Ben Beall, David
  Louden, Gil Caro
Cajun voice: Lance Montalto
"1-900-Bonephon" line voice: Beth Royals
Voice of reprimand: Hilda Rhoades (Mom)
Actual DJs making appearances: Ken Carson, Steve Mitchell, Steve
  Animal, Bob Bailey, Elaina Fox, Kevin Phillips, Rapid Rich, Rico
  Hadden

9. **RHOADES ALL OVER THE MAP** (CD); Release date: May 10, 2000;
No Big Deal Records
  Darryl Rhoades
  Recorded at Jim Boling's studio (Smyrna, Georgia)
  Produced by Jim Boling, Darryl Rhoades
  Engineer: Jim Boling

CREDITS:

Guitars: Johnny Carlton, Tommy Strain, Richard Smith, Rob Smith
Bass: Rex Patton, Sam Smith, Tommy Vickery, Gary Land (upright)
Keyboards: Don McBroom, Jim Boling, Rev. Billy Wirtz
Saxophone: Jonny Hibbert, Wally Tirado
Trumpet: Jim Boling, Dave Ferguson
Flute: Jim Boling
Trombone: Jimmy Royals
Harmonica: Jimmy Royals
Pedal steel: Randy Sorrells
Drums and vocal: Darryl Rhoades
Memphis on air crew: Tim, Bev, Bad Dog
Narrator: Steve Mitchell
Background vocals: Dave Ferguson, Wally Tirado, Darryl Rhoades, Trint Cole
Duet vocals: Kim Williams, Darryl Rhoades, "That's What She Said"
Spanish translator: Suzanne Deaton, "Bonus Dias"

10. THE SHADOW YOU CAST DEPENDS ON WHERE YOU STAND
(Double CD); Release date: May 1, 2003; No Big Deal Records
Darryl Rhoades
Recorded at Jim Boling's studio (Smyrna, Georgia)

Produced by Jim Boling, Darryl Rhoades
Engineer: Jim Boling

TRACKS (CD ONE):

1. The Most Dangerous Man in the World (Has Got Nothin' to Lose)
2. The Wait of the World
3. A Big Cloud
4. I'll Never See the Sun
5. My Radio Sucks
6. Biography
7. Caffeine
8. Don't Let the Door Hit You
9. Fade Away
10. Love Nor Money
11. A Coat Without Pockets
12. A Deeper Blue
13. I'll Come Back to You

TRACKS (CD TWO):

1. The I of the Ego
2. The Failures of Success
3. A Street Where No One Lives
4. I Don't Believe
5. Can't Be That Good
6. Up in Heaven
7. My Clone
8. In '68
9. The Old Men of War
10. Savior Self
11. A Troubled Mind
12. When Forgiveness Ain't Enough

CREDITS:

Guitar: Corky Hughes, Tommy Strain, Johnny Carlton, George Coats, Edward Tanner
Bass: Tommy Vickery, Rex Patton, Gary Land (upright)
Harmonica: Jamie Russell, Jimmy Royals
Percussion: Jim Boling, Darryl Rhoades
Keyboards: Jim Boling, Dean Daughtry, Rev. Billy C. Wirtz
Drums: Darryl Rhoades
Strings: Jim Boling (The Smyrna Sinfonia), sitar, marimba, shamisen
Saxophone: Jonny Hibbert
Trumpet, trombone: Jim Boling

Fiddle, mandolin: Randy Smith
Dobro: Tommy Dodd, Tommy Strain
Pedal steel: Tommy Dodd
Bagpipes: R. J. Grady
Bandoneon: Mario Peralta
Voiceover: Steve Mitchell
Lead vocal: Darryl Rhoades, except Tommy Vickery, "A Deeper Blue"
Background vocals: Jimmy Royals, Jim Boling, Darryl Rhoades, Dean Daughtry, Jimmy Hammond, Claire Poole, Tommy Vickery, Kim Williams
Trio vocals "Caffeine": Darryl Rhoades, Claire Poole, Jimmy Royals
Duet Vocals "In '68": Claire Poole, Darryl Rhoades

11. RAPARATIONS (CD); Release date: June 25, 2005; No Big Deal Records

Darryl Rhoades
Recorded at Jim Boling's studio (Smyrna, Georgia)
Produced by Jim Boling, Darryl Rhoades
Engineer: Jim Boling

TRACKS:
1. The Rap Institute of America (uncensored)
2. The Man in My Windshield
3. Buster Love for Mystic Moods
4. Screech Doggy Dogg
5. Chokin' on Love
6. Showtime at The Apollo with Louis Farrakhan
7. Country Music Heaven
8. The Loggin' Song
9. Amerikan Woman (Part 2)
10. Live in Louisville at The Comedy Caravan (February 6, 2004)
11. Arkansas the Musical
12. The Puppy in My Pants
13. Be Kind to the Animals
14. Livin' Large
15. A Change of Life
16. If That's Love
17. A Do Right Woman (With a Can't Do It Right Man)
18. Cockblocker
19. The Rap Institute of America (censored)

Guitar: Tommy Strain, Johnny Carlton, Edward Tanner
Bass: Tommy Vickery, Gary Land
Keyboards: Jim Boling, Jeff Crompton, Dean Daughtry
Drums: Darryl Rhoades
Flugelhorn and oboe: Jim Boling
Saxophone: Jonny Hibbert
Pedal steel: Tommy Dodd
Announcer: Steve Mitchell
Lead vocal: Darryl Rhoades, except Claire Poole, "Amerikan Woman"
Background vocals: Claire Poole, Darryl Rhoades, Jim Boling, Jimmy Royals, Jessica Royals, Kay Boling, Jasper The Wonder Dog
Impressionist: Chris Dubail

12. **WEAPONS OF MASS DECEPTION** (CD); Release date: October 31, 2008; No Big Deal Records
Darryl Rhoades
Recorded at Jim Boling's studio (Smyrna, Georgia)
Produced by Jim Boling, Darryl Rhoades
Engineer: Jim Boling

TRACKS:
1. Addiction to Friction
2. I'm in a Bad Mood
3. The Sins of the Father
4. Let My People Go
5. The Edge of the World
6. Alcoholocaust
7. Birds on a Wire
8. Someone Must Have Hurt You
9. Betrayed
10. An Eye for an Eye (Leaves Everyone Blind)
11. The Music Brought 'Em Together (But the Business Tore 'Em Apart)
12. August 29, 2005
13. Lost in America
14. Living Without
15. A Grave Mistake

CREDITS:
Guitar: Tommy Strain, Johnny Carlton, Peter Stroud, Rick Richards
Bass: Tommy Vickery

Saxophone: Johnny Hibbert, Jeff Crompton
Clarinet: Jeff Crompton
Dobro: Peter Stroud
Keyboards: Jim Boling, Jeff Crompton
Fiddle, mandolin: Randy Smith
Banjo: Casey Dean
Drums: Darryl Rhoades
Horns: Jim Boling
Concertina: Jim Boling
Percussion: Sal Padillo, Jim Boling, Darryl Rhoades
Narration: Col. Bruce Hampton
Lead vocal: Darryl Rhoades, except Pete George, "Living Without"
Background vocals: Deborah Reece, Jimmy Royals, Jim Boling, Darryl Rhoades, Tim Smith, Rhonda Carter

13. DARRYL RHOADES PRESENTS SONGS FOR TEENAGERS IN HEAT
(CD); Release date: April 15, 2014; No Big Deal Records
Darryl Rhoades
Recorded at 800 East Studios (Atlanta, Georgia)
Produced by Martin Kearns, Darryl Rhoades except "Up to My Knuckles in Love" produced by Jim Boling, remixed by Martin Kearns
Engineer: Martin Kearns
Recorded and mixed at Songbird Studios: "It's Wiggy"

TRACKS:
1. American Music
2. She Likes Girls
3. Teenagers in Heat
4. Don't Take This the Wrong Way
5. Livin' Large (Live at The Variety Playhouse Theatre)
6. Asshole
7. The South Georgia Border Karaoke King
8. It's Wiggy
9. My Boyfriend's Black
10. Your Husband Is Gay
11. Up to My Knuckles in Love
12. The Lesbian Song (Thinkin' Outside the Box) Live in Louisville
13. The Band House (I'm an Entertainer)
14. I'm Having Trouble (Live at The Variety Playhouse Theatre)
15. It's Not My Cup of Tea

16. Bean Me (Live at The Rosie Palm Lounge)
17. Caulk
18. Torch Songs Burn a Hole in My Heart

CREDITS:
Guitar: Tommy Strain, Rick Hinkle, Edward Tanner, Bob
    Cunningham
Bass: Bob Glick, James Cobb, Tommy Dean (upright), Jason Keane,
    Rex Patton
Saxophone: Jeff Crompton, Jonny Hibbert
Trumpet: Ken Gregory
Drums: Darryl Rhoades; except Dino Donald, "I'm Having Trouble"
    (Live)
Keyboards: Martin Kearns, Blair Tanner, Jimmy Royals
Horn section: Jim Boling, "Up to My Knuckles in Love"
Strings: James Cobb, "Torch Songs Burn a Hole in My Heart"
Mandolin, dobro, pedal steel, banjo: Ben Holst
Accordion: Martin Kearns
Song intro: Mary Ann Deaton, "The Band House"
Karaoke Announcer: Johnny Carlton
Announcer: Daz Ikue, "Bean Me"
Lead vocal: Darryl Rhoades, except Jessica Royals, "Torch Songs Burn
    a Hole in My Heart"
Background vocals: Jimmy Royals, Darryl Rhoades, James Cobb,
    Deborah Reece, Jessica Royals, Rick Dovi

14. **THE LAST GOODBYE** (CD);Release date: October 15, 2017; No Big
Deal Records
Darryl Rhoades
Recorded at 800 East Studios (Atlanta, Georgia)
Produced by Martin Kearns, Darryl Rhoades
Engineer: Martin Kearns

TRACKS:
1. They're Killin' Jesus Again
2. You've Missed Your Last Goodbye
3. When You Feel Blue
4. The Little Hand Was on Goodbye
5. I've Been Played Again
6. The Trouble with Guys Like Me
7. Cool Ain't Payin' the Bills
8. People Do Crazy Things
9. Rain & Stone

10. I've Got a Problem
11. Blinded
12. The Not So Incredible Shrinking Man
13. When Blue Was Just a Color
14. I'm Not Dying Anymore
15. Aces & 8s
16. The Kiss of Judas
17. Between Forgotten & Unknown

CREDITS:

Guitar: Tommy Strain, Gary Limuti
Bass: Bob Glick, Kari Cabral Simmons, Tommy Vickery, Randy
    Smith (upright), Gary Limuti
Keyboards: Martin Kearns
Drums: Darryl Rhoades
Percussion: Colin Agnew
Mandolin, fiddle: Randy Smith
Accordion: Martin Kearns
Saxophone: Jeff Crompton
Harmonica: Jimmy Royals
Banjo: Rev. Jeff Mosier
Lead vocal: Steve Barker, "You've Missed Your Last Goodbye," "The
    Not So Incredible Shrinking Man"
Lead vocal: Martina Albano, "When You Feel Blue," "Rain & Stone"
Duet vocals: Deborah Reece, Darryl Rhoades, "People Do Crazy Things"
Background vocals: Jimmy Royals, Martina Albano, Steve Barkers,
    Darryl Rhoades, Deborah Reece, Richard Hayden, Tyler Hayden,
    Daz Ikue, Guy Goodman

15. TEST SPECIMENS (LP); Recorded September 16, 1982; Dance-A-
Thon/Hottrax Records (Atlanta, Georgia)
Various artists
Recorded at Bert Elliott Sound Studio (Atlanta, Georgia)
Produced by: Aleck Janoulis
Engineer: Bert Elliott

CREDITS:

"Leprosy Queen"
Guitar: David Michael, George Coats
Bass, cello: Andy West
Lead vocal: Darryl Rhoades
Background vocals: Debbie Thompson, Judy Argo

I could write a book about the difficulties of writing a book. There are multiple similarities between this project and recording albums. Both rely on others with talents and skills I am unable to grasp. Without the help of so many, this book would have been nothing more than another idea I didn't follow up on.

I want to thank Michelle Hiskey, writing coach, for her guidance along the way. Without Anne Richmond Boston's expertise in book design, I'm not sure this project would have come together. Thanks to both of these incredible women for their talents and patience.

Special thanks to my friend, Jonathan Patterson, for putting the book cover design together.

I went through literally thousands of photos over a sixty-five-year period which was an emotional journey to say the least. I couldn't see putting out a book without some visual references but pairing them down to a section was difficult. I wanted to highlight pictures of so many bands who influenced my early days in Atlanta but I may be one of the few that held onto photos from those times.

PHOTOGRAPHS: Front cover photo (2009) and back cover photos (2015), courtesy Mark Kocher; The Great Southeast Music Hall with The Nighthawks, July 4, 1977, courtesy Linda Skvasik Green; Lakeside High School Biafra Charity Dance 1970, and Sex Pistols' American debut, January 5, 1978, courtesy Murray Silver Jr.; Early Hahavishnu Orchestra promo shot 1976, and Rock 'n' Bowl NARAS event, August 15, 1981, courtesy Rick Diamond; The Bag at the Catacombs 1967, and Banana promo shot Piedmont Park 1968, Haynes McPhadden.

Thanks to Steve Mitchell and Harrison Citron for their work on the photo section.

POSTERS, BROCHURES, AND OTHER PHOTOS: Darryl Rhoades archives.

ILLUSTRATIONS: "Jesus is Screamin' on my TV" by Jerry Frazee; "Cowboy Country" by Mark Burger; "Epitaph Without a Stone" and "Guns" by Steve Mitchell.

"THE EDGE" BY FRANKIE BASTILLE: Reprinted with permission from family members: Dominick Bastio, Rosemary Bastio-Lindley, and Anthony Bastio.

Right

The right hand on the bible
The right side of the law
I'm told quite rightly so
Pride goes right before the fall
You may have the right of way
But get run over late at night
And the next day, your headstone will say
That you were still dead right
Join the right club and shake the right hand
Have the right look and make the right friends
Take the right stand on the right side of the line
But lookin' in the mirror now, you're on the other side
My left will be your right
So pick your battles and choose your fight
Cause two wrongs never make a right
You can spray right guard and use the right stuff
Do the right thing but still not have enough
Get right back in the saddle and get in the right frame of mind
You can be right on time and still be left behind
You can be right-wing but still not fly
Be right to life and one day die
Be right to work while unemployed
Push the right button and be destroyed
My country right or wrong
Use the right words but sing the wrong song
Right to bear arms, right to free speech
Never let your grasp exceed your reach
Walk the right walk, or you'll cross that line
Get so close and never find
Your do right woman or do right man
Still singin' the gun is the devil's right hand
The right words in the right ear
At the right time just might hear

You can get right with Jesus
Be right as wrong can be
Be right before your eyes
But still not see
When it doesn't look right
It doesn't feel right, it doesn't seem right
When they don't act right, they don't talk right
You can fight for right and be crucified
When rights delayed are rights denied
You can succeed where many have tried
You got the right string baby but the wrong yo-yo
Between the right to privacy and the right to know
To get the right angle and stay right on top
Go left, yield right but know when to stop
You can flex your muscle and show your might
But the Customer is not always right
It's your Right to win, right to lose
Step right up for the right to choose
You can right-click to get the news
Argue over civil rights
To win peace you vow to fight
A right to remain silent that you never use
With human rights that get abused
And it's important to be right on the money
Right on the button, right on the nose
Use volume over logic to argue with might
Shielding the truth while you dim the light
Using your God for a reason to fight
While blocking all reason and with a blinding sight
In your soul you know . . .
It ain't right . . .

RIGHT ©2022 DARRYL RHOADES (SPOKEN WORD)